Portsmouth
An Old Town by the Sea

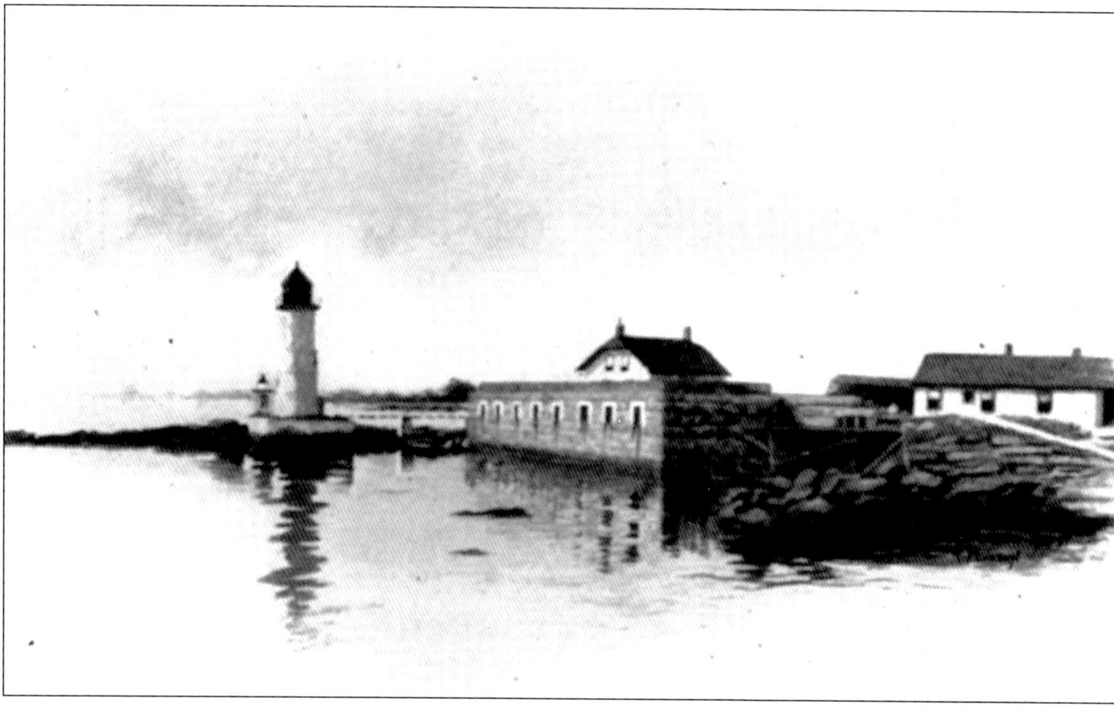

This view of Fort Constitution and the lighthouse show how they appeared a century ago. The site looks remarkably the same today, as visitors to the fort can testify. (From Helen Pearson, Vignettes of Portsmouth.*)*

THE MAKING OF AMERICA SERIES

PORTSMOUTH

AN OLD TOWN BY THE SEA

RUSSELL M. LAWSON

ARCADIA PUBLISHING

ISBN 978-0-7385-2427-6

Published by Arcadia Publishing,
Charleston, South Carolina

Printed in the United States of America

Library of Congress control number: 2003106057

For all general information contact Arcadia Publishing at:
Telephone 843-853-2070
Fax 843-853-0044
E-Mail sales@arcadiapublishing.com
For customer service and orders:
Toll-Free 1-888-313-2665

Visit us on the Internet at www.arcadiapublishing.com

DEDICATION:

FOR SHIRLEY

Front cover: *The transport ship* Baboosic *was launched from the Portsmouth Naval Shipyard during World War I. (Courtesy Strawbery Banke Museum.)*

Contents

Prologue

The history of Portsmouth and the Piscataqua River Valley is synonymous with the history of America. Native American hunters and fishermen, English explorers and colonists, shipbuilders and captains, merchants trading in lumber and fish, industrialists, military strategists and diplomats, and tourists, have long been attracted to the beauty, power, harbors, location, and economic resources of the Piscataqua River and the port at its mouth. Early English explorers such as Martin Pring and John Smith saw the endless potential of a shoreline dotted with wild strawberries adjacent to a deep harbor secure from the currents of the broad and hurried Piscataqua. "Strawbery Banke," as the site came to be known, could be easily defended from attack and was the most likely spot in northern New England to host the vast commercial opportunities of the lumber, shipbuilding, fishing, and fur industries. During the seventeenth century, Strawbery Banke realized its potential to become the economic, social, and cultural hub north of Boston.

The city's heyday came during the years before the Revolutionary War. Portsmouth merchants found a ready market in Europe and the Caribbean for cod and other fish caught off the coast of America at the Gorges Banks. Naval stores and lumber from the vast inland forests of New Hampshire supported the lucrative regional shipbuilding industry. The British government, desperately in need of masts to outfit the frigates and cruisers of the Royal Navy, arbitrarily reserved the tallest, straightest, and most massive white pines for the King. The masts were floated downstream to Portsmouth harbor, where they were loaded and sent overseas. The extensive wharves and beautiful mansions of Portsmouth's merchants indicated their interest in promoting the wealth of the British Empire.

The American Revolution silenced the busy sounds of the harbor. Portsmouth, like most American ports unable to replace their trade with England, suffered a crushing economic blow. The city promptly rebounded after the war, enjoying some of its best years of trade, shipbuilding, and wealth. It was during these years that the Portsmouth Naval Shipyard, located on the north shore of the Piscataqua, adjacent to the Maine town of Kittery, began its long service of building and repairing America's ships of war. Yet Portsmouth's claim to regional prominence slowly declined after the economic dislocation caused by the War of 1812. Even so, Portsmouth shipbuilders turned out the best of the clipper ships that marked the age of sail during the nineteenth century.

The significance of Portsmouth during the twentieth century, and today, lies in its singular anachronistic appeal. Of all the cities and villages dotting the New England coast, Portsmouth invites the visitor to enter into the early American past, to walk the same lanes as Governor Benning Wentworth and John Langdon, signer of the Declaration of Independence; stay at the same inns as John Paul Jones while he awaited the construction of the ship *America*; and to sail the same waters as Samuel de Champlain and Captain John Smith.

Portsmouth recalls the past for the visitor of today walking its narrow lanes overhung with brightly colored salt-box homes and Federalist mansions. Ancient cemeteries, such as the Point of Graves, overlook the harbor. Fishing trawlers and tugboats navigate the churning river currents that rarely freeze. Church spires serve as seamarks for sailors, who might wander through the doors of the Old North Church dominating Market Square, the spot where Reverend Joseph Buckminster once held sway. Here at the market center, one still senses the American past and feels the unending call of the sea.

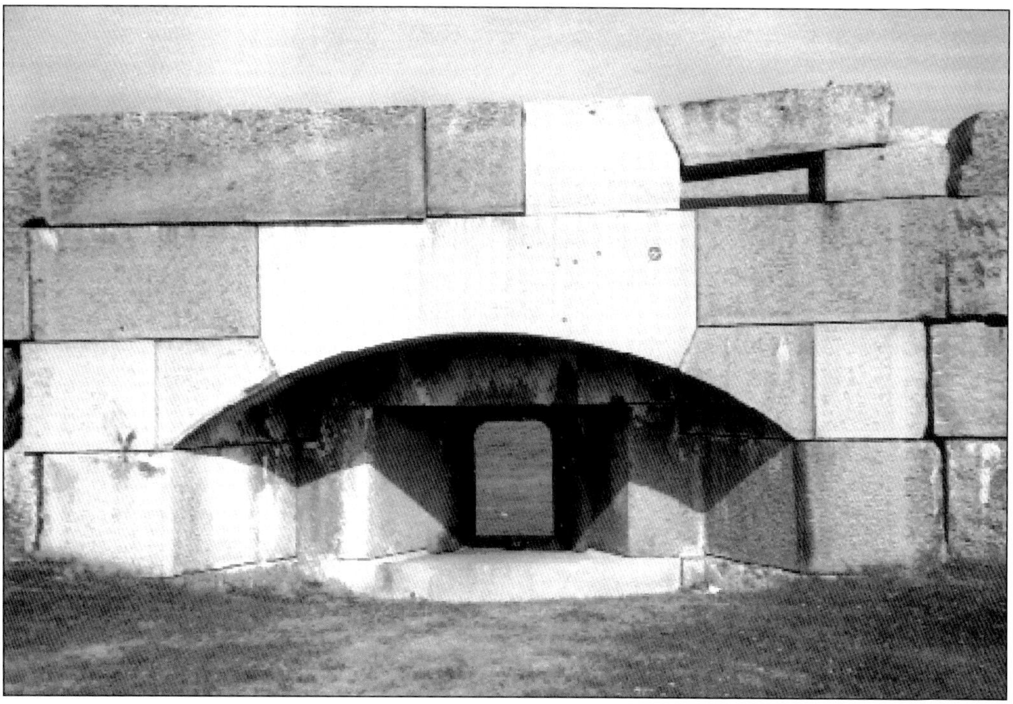

Cannon once peered ominously through the many gun turrets at Fort Constitution. Once called Fort William and Mary, the fort has protected Portsmouth harbor since the initial settlements of the 1630s. (Photo by Benjamin Lawson.)

1. The Piscataqua

Seekers of the Northwest Passage, an elusive waterway connecting the Atlantic Ocean to the Pacific, were the earliest European explorers of the northern New England coast. Giovanni Verrazzano, sailing for the French in 1524, skimmed the cool Atlantic waters north past the sandy beaches interspersed with lofty bluffs of the New Hampshire coast. Perhaps Verrazzano and his men, sailing the *Dauphine*, could feel, smell, and taste the fresh water pouring from the gaping mouth of the Piscataqua River, as it merged with the sea. Or perhaps John Rut, sailing for the English and King Henry VIII, passed by the mouth of the Piscataqua on his journey south from Newfoundland in 1535. More doubtful is the claim that in 1497 John Cabot, the Italian who sailed for the English and King Henry VII, would have steered the *Matthew* south of Newfoundland and Nova Scotia toward the New England coast and the Piscataqua River. Even the Vikings have their backers, antiquarians who believe that Norse navigators coasted the rocky Maine shore until they spotted and went up the broad Piscataqua, rowing their open wooden boats.

More likely, the first Europeans to explore the harbors, islands, currents, and shoals of the Piscataqua River were the many anonymous sixteenth-century Portuguese, Basque, French, and English fishermen. News of waters teeming with fish off the coast of Maine and New Hampshire spread quickly among fishermen, who eagerly frequented the shallow waters and banks during the spring, hauling aboard tons of cod. During the warm summer months, fishermen formed temporary camps, particularly on islands, where they split open, salted, dried, and packed the fish ready for market. In early autumn, they either departed for other ports or home.

On these clear summer days, sailors could spy eight tiny islands shimmering on the surface in the distance. One cannot help but assume that the islands, like sirens, beckoned sailors toward their rocky shores and still coves. Although Captain John Smith claimed that he was the discoverer of the Isles of Shoals, lying a few miles off the New Hampshire coast, the French explorer Samuel de Champlain noted them on his voyage of 1605. Indeed, experienced seamen and fishermen would hardly pass by such a likely place for making port, resting, repairing boats, and preparing fish.

During the reigns of Queen Elizabeth I (1558–1603) and James I (1603–1625), there was sufficient enthusiasm among merchants and sailors—and enough royal support to encourage their adventures to America—that quite a few ships were outfitted for trade and fishing, even colonizing. Speculators in the west English towns of Bristol and Plymouth, intent on profit and promoting England's power, sponsored the voyage of Martin Pring in 1603. Pring sailed along the same path as Bartholomew Gosnold. Captain Gosnold cruised the New England waters in 1602, named Cape Cod, and attempted to create a colony on the island of Cuttyhunk, south of Rhode Island. Captain Pring led two ships and crews along the coast, where they hoped to trade clothes, tools, and baubles to the native inhabitants for the wealth of the country. Pring and his men especially sought sassafras, which was thought to cure disease and restore health. The two boats, the ship *Speedwell* and the bark *Discover*, rowed up the Piscataqua, making port at places to refresh themselves and to locate the local inhabitants. Although they saw traces of the Indians, they could find none to trade with, the Indians having gone upriver to fish and hunt. Besides, the Piscataqua (Pascataquack), Newichewannock, and Squamscott tribes had learned by experience to avoid contact with the strangers who came forth in the bulky mast ships. Disappointed, Pring and his men were nevertheless astonished at the incredible bounty of animals, fish, and trees that met their eyes.

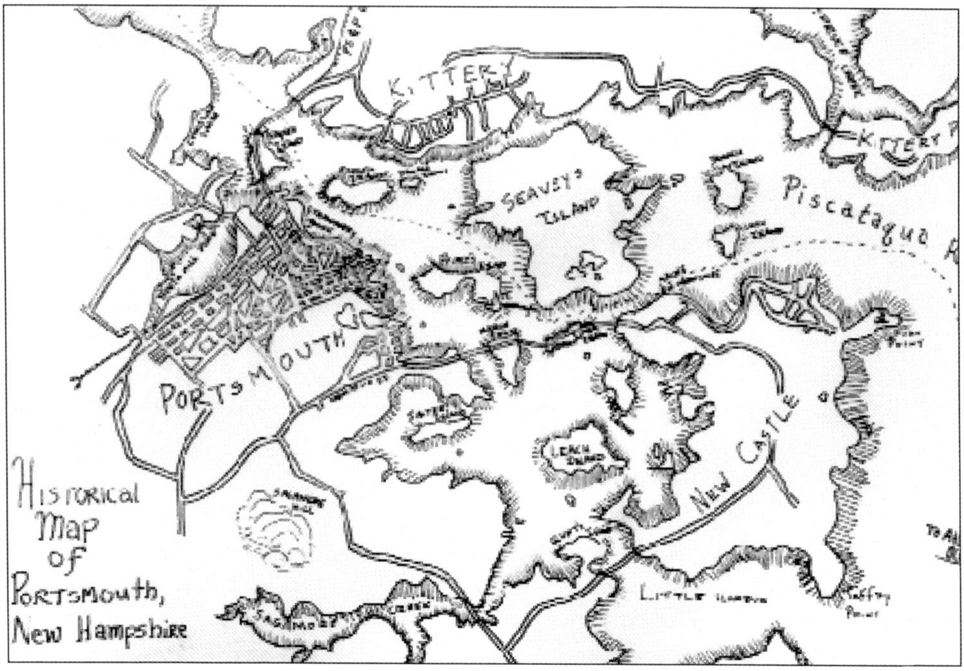

Portsmouth, originally called Strawbery Banke, occupies the southern shore of the Piscataqua River near the river's mouth. The site invited early American colonists seeking fair harbors safe from the storms at sea and rapid river currents. (Drawing by Benjamin Lawson.)

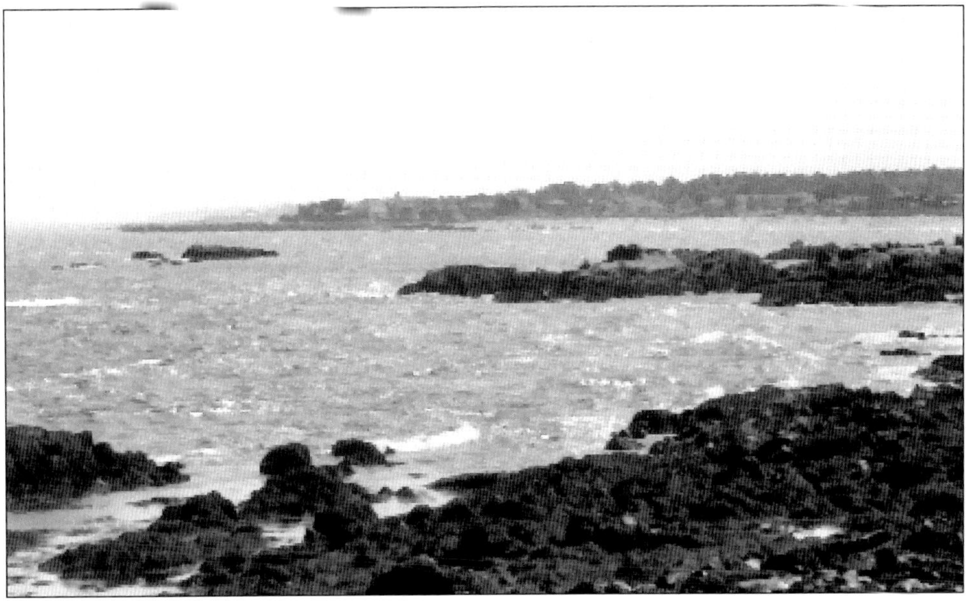

The New Hampshire coastline, shown here looking south, is narrow but beautiful. Sandy beaches alternate with outcrops of rocks and dangerous shoal water. (Photo by Benjamin Lawson.)

Captain John Smith, who explored these parts 11 years later, was so impressed by the promise of the forests, valleys, rivers, coasts, and harbors of New England that he wrote several pamphlets promoting their settlement and development as colonies for garnering the vast resources of America. Smith ranged the coast of New England in a small pinnace with eight other crewmen during the summer months of 1614 and explored the coastal waters from Penobscot Bay to Cape Cod. He recognized the apparently endless numbers of fish and fur-bearing animals. John Smith's goal when he arrived at the northern New England coast was to discover and map the coastal waters, identify the resources upon which trade could be developed, and establish nominal relations with the native inhabitants. Smith claimed that he conversed with them in a "broken language to my understanding;" he had learned a similar Algonquin dialect seven years earlier in Virginia as part of the Jamestown settlement. The New England Algonquians, consisting of the Piscataquas, Squamscotts, Penacooks, Newichewannocks, and Abenakis, told Smith of their "mortal enemies," the Tarratines and Penobscots to the east and the Mohawks to the west. They also compared the fish in the sea "to the hairs on their heads." Smith wrote in his *Description of New England* (1616) that "worthy is that person to starve that here cannot live." Smith had never seen such abundance. He could not help but compare the land to Eden: "This is only as God made it, when he created the world." Here one could lower a basket and raise it filled with glistening cod, load a boat with thousands of clams and lobsters, or drink from the "most pure" streams "proceeding from the entrails of rocky mountains."

Smith explored the region of the Piscataqua Valley: the "sandy Bay" of York and the "convenient Harbours of Accominticus and Passataquak," known later as Portsmouth and Kittery on the Piscataqua River.

An observant ethnographer, Smith learned of the good lives these natives led, of the plentiful food grown in the fertile soil of the valley—maize, pumpkins, squash, beans, and gourds. They caught pickerel, pike, trout, salmon, herring, and cod in the river and sea, and the forest provided bear and venison. Smith saw, and perhaps stayed in, the snug Algonquin lodges built of birch-bark insulated with a mix of beaver, lynx, mink, and otter pelts. He admired their quick and light canoes, made also of the bark of the white birch. These birch-bark canoes could ascend the Piscataqua and the rivers that feed it as well as range the coast, going even so far as the Isle of Shoals.

One warm June day, Smith and his crew navigated their small boat in and about the rocky islands of what would become known as the Isles of Shoals. The eight islands looked more like one or two, "a heape together," in Smith's words, floating on the sea. As the boat approached, the islands took shape: small rounded humps rose forbiddingly from the water, which was shoal, demanding careful seamanship. The crew moored their boat next to one after another of the islands for closer inspection. They were rocky and treeless, save a few tall bushes lording over the barren landscape. Yet when Smith first spied these eight islands lying a few miles off the coast of New Hampshire, he envisioned an outpost that would ensure his own fame and fortune, as well as the successful colonization of New England. Before they became the "Isles of Shoals," they were "Smyths Isles," the namesake of the captain who recognized in these desolate islands his vision of the future.

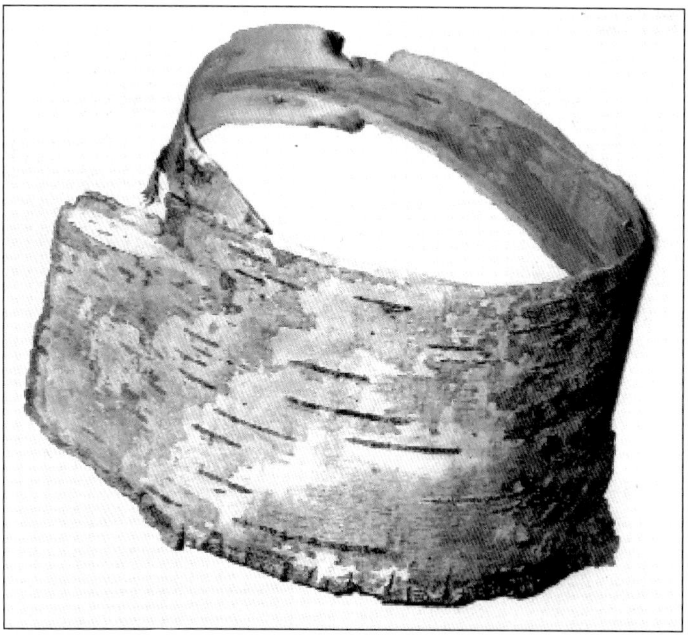

The native Algonquin tribes of New England fashioned functional huts and canoes with the remarkable bark of the white birch tree. The birch is a deciduous tree that dominates the northern forest. (Photo by Benjamin Lawson.)

The eight islands of the Isles of Shoals are shown here in a map from John Jenness's study, The Isles of Shoals, *published in 1875. The town of Gosport was located at Star Island.*

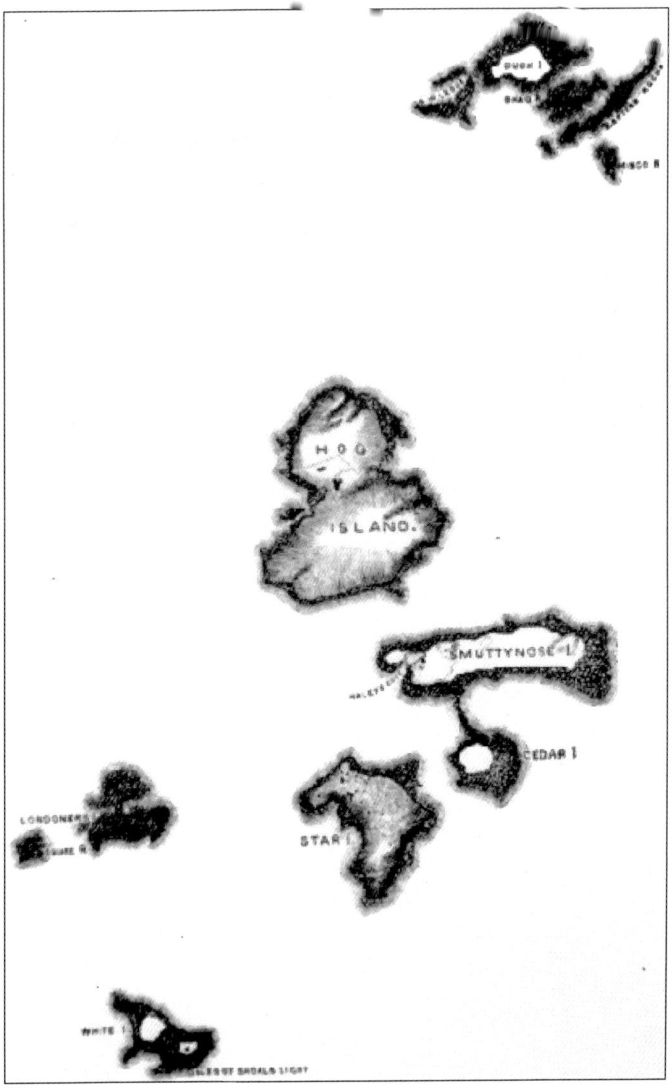

Before the English arrived, the native inhabitants in and about the Piscataqua Valley shared a common language, culture, and history. They were also loosely connected under regional political hegemonies. Smith learned in 1614 that "the Bashabes of Pennobscot" was "the chiefe and greatest" sachem. In subsequent years, the Bashabes found a challenger in his counterpart Passaconaway, sachem of the Pennacook tribe of the Merrimack Valley in central New Hampshire. Passaconaway's reputation as a great and wise religious leader garnered him the respect and support of the region's tribes, from the Piscataqua to the Merrimack.

Early American Algonquin tribes joined political and religious leadership in the person of the sachem, who besides being a great warrior and wise leader, had insight into the realm of the spirit. This shaman astonished his people with the ability

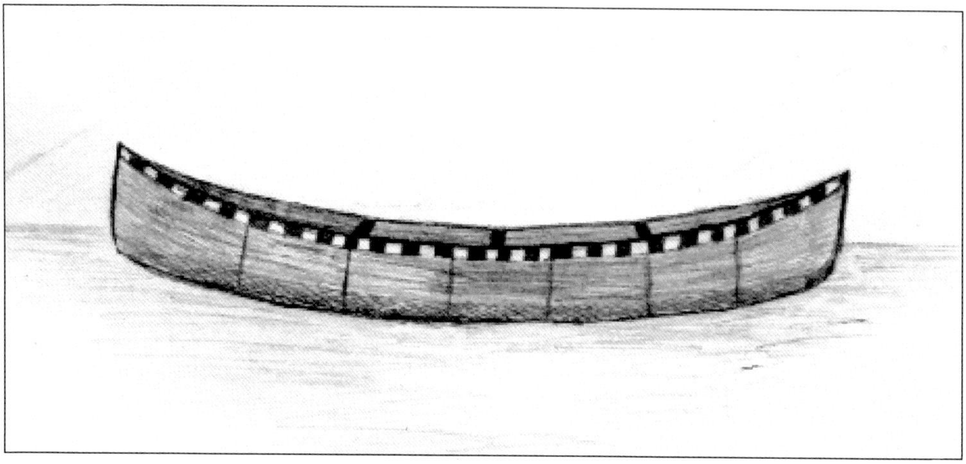

Early Americans learned how to make birch-bark canoes from the Native American tribes. The canoes were swift and light, perfect for navigating the shallow mountain streams of the northern forest as well as the rapid rivers near the coast spilling into the sea. (Drawing by Benjamin Lawson.)

to manipulate the natural environment through magical means. Passaconaway, at least, convinced the Algonquians of northern New England that he could enlist the aid of the spirit world to achieve his temporal aims. Passaconaway's world was a pantheistic and animistic one, where a supreme spirit transcended human time and place, and went beyond the particular realms and activities of the multitude of spiritual beings inhabiting forests, mountains, lakes, rivers, and seas. Nature and all of its attributes were divine, holding secrets to the particular powers inherent in each phenomenon; the shaman knew how to unlock the power of the spirit world to benefit his tribe and repel his enemies.

According to legend, Passaconaway was present at Plymouth when the Pilgrims arrived aboard the *Mayflower* in the fall of 1620. Even if the legend is false, it indicates the Algonquin's growing awareness that the random explorers and fishermen who arrived in the spring and departed in the fall were to stay. The decision had been made soon after the accession of James I to the English throne in 1603 to aggressively pursue the establishing of colonies in the vast land that the English called simply "Virginia," which lay between 45 degrees and 32 degrees North latitude. Merchants and speculators of Plymouth and Bristol focused on the northern tract of this land. The Council of New England, particularly its members Ferdinando Gorges and John Mason, organized voyages of exploration, and later colonization. Gorges and Mason obtained a grant in 1622 for the territory that they christened "Laconia," which lay between the Merrimack and Kennebec Rivers from the seacoast extending north to the lakes and rivers of Canada. The extent and quality of Laconia being unknown to Gorges, Mason, or anyone else, the two proprietors sent agents on their behalf to explore, settle, and make profitable this venture in land speculation and trade.

David Thomson, a longtime employee of Ferdinando Gorges and an experienced seaman, was the first English settler of the Piscataqua Valley. Thomson arrived in 1621 with orders to build a fortified trading post at the mouth of the Piscataqua River, from which his men could engage in their tasks of fishing (from a base at the Isles of Shoals), lumbering, and trading with the local tribes. By 1622, the fortifications were completed at a rocky, elevated point of land jutting into the Atlantic. Today the spot is called Odiorne's Point; in 1622, it was known as Pannaway. Notwithstanding the fortified buildings and cannon that protected the entrance of the river, it was (and is) a beautiful spot. Cleansing sea breezes blow from the east mingling with the smells of the salt sea, marshes, and tide pools. To the north, one's view surveys the immense mouth of the Piscataqua River. With the help of a fertile imagination, one crosses the deep river from Pannaway a mile north to small rocky islands that guard the mouth, then further to Gerrish Island and the Maine side of the Piscataqua. Land hems in, but cannot halt, the flow of rushing river water outward and seawater teaming inward. Morning can bring an eerie fog to dampen and hide everything while an invisible sea crashes and the wind moans; one hears the creaks of sails and rope of that chance schooner feeling its way along. Danger, wonder, beauty, and mystery engulf the senses.

In the wake of Thomson others came, ascending the Piscataqua past Pannaway and upriver to Bloody Point, Dover Point, and beyond. Edward Hilton penetrated to a point of land that juts between the descending waters of the Piscataqua to the east and the converging waters of the Back, Oyster, Lamprey, and Squamscott Rivers to the west. The Indian name for Hilton's Point (now Dover Point) was Winnichahannat. Hilton, his brother, and associates set up a fishing colony; they built stages to dry the fish, plus houses and a meetinghouse. Hilton's point

The Isles of Shoals were the center of fishing operations in northern New England. European fishermen of the 1500s and early 1600s set up fishing camps for the summer months. (From Jenness, Isles of Shoals.*)*

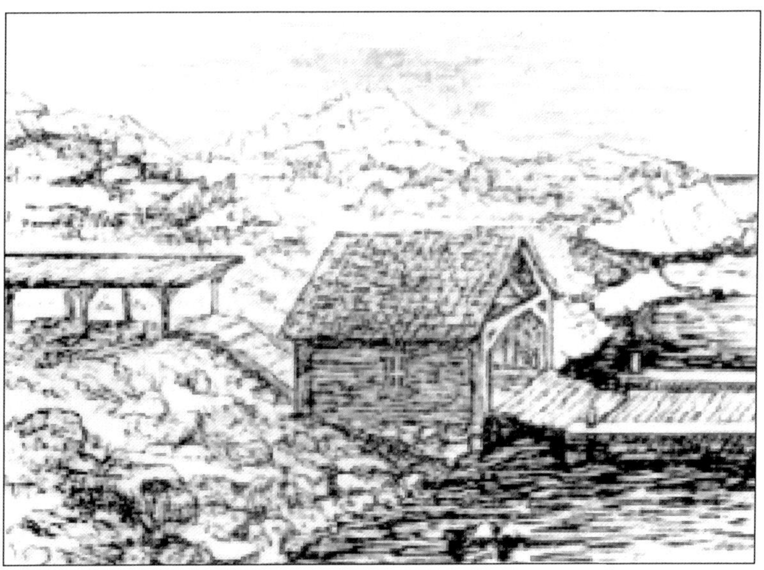

commanded the upper Piscataqua with its rising peninsula, sloped "like a ship's deck" in the words of the historian Jeremy Belknap. Thomson and Hilton sent word back to the lords and ladies of England that the Piscataqua Valley was like an untouched garden ready to be harvested. The islands and currents of the Piscataqua provided natural defenses against raiders from the sea, and local tribes appeared more than willing to share the wealth of the land. The Indians had no choice because the English clearly had more advanced technology, and because disease had brought an unparalleled mortality to the tribes of the New England coast. The English considered these epidemics the product of God's favorable will toward building Christian plantations in the New World. That was, at least, the ostensible reason for the shark-like hunger for patents and land that English speculators and adventurers exemplified during the decade of the 1620s. The most energetic were Mason and Gorges, who obtained several, often redundant, grants of land in and about the Piscataqua Valley. Their motive was greed, of course, as well as an image of America as a haven for English lords and grandees in case they thought to pop over to the New World for a visit. The dreams of Mason and Gorges were in the end ephemeral; neither man journeyed to America, rather they sent agents to do the real work of colonization.

One of these agents was Captain Walter Neal, who arrived aboard the *Warwick* in March 1630. Neal and others, including Humphrey Chadbourne, Thomas Wiggin, Edward Godfrey, Ambrose Gibbins, Richard Vines, and Henry Josselyn, sought to establish a trading and fishing colony at the mouth of the Piscataqua to make this province of Laconia profitable. Neal set up his headquarters

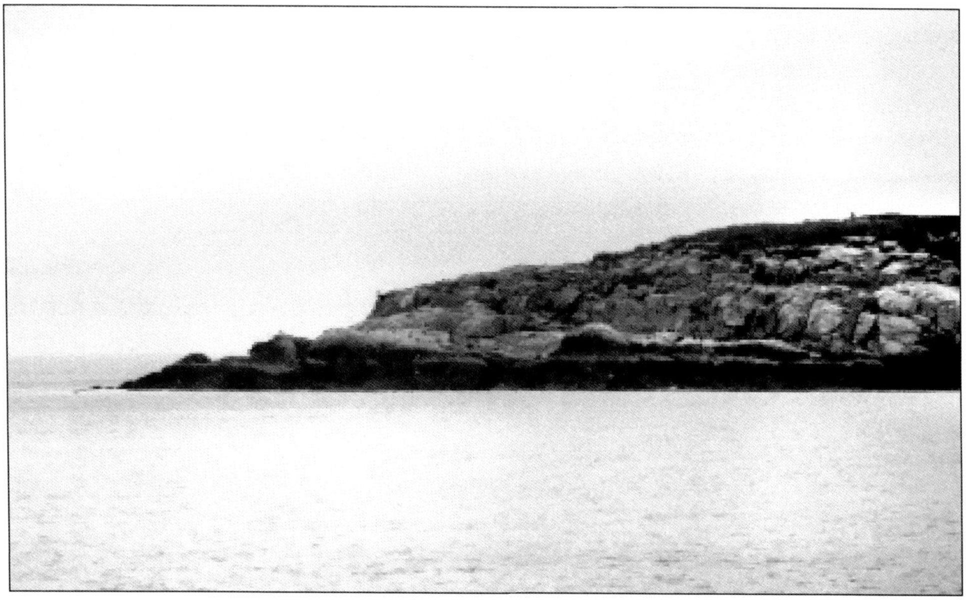

This photo, by the author, shows one of the rocky islands of the Isles of Shoals. The day is cloudy and rainy, though the sea is calm.

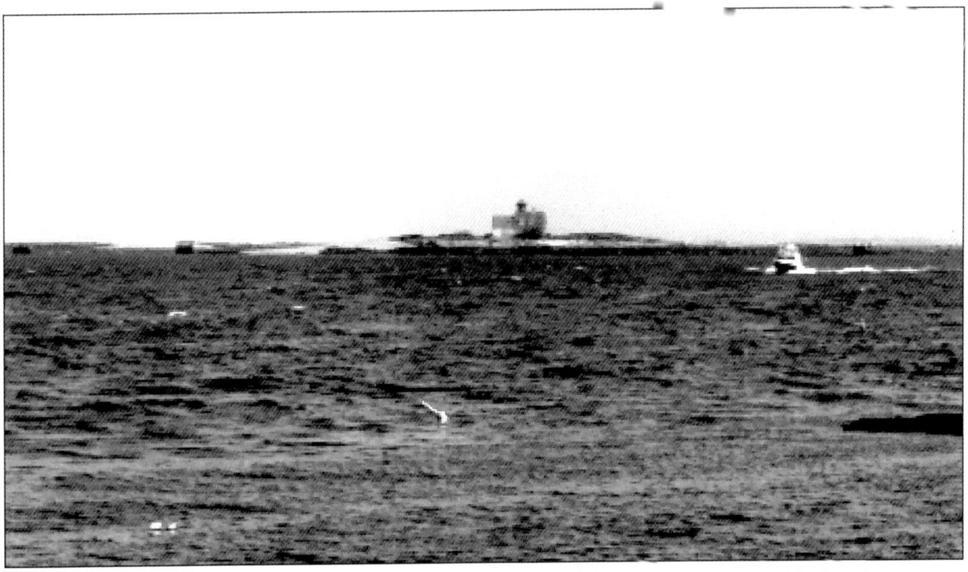

Numerous islands dot the mouth of the Piscataqua. Tidal currents merge with the river water spilling into the sea, creating treacherous currents. (Photo by Benjamin Lawson.)

at Little Harbor, adjacent to Pannaway and just across from the Great Island (Newcastle). He directed the fortification of the Great Island, a precursor to Fort William and Mary, and appointed Godfrey to organize the fishery. He also engaged in diplomacy with the local tribes for trade and land rights, and explored the interior, following rivers north beyond the fall line to the distant White Mountains. Meanwhile, Thomas Wiggin and Ambrose Gibbins established trade and fortifications upriver at Dover Point and Newichwannock, and Richard Vines and Henry Josselyn took charge of Gorges's Maine operations. Humphrey Chadbourne built a "Great House" along the south banks of the river, made appealing by outcrops of Strawberry plants. That the Great House was rather like a fortified English keep is shown by the list of "arms and ammunition" at Piscataway in 1635:

> 3 Sakers, 3 minions, 2 faulcons, 2 rabenets, 4 murthers, 2 chambers, 22 harquebusses, 4 muskets, 46 fowling pieces, 67 carbines, 6 pair of pistols, 61 swords and belts, 15 halberds, 31 headpieces, 32 beaver spears, 50 flasks . . . pair of bandaleers, 13 barrels of powder, . . . iron bullets, 2 firkins of lead bullets, 2 hogsheads of match, 955*lb*. of small shot.

The supplies also included "2 drums, 15 recorders and hautboys" for the requisite martial music.

"Strawbery Banke" became the colloquial nomenclature for this first settlement on the Piscataqua River. Summers along it are mild and wet, a perfect environment to host flowering shrubs and vines. Oaks, maples, birch, beech, and especially fir trees line the shore, hovering over the water, although the massive white pine towers above all else. Water fowl is abundant, and besides the ubiquitous seagull screaming overhead, the harbor is dotted with the sleek cormorant, or the "sea crow," that slips under the surface for long spells of fishing before reemerging with the catch. This unique and beautiful environment suggests peace and tranquility, a perception encouraged on those moist days when the dense and haunting fog, "like a line of phantom breakers," rolls in to blanket the river and harbor. "There is a fitful saline flavor in the air," wrote Thomas Bailey Aldrich, which constantly awakens visitor and resident alike. The moist, stark reality of the cold sea air competes with the dream-like quality of "the strangely shifting magic lights of sky and water." Islands dot and interrupt the channel of competing currents of descending freshwater and ascending tidewater that rarely freeze, even during the coldest winters. The tide rises to 7 feet for miles inland, where rivers rise and fall, host a variety of fresh and brackish wetlands, freshen the air with salt, and suggest to the enterprising mind the possibilities of shipbuilding. The marine environment of the sea dominates the entire region of the Piscataqua Valley, which includes the Salmon Falls (Newichwannock) River that marks the border with Maine; the Cocheco, which gently descends and combines with the former to mark the Piscataqua's beginning; the Squamscott, which winds beautifully to the Great Bay amid rich marshland; the Oyster, 10 miles from the coast yet perfectly commensurate with the repetitive movements of the sea; the Lamprey, a deep, dark river of cold, swift water; and the Back (Bellamy), which along with the others combine to form the estuary of the Great Bay.

The first settlers were impressed by the wide, inviting mouth of the Piscataqua, where shoal water is rare, though the current is treacherous. The water is deep, the anchorage generally secure, and the tide ranges from 10 to 14 feet. Seamarks along the coast and inland helped sailors find their way to port. They knew that Mount Agamenticus, a small hill near York, Maine, "lies four leagues due north. Pigeon hill, on Cape Anne, bears due south, distant ten leagues; and the highest of the Isles of Shoals bears S. E. by S. distant three leagues from the entrance of the harbour." After the Newcastle lighthouse was constructed in 1771, captains under most conditions could enter the harbor following the directions provided in Jeremy Belknap's *History of New-Hampshire*:

> Ships coming from the East, should keep in twelve fathom, till the light bears N. half a point E. or W distant three miles; (to avoid a ledge of rocks which lies off the mouth of the harbour;) then bear away for the light, keeping the western shore on board, and coming no nearer that shore than the depth of nine fathoms; giving the light a proper birth, and standing over to the northern shore of the river; when they may anchor in nine fathoms, abreast of Sparhawk's point. Ships coming from the southward, should observe the same directions, respecting the light, and keep in nine fathoms on the western shore.

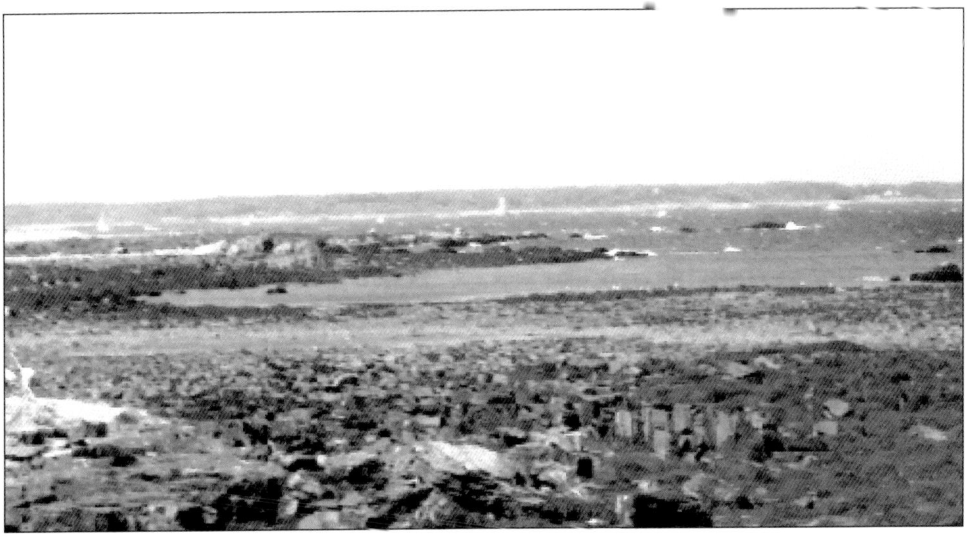

This photo, taken from the New Hampshire coast just south of Odiorne Point, shows the mouth of the Piscataqua River. The Maine coast is in the distance. (Photo by Benjamin Lawson.)

Today, the glare of lighthouses guarding the mouth of the river can be seen even from the rocky Isles of Shoals 6 miles out. Before the age of lighthouses, when seamanship and luck were in more demand, mariners knew that of the two entrances to Portsmouth harbor, the southern (entering near Pannaway into Little Harbor) was to be avoided. The northern entrance, between Great Island and Kittery Point, was the optimal path. The route then became more challenging, as a boat must skirt past Great Island and sail the channel between Seavey's, Goat, and Peirce's islands. "Here the stream is contracted to a very narrow passage, and the tide is extremely rapid; but the water is deep, with a bold rocky shore on each side." Once past Peirce's Island, Strawbery Banke came into view. South of Goat Island was a deep, quiet anchorage called The Pool, where large ships were safely moored. Strawbery Banke, just upriver, hosted anchorage for ships large and small, and as time passed the wharves at Puddle Dock were constantly busy with sailors loading and unloading cargo.

Strawbery Banke was the location of the Great House, built on the orders of the absent proprietor Captain John Mason, which continued in use for years after his death in 1635. Before he died, Mason named his proprietorship "New Hampshire" after his home of Hampshire, England. He arranged in his will to have his heirs continue to pursue his aristocratic dream, even as America was moving beyond the old social disparity between lord and peasant. Mason's heirs, Robert Tufton Mason and John Tufton Mason, would be thorns in the side of Piscataqua inhabitants for over a century. Nevertheless, the dissolution of the Laconia Company, confirmed by Mason and Gorges's respective deaths, encouraged the inhabitants of Strawbery Banke to form a social covenant among themselves for mutual benefit and protection. Life was precarious enough

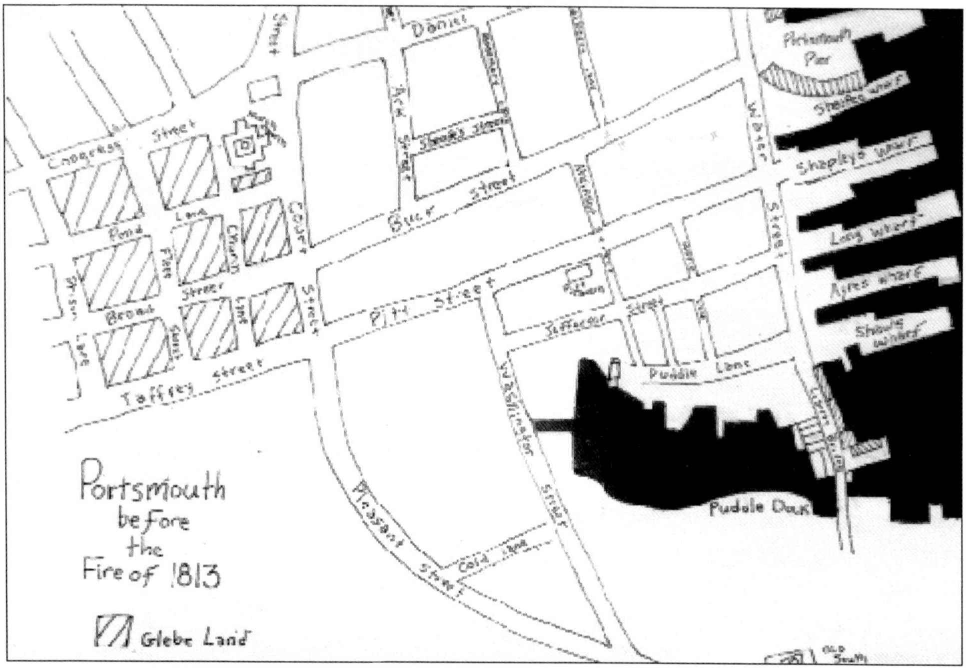

Portsmouth during the eighteenth century was centered around Puddle Dock and the Glebe. The Glebe, set aside at the beginning of the settlement in the seventeenth century, was land reserved for the parish, used by the town. (Drawing by Benjamin Lawson.)

to insure that this covenant emphasized the means and manner of Christian worship. The inhabitants of Strawbery Banke granted lots and formalized property boundaries, reserving choice acreage for the glebe, parsonage, and chapel. In conformance with the state-supported Church of England, the pious inhabitants, seeking to advance "the honor and glory of God," obtained The Bible (King James Version), the Book of Common Prayer, plates, and linens, and looked for a proper vicar. The 50-acre glebe reserved for the church was an anachronistic salute to the Medieval English past. Two leaders of Strawbery Banke, Thomas Walford and Henry Sherburne, were named "feoffees in trust" (church wardens) over the glebe and were in charge of governing it for the good of the church. During the entire colonial period, and after, the wardens leased the 50 acres to the town and individuals. Nevertheless, Portsmouth was founded at a time when the traditional mentality of landed wealth (feofs) and the privileges of noble birth were being challenged by new ideas of individual merit and the entrepreneurial spirit. The illusory hopes of the likes of Gorges and Mason vanished in the reality of a land that required not good birth, but perseverance and hard work.

The glebe became the center of what would become the town of Portsmouth. Those 50 acres formed a square bounded by Court, Pleasant, Congress, and Chestnut Streets. Church wardens reserved land for a parsonage near the South

Mill Pond. The northeast extreme of the glebe would become the market center of the town.

As Strawbery Banke was organizing itself into a settled community, other immigrants from England and Massachusetts similarly occupied lands in the Piscataqua Valley, and ostensibly purchased or otherwise gained permission from the local Algonquin tribes to develop the land. In the process, they founded the towns of Dover, Exeter, and Hampton. Dover emerged from the remnants of Hilton's patent at Dover Point and the work of Thomas Wiggin and Ambrose Gibbins at the so-called "upper plantation." The initial settlement at Dover Point, which is separated from Bloody Point (Newington) by diverse currents (denoted the "horse races") and divides the descending rivers that form the Piscataqua, was inextricably abandoned in favor of the Cocheco River. The falls of the Cocheco soon hosted sawmills and the hum of blades cutting pine boards for homes and ships. The timber and shipbuilding industries would become the basis of Dover's economy.

Dover and other Piscataqua towns, mirroring the tendencies of the age and the peculiarities of New England, were the sites of some remarkable religious

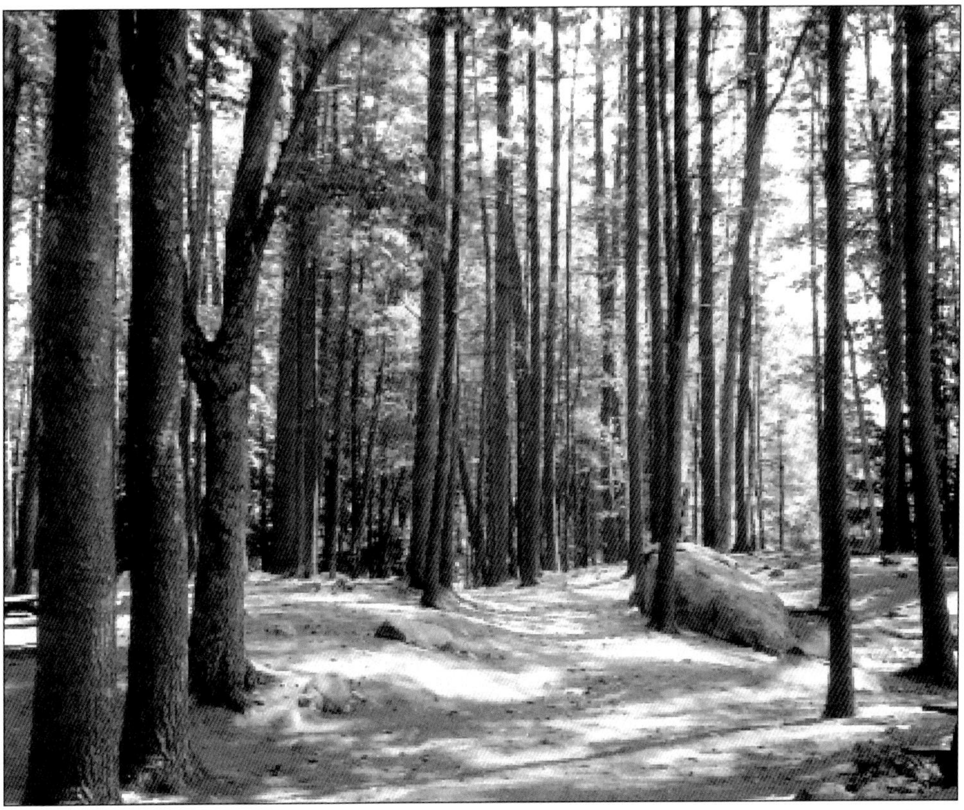

The pine forests of New Hampshire built the Piscataqu shipbuilding industry and fueled Piscataqua trade. The dominant tree of the northern forest, the white pine, supplied the masts of the British Navy during the colonial period. (Photo by Benjamin Lawson.)

controversies during the 1630s and 1640s. The Church of England, favored by the established citizens of England and America who wanted order, decorum, and stability, was challenged by a brand of Calvinism that wanted to purify the Church of England of its "Catholic" or "high church" tendencies. These Puritans, such as the Pilgrims of Plymouth and the followers of John Winthrop at Massachusetts Bay, felt that God sent them on an "errand into the wilderness" of America to establish a "New Jerusalem" to mold communities founded upon God's word and law. One could expect controversy erupting in New England between the stalwart defenders of the Church of England and the rebellious reformers who aimed to build a glowing "city upon a hill." Similar conflict in England resulted in the execution of Charles I and the subsequent English Civil War. Nothing so dramatic happened in New England and the Piscataqua Valley, yet tensions over religious beliefs did frequently spill over into political matters.

A particularly fervent expression of Puritanism, dubbed Antinomianism, which focused on the ability of each believer to find salvation within his own heart, caused a stir in Boston during the 1630s, then spread to New Hampshire. Anne Hutchinson challenged the authority of Massachusetts Bay and got herself banished; her brother John Wheelright was similarly banished from Massachusetts. He led the disillusioned and disconcerted north to the banks of the Squamscott River. According to legend, Wheelright bought the rights to the land from various Indian sachems, such as Passaconaway; however it occurred, the Puritan refugees established the town of Exeter.

Other settlers arrived from England and took possession of the rich salt marshes along New Hampshire's sandy coast. The few Indians who lived there called the place Winnecunnet, but immigrants, led by Stephen Batchelor, changed the name to Hampton. The people of Hampton were Puritans who engaged particularly in fattening their cattle with the rich marsh hay. They were not interested in theological or political disputes, and considered themselves under the jurisdiction of the government at Massachusetts Bay. Royal patents granted to proprietors originally governed Strawbery Banke and Dover, but by 1640 these settlements lacked proprietary leadership or provincial government. Town leaders decided to join with their rich and powerful neighbor to the south, which would provide them with economic and political security. Exeter agreed with the strategy and soon followed suit. The four towns of the Piscataqua region—Strawbery Banke, Dover, Exeter, and Hampton—were under Massachusetts Bay authority by 1642. The Massachusetts General Court in 1643 designated these towns, along with Salisbury and Haverhill in Massachusetts, as comprising the "Shire" of Norfolk.

The Massachusetts General Court imposed a gentle will upon Piscataqua towns, not basing civil rights on church membership, which could hardly be expected in these burgeoning fishing and trading towns where religion was second on the list and ministers were often corrupt, apathetic, or transient. Quite a number of Piscataqua inhabitants lived in fishing camps on Great Island or the Isles of Shoals. They spent their days fishing or drying their catch of the

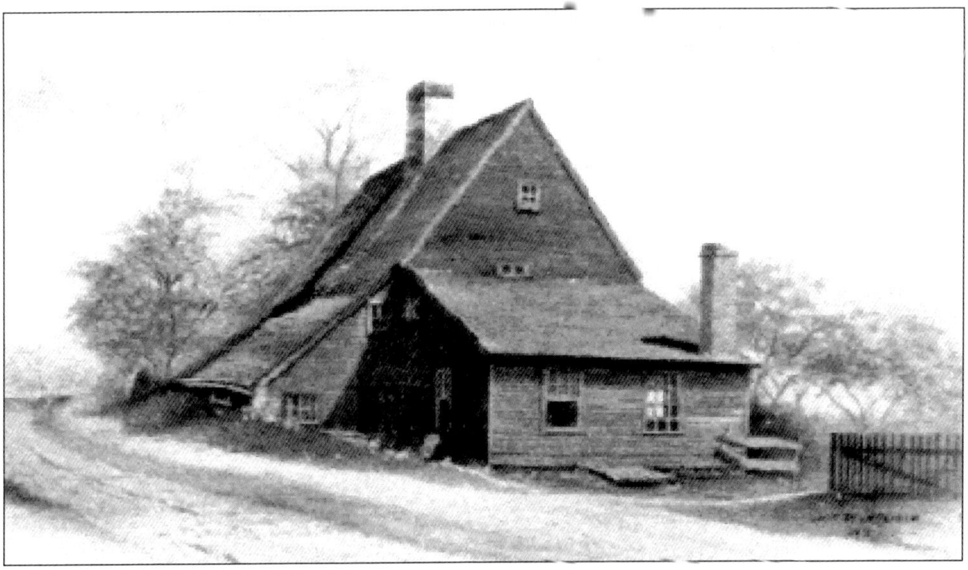

The Jackson House is the oldest wood structure in the Piscataqua Valley. Richard Jackson built the house in 1664. (From Vignettes of Portsmouth.*)*

day before mending nets and patching boats. They were fond of drinking, used profanity frequently and with gusto, were concerned with prosperity rather than piety, and were often lonely as few women lived in the harsh conditions of the fishing village.

Once called Smyth's Isles, at least by John Smith, then renamed sometime before his death in 1631 (by whom it is not certain), the Isles of Shoals were beautiful and romantic in their isolation and utter dependence upon the sea. They were misshapen rocks with a little soil to host the most adaptable plants; if the Isles were not a place for the farmer or herdsmen, they were the perfect base for a fishing industry. A few of the islands, such as White, Lunging, Shag, and Duck, were uninhabitable except by the hardy soul with plenty of potable water, food rations, sturdy lodgings, and patience. Hog, Smuttynose, Cedar, and Star Islands were hardly better, yet they were larger and more secure from the harsh realities the sea offered. From the beginning, fishermen of the Isles of Shoals were drawn to the Piscataqua for food, supplies, companionship, and the hope for a less rigorous life. Few fishermen were sufficiently successful in giving up fishing for trade and property management. Such were the origins of the Pepperrells and the Cutts, two great families of Kittery and Portsmouth.

A more humble, yet typical, example was that of Andrew Newcombe, who captained a fishing vessel at the Isles of Shoals from 1666 to 1673, making his home at Hog Island. His wife Sarah bore six children while living at the Shoals. He was frequently gone during the long winter nights, but earned such a good living that he could afford to purchase property on a point of land at Kittery that jutted into the Piscataqua. Andrew was a constable and, in serving a warrant or

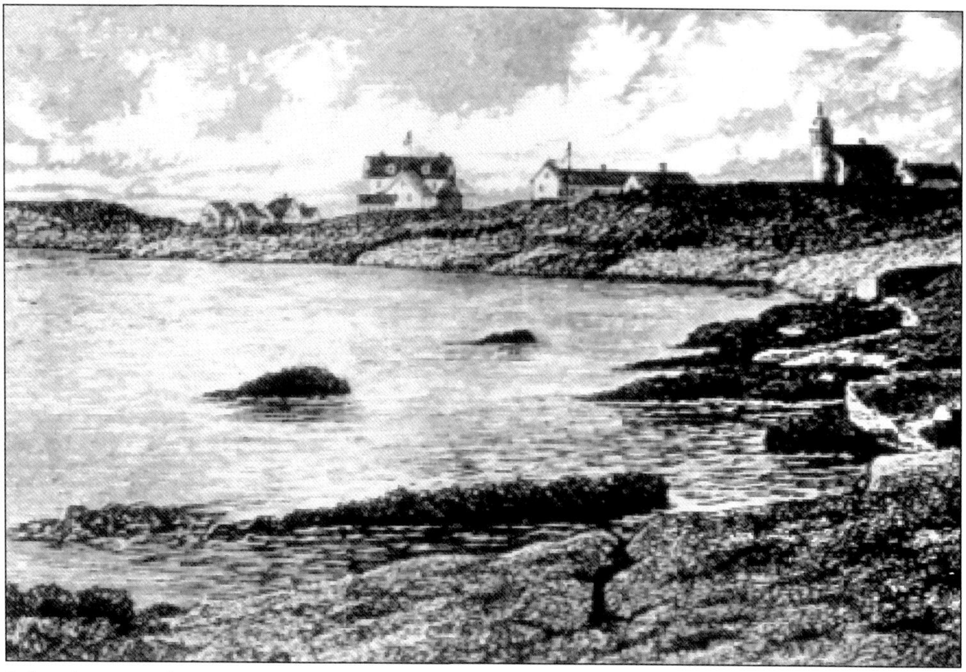

This drawing, from Isles of Shoals, *shows the rocky isolation and sparse habitations of Star Island. The Gosport parish steeple is located in the upper right hand corner.*

demand for payment to one Shoaler in 1671, was told by Mark Roe that he would "break his bones." The threat proved idle. Andrew and Sarah sold their property in Kittery and Hog Island to remove to Martha's Vineyard two years later.

Meanwhile, the community at Strawbery Banke in the 1640s and 1650s was maturing and becoming less like a frontier outpost or temporary fishing village and more like an actual town. Besides the hardy and gruff fishermen there were merchants, grocers, craftsmen and their wives, children, servants, and slaves. Stability begets a desire for order, which requires structures and institutions that promote morality, prosperity, learning, and harmony. Towns must have government constructed under the authority of the best men, the selectmen, chosen in assembly by freeholders, the citizens who by virtue of their property have a stake in the future of the town.

In 1652, when the surviving town records begin, Strawbery Banke had 200 to 300 people and 50 or 60 families. A simple clapboard meetinghouse had been built to accommodate meetings on the Sabbath as well as town assemblies, which were sporadic. Like most New England towns during the colonial period, the town moderator kept order during, and set the agendum for, the town meeting. It was a venue to consider the most compelling issues facing the town. Of prime importance were the rights of inhabitants to property, its distribution, and the setting and regulation of boundaries. Next in importance were the town's expenses and raising revenue. Fines of various sorts and poll and property taxes were disbursed for constructing public buildings (such as the meetinghouse) and their periodic maintenance; building roads and accompanying surveying costs; and the relief of the town poor. The assembly passed laws by majority vote of present citizens. They accepted nominations for town posts, candidates were voted on, and victors declared in one meeting. Serving the town was required and those who refused to do so were fined. Several constables were chosen to collect fines and taxes, to keep order at meetings and on town thoroughfares, and to fine (and if need be, run out of town) foreigners, and ne'er-do-wells. Positions that were determined at these meetings included fence-viewers to mark out property boundaries and to settle disputes between neighbors; hog-reeves to keep the town pen to restrain errant hogs disturbing the peace, as well as goodwives' gardens; and the surveyor of roads, whose job was to plan for new roads and to maintain the old. The town appointed ad hoc committees as needed to consider and act upon compelling issues and disputes. Three citizens in March 1655 were appointed to supervise building a parsonage for the minister, Reverend Browne, whose temporary status was becoming more permanent. The town declared that the decision of the committee would "stand firm as the acte of the wholl town for ever." On another occasion, in 1661, three men were appointed to an ad hoc committee to negotiate a boundary with the neighboring township of Hampton.

At the assembly of April 5, 1652, inhabitants voted on the town's first selectmen, who were authorized to take care of town business "as though our selves the wholl Town wear Presente." The selectmen ran day-to-day affairs of the town, though overall "the Power . . . Remains to the Wholl Towne." The assembly determined the seating by social rank and the divisions by gender and age at Sabbath meetings; the selectmen enforced assigned seating with fines imposed on transgressors. Those who were at that meeting granted John Webster permission "to keep an ordinary;" it was the selectmen's responsibility to regulate what the tavern sold and who it served. It was up to the town as a whole to receive John Harte in 1658 "as an inhabitant of this Towne and to have a house lott of eight accers as other inhabitants have." The job of the selectmen was to determine whether or not the applicant was a "stranger" of unknown wealth and character, or an honest "tradesman" who would not be a financial burden to the town. The selectmen also composed petitions to the provincial government based on directions of the town in assembly.

One of the first petitions drawn up by the selectmen in 1653 to the General Court of Massachusetts concerned the proper name of the town. Strawbery Banke sounds wonderfully poetic to the modern resident and visitor, but to the goodmen and goodwives of mid-seventeenth-century Piscataqua, it appeared inaccurate and not at all descriptive of the town. The first explorers, such as Martin Pring and Walter Neal, had noted the presence of wild strawberries on the Piscataqua's banks. This was the Common Strawberry (*Fragaria virginiana Duchesne*), a prolific plant that adapts to a wide variety of soils, including sandy and generally infertile plots. The native Piscataqua tribe used the berries to prevent scurvy, made tea of the leaves to calm the anxious, and used the root to also make a tea for general stomach and intestinal disorders. Initially, however, explorers were attracted to the Piscataqua because of the herbs that reputedly grew on its banks. Martin Pring's voyage of 1603 aimed to return to England with a load of sassafras, gathered or traded for with the Indians. The natives ingested sassafras (*Sassafras albidum*) as a tea or a soup to treat a host of stomach, kidney, bowel, and arthritic ailments. Yet the area never became a sassafras export center, and residents of Strawbery Banke knew the reason: the soil was too poor to produce large yields of anything edible. Thus citizens of Strawbery Banke turned to the wealth of the river and the sea for inspiration in generating a name. "A name most suitable for this place," petitioners wrote, "it being the river's mouth," with a harbor as "good as any in this land," was Portsmouth. The Massachusetts General Court agreed, and Strawbery Banke became Portsmouth.

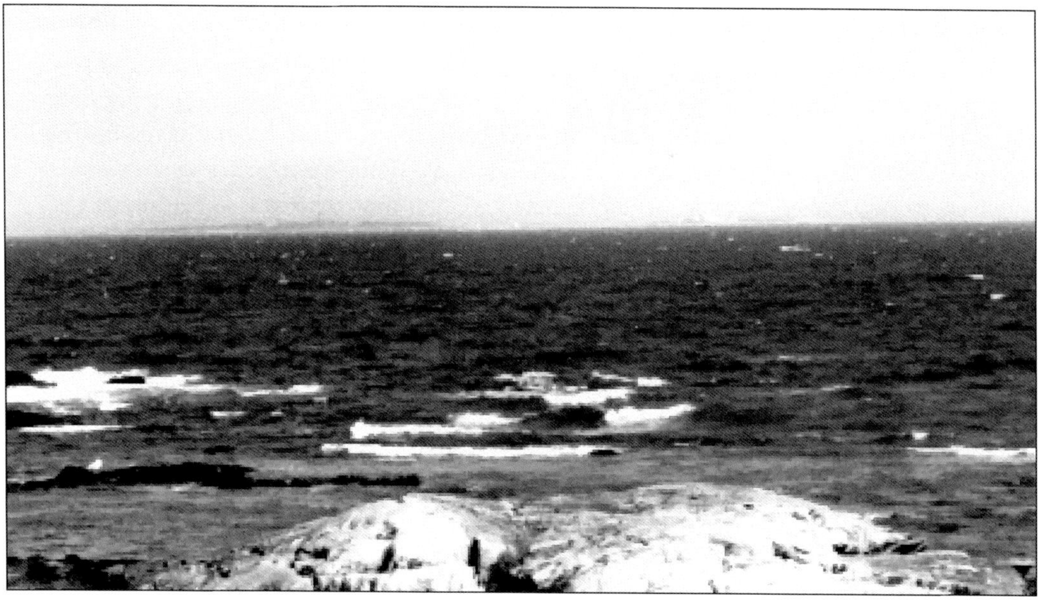

The observer standing on the New Hampshire coast looking east across the Atlantic can spy the Isles of Shoals on a clear day. Other days fog completely envelopes the islands, hiding them from the land and ships at sea as well. White Island hosts a lighthouse for such days. (Photo by Benjamin Lawson.)

2. The Search for Order

Portsmouth is in a strange sense the land of the dead, at least when one considers the many cemeteries and burial grounds that dominate portions of the city. The town's age is revealed in the narrow streets, clapboard homes, old churches, and particularly in the old graveyards marked by ancient monuments covered with lichen and toppled granite headstones, old mislaid tablestones, and forgotten tombs. One of the grandest records of Portsmouth history is the North Burial Ground near the North Mill Pond. Buried there are some of the great leaders of Portsmouth's past, such as Governor John Langdon, signer of the Declaration of Independence and delegate to the Constitutional Convention; Woodbury Langdon, John's brother and merchant; Joseph Whipple, merchant and adventurer; William Whipple, Joseph's brother and signer of the Declaration of Independence; Prince Whipple, who gained his freedom during the Revolution; and Captain Thomas Thompson, who sailed the *Raleigh* against British warships during the Revolutionary War. The headstone of Dr. Clement Jackson, Portsmouth physician, reads:

In Memory
of
Clement Jackson, Esqr
Eminent Physician of this Town
who died October 10th, 1788
aged 83 years
His whole Life was one continued act
of
Benevolence & Charity.
The man who raises a monument
by his virtuous actions,
Will be held in grateful rememberance
When the boasting Marble & flattening Brass
are moulder'd to Dust.

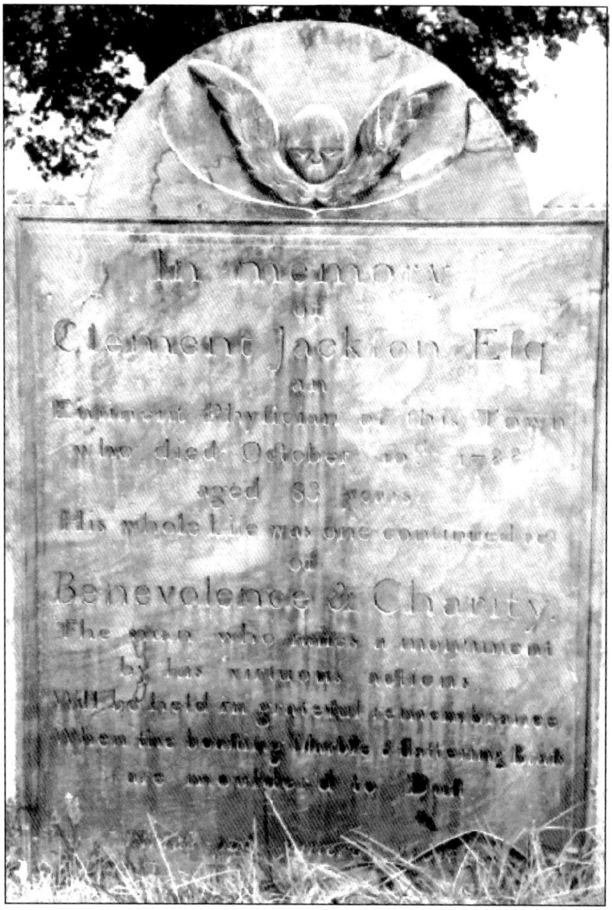

An angel casts its wings over the epitaph of Clement Jackson at the North Burial Ground. Jackson was a Portsmouth physician. (Photo by Benjamin Lawson.)

St. John's Episcopal Church in downtown Portsmouth, overlooking the harbor, features an old burial ground from its days when it was known as Queen's Chapel before the Revolutionary War. The inquisitive traveler along Bow Street can spy between the parked cars and parking meters the old brick and stone tombs of Portsmouth's eighteenth-century merchant elite. There lies Theodore Atkinson, a graduate of Harvard College, Collector of Customs, naval officer, sheriff, counselor, merchant, and philanthropist. Atkinson, an infamous Tory, quietly died in 1779, an outspoken opponent of the colonial rebellion.

Then there is the Point of Graves, an out of the way place of unequaled peace and beauty, of aged oaks and maples, providing verdure cover for those quietly resting. Anne Jaffrey is buried there, looking out over Portsmouth harbor where once her husband's ketches, schooners, and barks rode at anchor; the birth of her son George took her life in 1682. William Button also lies there, an English merchant who accidentally drowned in the Piscataqua one fall day in 1693. Signs of the unexpectedness of death and fragility of life are everywhere. Little Sarah

Rogers lies next to her grandmother, victims of an October 30, 1704 fire. Sarah was the daughter of the Reverend Nathaniel Rogers, pastor of the North Parish, and his wife Sarah. Fifteen years later they were parents again to a lively five-year-old who was laid to rest as well, near his sister. The headstone features the grim winged skeleton so typical of colonial funerary art. Captain John Pickering, who donated the land for the graveyard, also rests there.

Death is the great equalizer, even if life, institutions, and cemeteries are not. On the road toward Rye and Hampton at the edge of Portsmouth, hidden amid tall trees and fallen leaves, is a small burial ground scarcely noticeable except for the rocks that enclose it, marking it as something memorable. Here the slaves of the Portsmouth elite are buried; a few blank headstones—really just rocks—mark their anonymous graves. Tall, unkempt grass covers the remains of Pomp, Hannah, Violet, and Nanne, one-time slaves owned by John Langdon and family.

Death, burial, cemeteries, headstones: macabre, perhaps, but such were the frequent themes of life in Portsmouth during the 1600s and 1700s. Thomas Bailey Aldrich, the Portsmouth antiquarian and writer, knew from experience that:

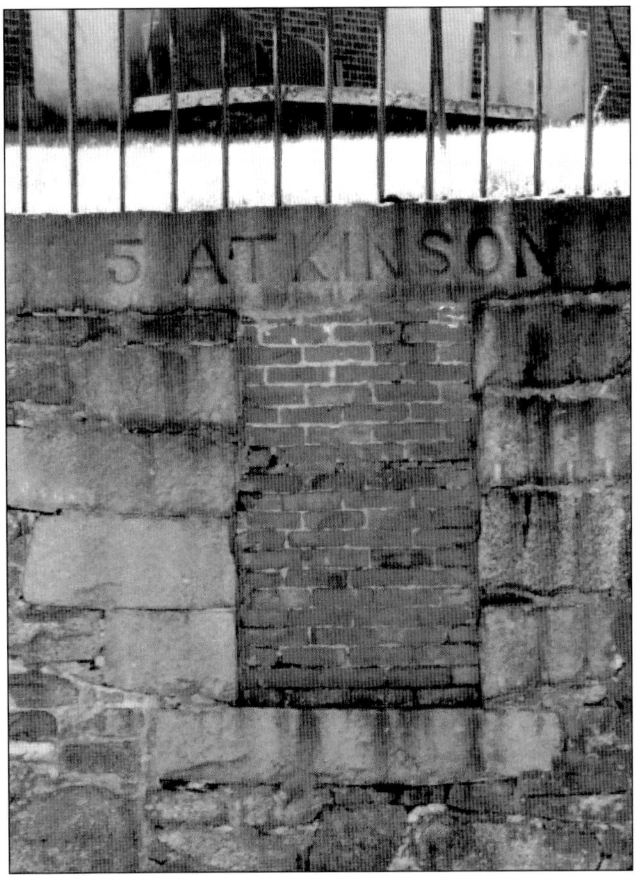

The Atkinson family vault holds the remains of eighteenth-century leader Theodore Atkinson. The vault is on the grounds of St. John's Episcopal Church. (Photo by Benjamin Lawson.)

> dwellers by the sea are generally superstitious; sailors always are. There is something in the illimitable expanse of sky and water that dilates the imagination. The folk who live along the coast live on the edge of a perpetual mystery; only a strip of yellow sand or gray rock separates them from the unknown; they hear strange voices in the winds at midnight, they are haunted by the specters of the mirage. Their minds quickly take the impress of uncanny things.

Ghosts wandered the nooks and crannies of the Isles of Shoals, and witches abounded in Portsmouth.

A famous witch of seventeenth-century Portsmouth was Goodwife Walford. The night of March 30, 1656, Susannah Trimmings was making her way home with a babe in her arms, as well as other items, when she heard a strange noise in the forest. There stood Goodwife Walford. The old and haggard witch begged for "a pound of cotton," which Trimmings refused to give. The old woman cursed her and departed "in the shape of a cat." Goodwife Trimmings immediately felt "a clap of fire on the back." She returned home in a sorry state. Her husband Oliver testified that:

> she passed by me with her child in her arms, laid the child on the bed, sat down on the chest, and leaned upon her elbow. Three times I asked

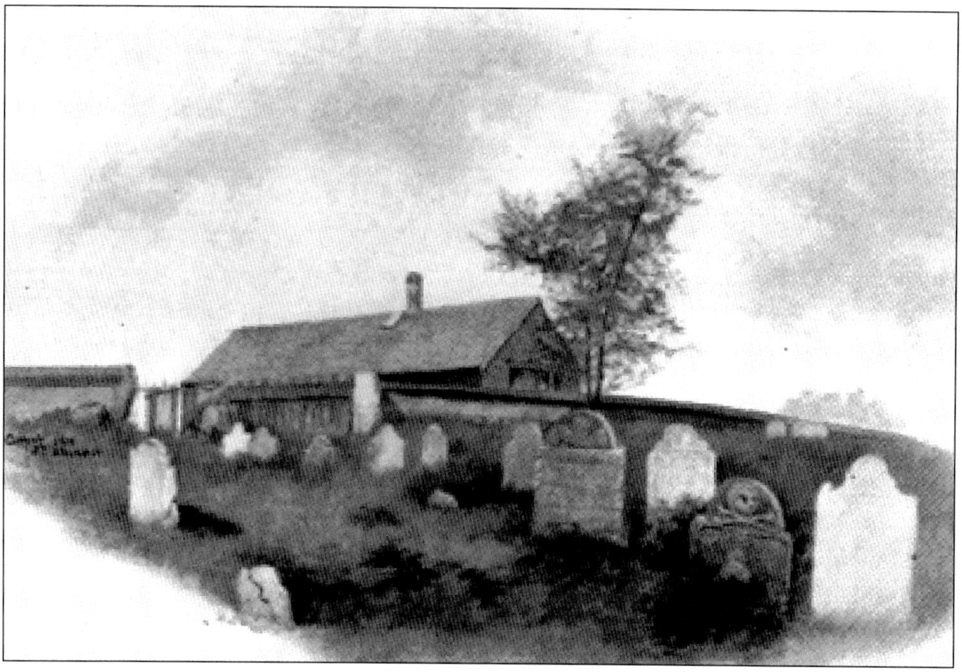

The Point of Graves is the most ancient of Portsmouth cemeteries. It is located next to the harbor on land donated by Captain John Pickering. (From Vignettes of Portsmouth.*)*

> her how she did. She could not speak. I took her in my arms, and held her up, and repeated the question. She forced breath, and something stopped in her throat, as if it would have stopped her breath. I unlaced her clothes, and soon she spake, and said, Lord have mercy upon me, this wicked woman will kill me. I asked her what woman. She said Goodwife Walford.

The wife further told the husband "that her back was as a flame of fire, and her lower parts, were, as it were, numb and without feeling. I pinched her, and she felt not." A friend, Eliza Barton, related:

> that she saw Susannah Trimmings at the time she was ill, and her face was coloured and spotted with several colours. She told the deponent the story, who replied that it was nothing but her fantasy; her eyes looked as if they had been scalded.

The evidence at court was not sufficiently convincing to convict Goodwife Walford. Yet all of her Portsmouth neighbors knew her to be a witch, and as the years passed, knew her daughter to be one too.

In 1682, George Walton experienced the effect of the powers of darkness. It began when for some inexplicable reason "showers of stones . . . thrown by an invisible hand" rained upon and emerged from within his house. The stones were red-hot; those coming from inside the dwelling smashed through the windows. The sound of "a dismal hollow *whistling* would be heard, and sometimes the *trotting* and *snorting* of a horse, but nothing to be seen." The sounds and stones and other bewitched items pursued the hapless man wherever he went. When he was sailing the Piscataqua, the boat's "anchor leaped overboard," caused by an invisible power for some hidden reason. "Several cocks of hay, mow'd near the house, were taken up and hung upon the trees" by the same force. Fortunately for Goodman Walton, the witchcraft left him as quickly as it had arrived, and in complete mystery. The great number of taverns furnishing strong drinks may have had something to do with Walton's experience. In 1725, John Spinney was returning home by boat from an evening's entertainment one dark night and saw a ghostly presence in the water, and thought perhaps it was Sarah Keene, a well-known witch.

Modern historians delight in explaining such episodes of witchcraft as the product of uncertainty and conflict. True, life was not simple on the Piscataqua, for winters were hard, the fishing uncertain, the sea unforgiving; death was a frequent visitor and French enemies and their Indian allies surrounded the British Americans of northern New England. When threatened with the chaos of time and place, both physical and spiritual, humans tend to join together to search for order. Seventeenth-century New Englanders were credulous, to be sure, yet they were stubborn, patient, practical, and persevering. They created institutions to respond to uncertainty and disorder, to provide as much as possible an anchor for their lives.

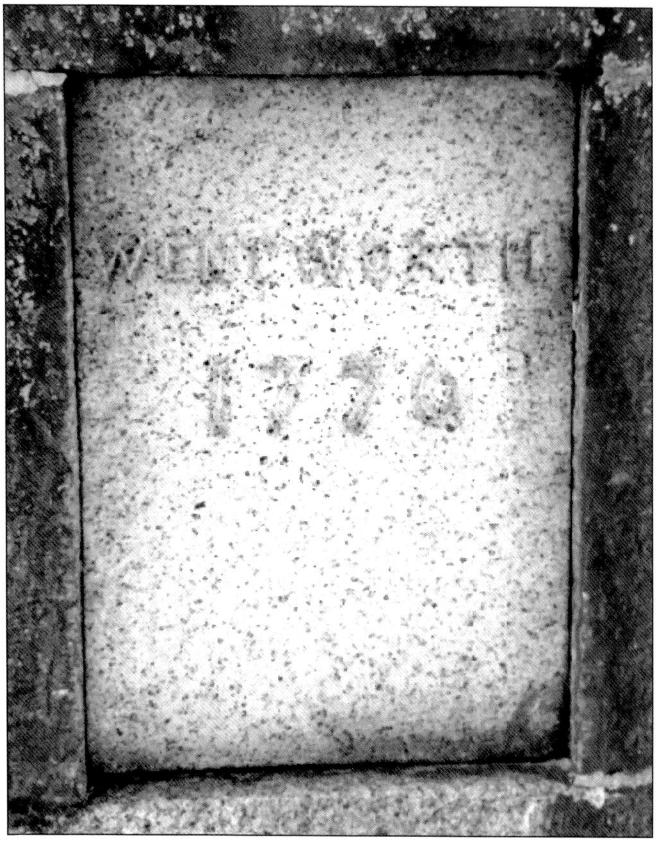

Before the American Revolution Queen's Chapel, later St. John's Episcopal Church, boasted the membership of some of Portsmouth's leading statesmen. The Wentworth family produced three colonial governors of New Hampshire. The Wentworth family vault is contained in the surrounding wall that contains the churchyard. (Photo by Benjamin Lawson.)

One such anchor was the system of "warning out." It was frankly quite difficult to become a citizen of Portsmouth if one lacked the proper credentials such as good breeding, a respected surname, and money in the pocket. A youthful community required residents who would be an asset rather than a burden. Any stranger who appeared on the streets of Portsmouth, who loitered about in a restless way, had to be persuaded to leave. It was the constable's unfortunate job to confront the stranger and demand that he post bond to indicate his financial ability and willingness to support the community. The town refused to accept vain promises or the youthful potential of strangers who could not make a material statement of their intentions, to guarantee "to keepe the Town harmless from being burthened in way of Charge."

This reluctance to accommodate immigrants derived in part from the seventeenth-century mindset, which saw the potential for evil in anything unusual or unknown. Tudor-Stuart England also fostered such insularity. The Act of Settlement of 1662 under Charles II required English parishes to return vagrants and strangers to their parish of birth. Each parish should care for its own.

Likewise, New England towns such as Portsmouth were willing to care for the orphaned, the sick, the aged, the disabled, and the widowed. The seventeenth-century town perceived itself as a large extended family, a cohesive community of friends and neighbors willing to participate jointly in the education, support, defense, and care of each other. Why should the inhabitant of one town end up as a burden on another town? Rovers and wanderers were not needed in New England, but rather upright farmers who intended to stay put and keep the family name connected with the land once they possessed property. "Strangers" were unknown, foreign, dangerous, and frightening, and it was much better to get rid of them before becoming a burden, or worse, a threat to the order of the town.

Records indicate that "warning out" was a ritual that protected the material resources of the town and enhanced the cohesion of the community. Once the constable warned out a stranger, the town required the person to depart. Frequently, however, the person covertly remained in the town since New England towns rarely had the apparatus to force the issue. There was no police force, and constables were not prepared to engage in anything beyond simple law enforcement. Persons who stayed in Portsmouth, who had not been legally accepted into the community, received no economic relief in food or shelter should the need arise. Strangers were never allowed a voice in town affairs. If they knowingly accepted such conditions and still sought to enjoy residency in Portsmouth, the town required them to pay taxes and perform duties like any other resident. In 1666, the town ordered all inhabitants including "any other residing in the towne" to assist with the upkeep of the fort on Great Island. The next year, the town declared that "every Inha[bi] tant and Dweller in the Towne" must contribute their portion toward the upkeep of the parish minister. Strangers therefore were taxed to pay for the upkeep of the town's deserving poor, the irony of which was not lost on the town fathers. Strangers assumed the risk of staying in town and if they prospered, paid their taxes, and acquired property, they still risked having themselves and their family labeled as "strangers" rather than "inhabitants" for many years to come.

The populace—that is, legal town residents—were responsible for insuring that strangers did not find a welcome place to stay in Portsmouth. In 1659, the town ordered inhabitants not to "entertain" strangers, for in so doing they "shall Secure the towne of all such charges at there one [their own] cost and damadges allsoe." Even so, husbands and goodwives of Portsmouth often fell to the temptation of "entertaining" strangers, particularly if they were family members, relations, or willing to pay well for their lodging. In July 1686, William Seavie, John Kelley, Peter Harvie, John Reed, and a Miss Stucker appeared before the selectmen "to give an acco[t] of there being in Town" and for "entertaining of strangers without Liberty." John Kelley, a husband and father of two children, "was warned by the Selectmen to give securety, for saveing the Town from any charge of himself and wife and children or to depart." John Reed, who had previously been warned out of town, found lodging with William Seavie. The town fined Seavie £40 for "entertaining" Reed for the past year. This was harsh treatment, as fines were generally imposed on a weekly or monthly basis, and at the comparatively small rate of 5 shillings per month. The selectmen demanded that Peter Harvie refrain from housing his sister and her children, which was "contrary to law." She and the children must return to Boston (their previous domicile) "or otherwise to be convaied by the constable from Town to Town till shee com their." When Roger Thomas requested admittance as resident in 1692, the town demanded security, which he did not have, so the constable warned him out of town. Two years later, Arnold Brick and wife were more fortunate. They had a friend in William Richards, who, to secure the town from financial liability, paid a deposit to allow the Brick family to reside in Portsmouth.

For all their good intentions, the inhabitants and selectmen of Portsmouth were losing their bid to prevent the strange and foreign from disrupting their perceived harmony and cohesion. As the population of New England expanded, so did the wealth of towns along the coast and the threat of enemies to the north and west. Immigrants who crossed the Atlantic to America were used to moving from place to place, and not against searching for the right spot to make their fortune. Portsmouth was a thriving seaport with many opportunities in fishing, trade, and shipbuilding. So why shouldn't the young and ambitious want to locate there? A significant reason was war, for conflict engenders mobility and the movement of peoples, many of whom seek the safety of a large town. When war broke out between France and England in 1689 (King William's War), there were raids along the New Hampshire and Maine frontier, and growing fear among the residents of frontier towns. Many fled to the safety of the seacoast. Even though these refugees were often met with a cold and unfriendly reception at Portsmouth, their numbers nevertheless grew, which required the town to rethink its policy toward strangers.

The welfare of the town demanded that all legal residents work for the benefit of the community until they could no longer work, when it became the duty of the town to provide relief for the aged and ill. Most of the residents of seventeenth-century Portsmouth came originally from England, which had a long tradition of towns and parishes caring for the indigent and the deserving poor. A series of laws enacted by Parliament, particularly the Poor Law of 1601 under Elizabeth I, made individual towns and parishes responsible for taking care of the aged and infirmed. The "haves" should care for the "have-nots;" the town served as the agent to fulfill this ideal.

The selectmen determined the taxes to be collected and monies to be dispersed to those requiring and deserving aid. The ongoing challenge was to achieve the community's inherent obligation toward its own at the least expense and trouble to the town and its members. The town chose relatively simple methods to help inhabitants not requiring direct personal care. According to the town records for 1668,"the Selectmen being informed of the povertie of Jos. Atkeson see it meete to remit his [tax] rate of foure shillings." In March 1670, as winter was drawing to a close, the hungry and poor such as "Widdow Sheaves" and her two children, who had "nothing to releive them," received a grant of 37 shillings from the town.

For those who could not care for themselves, the selectmen found inhabitants willing to house, feed, and care for the indigent in return for a stipend. A local landowner and surveyor of highways for the town, Thomas Peverly, was the first inhabitant on record to house and feed the poor, caring for Goodwife Evenes in return for £12 annually. Upon providing Thomas Williams with "his meat, drink, washing, lodging, firing [fuel] and attendance," William Richards received compensation from the town in the amount of 8 shillings per week. Richards was a local man of property who served as the keeper of the town pound in 1680. The town paid physician John Fletcher £5 to provide medical care for Thomas Williams. In 1676, Jennet "the Jarsey woman" and her child were put under the care of one Fry, who received 5 shillings per week in addition to an outright grant of 30 shillings. The next year, the selectmen paid Fry six "Bushels of Maize" in addition to almost £2 in cash. A caregiver such as Fry might receive £10 to £12 per year of which at least £8 were required to sustain the pauper—a profit of £2 to £4. When the selectmen learned "of the very poore and low condition of Goodm[an] Lucomb and his wife," they contacted the children, living and thriving in Boston, for financial assistance, warning them that otherwise the town would sell the elderly couple's land "for this purpose." Mariner Andrew Sampson, a husband and father temporarily lame and out of work, received 20 shillings of aid. John Barsham could apparently care for himself sufficiently, but the town's help of £1 notwithstanding, he was "Lyinge In A Languishing Condisction."

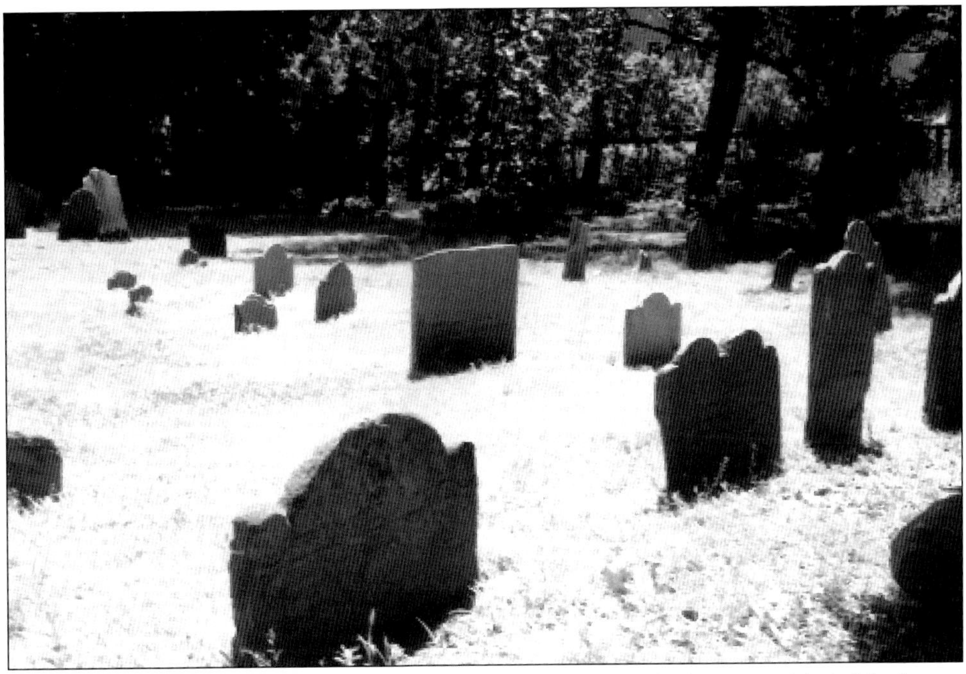

The Point of Graves, situated next to Prescott Park and the harbor, is a delightful place to stroll on a sunny summer day. Some of the earliest settlers of Portsmouth are buried here. (Photo by Benjamin Lawson.)

The Portsmouth town fathers were consistently benevolent in providing aid to the impoverished ill and dying. Daniel Duggins and his wife in 1689 earned £7 caring for Andrew the Dutchman, a resident of Portsmouth for 20 years. William Brooking and his wife agreed in 1692 to take care of the aged and crippled William Champernune for the remainder of his life in return for a complete remission of taxes. Champernune had come to Portsmouth without property, had been warned out, but had stayed, defying the selectmen and constables. The Brookings "entertained" him illegally. Yet compassion apparently overcame the letter of the law in this instance. The selectmen went so far as to grant Champernune "a shurt cloth" in return for his promise "not to trouble the town for two months time."

The town assembly in 1668 directed the selectmen to "take speedy care and course for the supplie of Roger Knight," who was sick and helpless. Knight was one of the original settlers of Strawbery Banke and an employee of Captain John Mason of the Council of New England. In 1633, he and his wife worked at "Pascatawa" under the authority of Thomas Warnerton. He later became a worthy landowner of long standing. Now battered by an unknown illness, the selectmen knew he had done his part for the community and it was time to care for him. This the town did, compensating Thomas Onyon, who became Knight's caregiver, £10 for one year and "Irish cloth, Coarse kersey," two dozen coat buttons, and thread in another year. Onyon was a farmer and property owner who was killed during an Indian raid in 1696 on the Portsmouth Plains.

Old "father Lewes," a former pioneer who worked for Captain Mason at the beginning of Strawbery Banke, was duly cared for by the town for five years, beginning in 1690. Each year a new family nursed the old man as his health declined—the lowest bidder always landing the contract. Goodwife Rowsley earned £12 in 1690, William Masson £10 in 1691, Goodwife Wacker £10 in 1692, and Goodman William Walker, a farmer, the same in 1694. Elishia Bryers, a town carpenter, earned 10 shillings in July 1695 for making "old Lewis['s] Coffin."

As the seventeenth century progressed, the cost of relief for the poor increased. The selectmen were under increasing pressure to balance their accounts and any funds made available were quickly used. In December 1692, the town granted the selectmen power to sell (or lease) any land within the township that is "Lying in Nocks and Corners" to help cover the costs of paying inhabitants to care for the needy. Yet Portsmouth, like other towns in New England and the communities of England before them, refused to relieve the undeserving poor. For decades, the English under the Tudors and Stuarts struggled to stop the tide of idleness and resulting crime that appeared to weaken the productivity and morality of their society. Likewise, New Englanders sought to stop the inactive, the "sturdy beggar," from indolently living upon the hard work of the conscientious and prosperous. In August 1686, when John Reed was brought before the selectmen for loitering and vagrancy, the selectmen ruled that he must bind himself in service to another or face expulsion from the town. Reed apparently responded with industry, as he became a proper, tax-paying resident within two years.

"Blessed are the poor," reads the Gospel of Matthew. If the indigent, deserving or undeserving, found the sturdy goodmen and goodwives of Portsmouth at times unwilling or unable to assist them, perhaps the local parish, the benevolent parson, or pious parishioner would help. Sometimes this was the case, as in 1671 when the fishermen of the Isles of Shoals agreed to contribute funds every Sunday for "the supply of their necessitys of poor, sick, aged and [diseased] or decreped persons." More often, parishioners emphasized the remainder of the Gospel passage, "poor in spirit," assuming that the poverty of humility before God made the material poverty before man more acceptable.

Humility, perseverance, and a willingness to abide by the will of God described Joshua Moody, who ministered to the "poor in spirit," the mariners and fishermen of Portsmouth. A 1653 graduate of Harvard College, Moody was trained like most graduates in the Puritan congregational way. The Puritans of Massachusetts were adherents to the teachings of John Calvin, who had taught his followers to establish independent congregations governed by godly men intent on working in concert with other such congregations to promote God's kingdom on earth. The pragmatic and earthy inhabitants of Portsmouth, however, were inclined toward the Church of England—or not inclined at all.

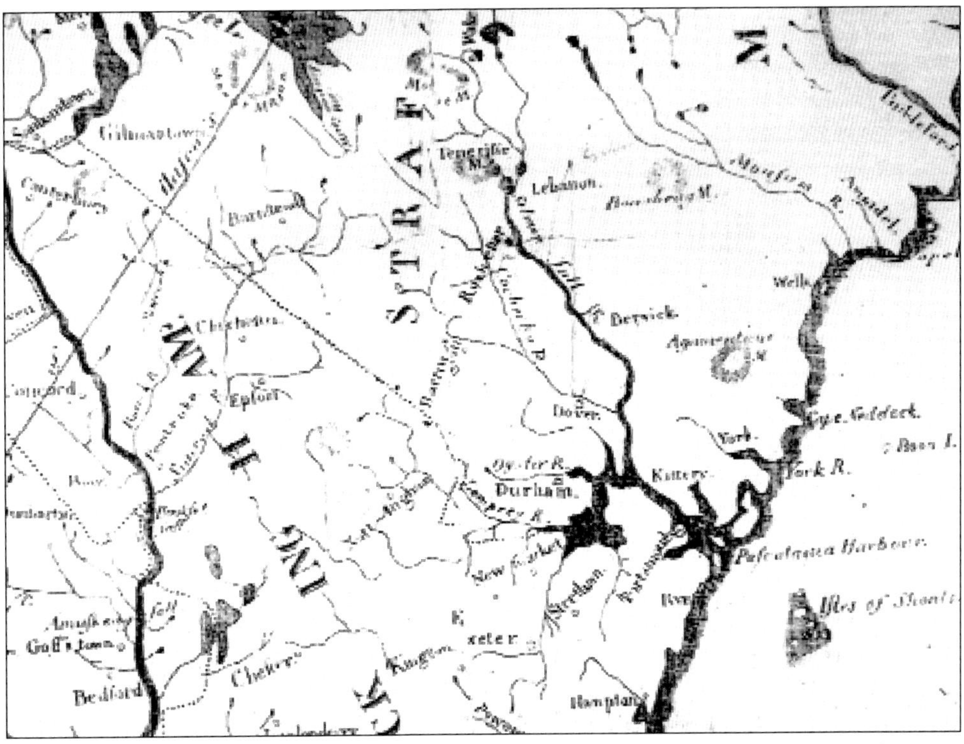

This detail from "A New Map of New Hampshire" appeared in volume two of Jeremy Belknap's History of New Hampshire *in 1791. Belknap served as minister to Dover's First Parish from 1767 to 1786.*

To Puritans like Moody, such Anglicans were perfunctory in their dedication to God's work.

He became something of a missionary in 1658, gathering lost sheep and leading them to the new meetinghouse (built in 1657) on the Lord's Day. Moody was an itinerant, as it were, traveling about between Portsmouth, Greenland, Newcastle, and Little Harbor, yet he resided all the while in the parsonage, the old meetinghouse. Under his watch there was some revival in piety and discipline, and the town passed laws requiring all residents to contribute taxes toward maintaining Moody's mission. Goodmen were appointed to keep children quiet at meetings, and the town strictly prohibited smoking or sleeping on the Lord's Day. Offenders spent a day of redemption in the "cage," a wooden structure similar to a jail, attached to a pillory set outside the meetinghouse. Here residents could scoff and shake their heads while heads of another sort, those of captured wolves, dripping with blood and nailed to the meetinghouse door, taunted the malefactors.

Reverend Moody was not the first parson in Portsmouth. The inhabitants of Strawbery Banke in the 1630s built a chapel and parsonage, which was inhabited for a brief time by the Reverend Richard Gibson, an Anglican. Gibson, whose sympathies toward the Church of England made him unpopular in Boston, was forced out by the Puritan authorities of Massachusetts Bay. In 1642, the fishermen of the Banke found another minister in James Parker, who was a Puritan and thus acceptable to the Massachusetts reformers. This created a minor religious awakening at Strawbery Banke until Parker moved to Barbados. During these early years, the harsh conditions and "very profane" and lax church-goers at the Banke brought only sporadic itinerants rather than stable ministers of the Gospel. Then Joshua Moody arrived.

Joshua Moody was a zealous apostle whose devotion and hard work paid off in the formation of the First Parish of Portsmouth in 1671. The first communicants were leaders of Portsmouth such as Richard Martin, who was a representative to the Massachusetts General Court; Elias Stileman, also a representative; Samuel Haynes, who would serve as Deacon of the First Parish; and the Cutt brothers, Richard and John, who were the most powerful family of seventeenth-century Portsmouth. John and Richard were upon a time fishermen at the Isles of Shoals before moving to Strawbery Banke to become leading merchants and landowners.

In 1680, during a turbulent time of power struggles in New England, as well as in England, John Cutt became president of the new royal province of New Hampshire. Robert Mason, grandson and heir of John Mason, still pursuing his grandfather's dreams of landed-wealth in the New World, found a sympathizer to such aristocratic pretensions in King Charles II. The King, upset with the ongoing obstinacy of the Massachusetts Bay Puritans, who sought to become an independent power in America trading with whomever they wished and worshipping according to conscience, separated New Hampshire from the authority of Massachusetts Bay to create a province under the direction of the Crown. Richard Martyn and Elias Stileman served under President John Cutt as counselors.

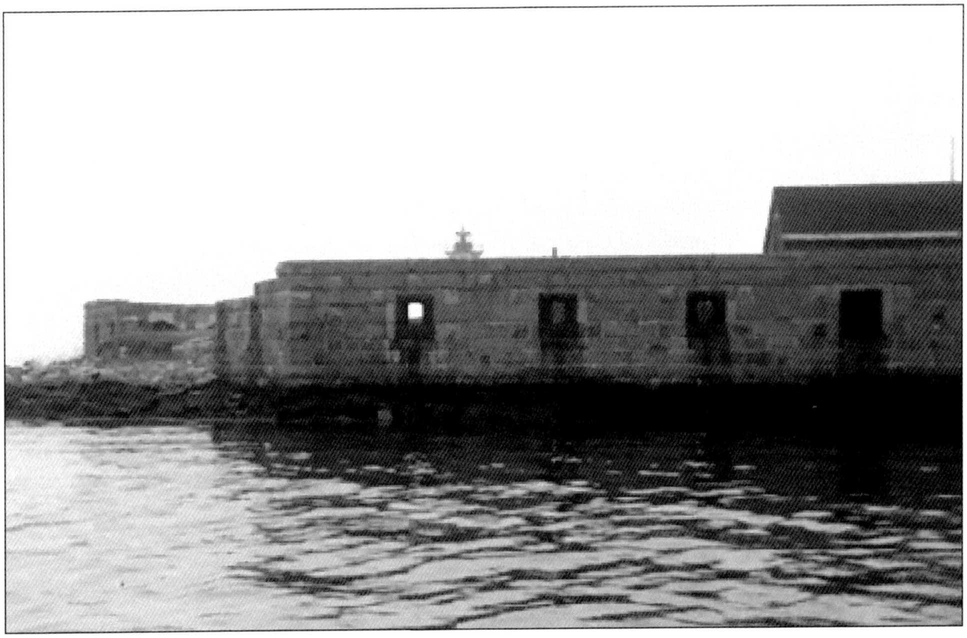

Fort Constitution (Fort William and Mary) guarded the mouth of the Piscataqua against unwelcome enemy ships during several wars. This photograph shows the fort as seen from the water. (Photo by author.)

These men, the elite of Portsmouth, resisted Mason's attempts to wrestle control of his supposed patrimony. Allowed by the King to assume the title Lord Protector, Mason caused havoc for a few months before departing for England in disgust at his failed coup. Edward Randolph, the Collector of Customs sent by the Crown to support Mason and supervise trade, made himself a nuisance, interfering with Cutt's administration by resisting the proclivities toward independence of the inhabitants of Portsmouth. Having died the year before, President Cutt missed the political shenanigans of 1682 when Edward Cranfield arrived as lieutenant governor.

Cranfield was Mason's man, intent on pursuing the erstwhile proprietor's claims to fame and fortune in New Hampshire. He made Walter Barefoote, another royal pawn, commander of the fort on Great Island; he demanded that the inhabitants of Portsmouth pay rent to the proprietor; he ran roughshod over the provincial assembly; he demanded that the rites and order of the Church of England be implemented. All of this raised the ire of Reverend Moody, who began to challenge Cranfield's authority. At one point in 1684, a communicant of the First Parish, George Janvrin, testified in court on a matter of customs, appeared to perjure himself, and arranged with Governor Cranfield to settle the matter behind closed doors. Moody responded by preaching a sermon on the seriousness of breaking the commandment, "Thou shalt not Bear False Witness." At length the parish pressured their fellow communicant Janvrin to express his guilt and ask forgiveness. He was forgiven, but Moody was not. Governor Cranfield decided to make an example of the reverend and the proclivity of the inhabitants to deny the authority of the Crown.

As the representative of the King, hence of the King's Church of England, Cranfield demanded that Reverend Moody cease from the dissenting ways of Puritanism and conform to the sacraments and liturgy as prescribed by the Book of Common Prayer. Moody, of course, could not go against his conscience and he knew what the result would be in refusal. Cranfield brought charges; Moody was convicted and thus sentenced to the gaol on Great Island. He stayed there for 13 weeks before being freed on condition of not serving as a minister in New Hampshire. Reverend Moody reluctantly moved to Boston, where he preached for nine years. Offered the presidency of Harvard College, he refused. In the meantime, the First Parish held together even though they were leaderless; Moody often visited, wrote letters, and otherwise counseled the parishioners to stay true and be patient. In exile, as it were, he consoled himself by writing such sermons as "A Practical Discourse Concerning the Choice Benefit of Communion with God in his House." Eventually Moody was able to return to Portsmouth in 1693 to take charge of the flock. He continued to preach there until his death four years later.

In the intervening years, Charles II died, succeeded in 1686 by James II, who decided to impose a general order on what he considered to be the disorderly New England colonies. The resulting Dominion of New England lasted only a few years. Portsmouth merchants welcomed the Glorious Revolution of 1689 that ousted James and brought William of Orange to the throne as William III. Parliament's assertion of control in respect to the Crown was an example not lost on Portsmouth leaders who were determined, even when New Hampshire was again made an independent royal colony in 1692, to exercise the rights of loyal New Hampshirans in local affairs.

Politics in Europe brought war to the continent—and to New England—between the years 1689 and 1697. The actions of great leaders (Count de Frontenac, governor of Canada, and Sir William Phips, who attempted but failed to conquer Quebec) became legend, and all of Portsmouth knew their stories. Closer to home, daily existence, if not legendary, was terrifying. Algonquin tribes, resenting past abuse, repeatedly raided Maine and New Hampshire towns that caused some deaths, much destruction, and waves of fear. Goodwives felt some reassurance hearing of work at the shipyards as the British 54 gun frigate, the *Faulkland*, was being built, yet that security vanished when news arrived of the destruction of York, 30 miles up the coast in Maine. The French and Indian raiders generally attacked frontier settlements, such as at Oyster River (Durham), Lamprey River (Newmarket), Dover on the Cocheco River, and Salmon Falls. The Native Americans also managed to launch an attack on Sandy Beach (Rye) in September 1692, killing and capturing 21 people. War always brings suffering to the innocent, an example of which was the smallpox epidemic that spread throughout Portsmouth during the same year. Crowded conditions and illness aggravated the already increasing numbers of poor and town dependents.

Even during war, people attempted some degree of normalcy. Inhabitants of Great Island were incorporated into the town of Newcastle and charged with the responsibility of maintaining the defense of the harbor. In the same year, 1693, Portsmouth hosted the new provincial post office. Residents refused to allow war to disrupt their preoccupation with wealth and status. In April of that year, the town charged the selectmen with organizing and assigning pews in the meetinghouse according to prestige, wealth, family, and status. Men, women, and children were segregated and only the most powerful males obtained seats near the pulpit. Those of importance, such as selectmen Captain Walter Neal and Mr. Richard Martin, sat in "the front seat before the Minister" Joshua Moody. Mrs. Martin was honored with the front position in the women's pews next to Mrs. Moody. Each man and woman received precise assignments as to the row in the front gallery, the side gallery, and the seats "below stairs." "The room over the women's staires" was for

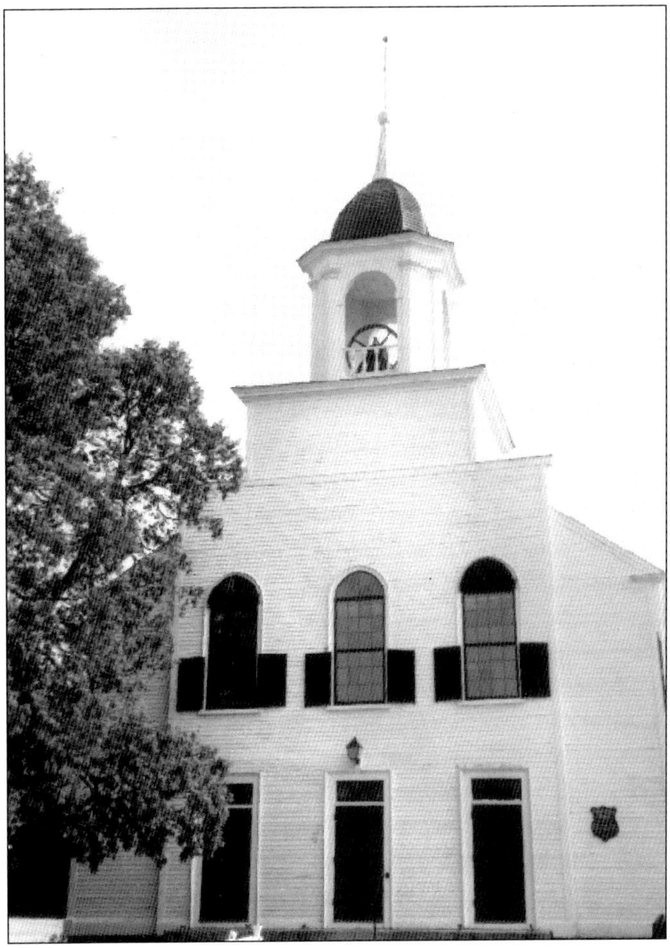

Once known as Great Island, Newcastle was an important fishing center during the seventeenth century. This photo (by Benjamin Lawson) is of the First Parish at Newcastle.

widows and wives of "mechanics" and other laboring types. "The 5th seat being the back seat is left for young persons about 14 years of age, unmarried." Those attempting to sit out of order received heavy fines.

The widow (and second wife) of former president John Cutt, Ursula Cutt, sat in the first row "in the Women's seat in the Gallery"; this was quite a drop in seating (and status) from 15 years prior. Mrs. Cutt lived just outside of town, up the Piscataqua on a fine farm; she still worked the fields in the morning and entertained in the afternoon at dinner. One summer morning, Mrs. Cutt was expecting Colonel Richard Waldron and family for dinner. The colonel was a provincial counselor and scion of one of the oldest and most respected families of the Piscataqua Valley. Recent native attacks had convinced many farmers to retreat to town for protection, but Mrs. Cutt was determined to finish mowing the hay with her paid laborers before the morning was out. Waldron, his wife, and child, were stopped on the road and warned of impending danger and decided not to make the dinner date with Mrs. Cutt. While eating at another friend's house they heard the dreadful news that Indians had attacked the Cutt farm, killing Mrs. Cutt and her three workers.

Two years later another disaster occurred at Portsmouth, this time downriver. Indian attackers beached their canoes at Sandy Beach, then proceeded to Little Harbor, near Pannaway (Odiorne's Point), where they attacked and killed 14 unsuspecting farmers. The militia, led by Captain William Shackford, pursued the attackers south to Breakfast Hill, but they retreated down the hill (by *rolling*, not running) and escaped to their canoes. Captain Gerrish led several small boats to blockade the canoes as they attempted escape north up the coast under cover of darkness, yet the Indians outmaneuvered the colonials, paddling out and around the Isles of Shoals to York, Maine.

The following year, in 1697, brought news that the French planned on sending an armada of ships down the coast to the Piscataqua. The inhabitants prepared for the worst, only to find that the attacking expedition never materialized. Fortunately the Peace of Ryswick ended King William's War, bringing a temporary end to such terror.

Domestic politics of the 1690s were not terrorizing, merely uncertain. The heirs of Captain Mason continued to seek profit from rents and to control lands along the Piscataqua, especially at Portsmouth. Robert Mason's heirs sold their interest to Samuel Allen, a London merchant, who proceeded to act upon his claim for power in Portsmouth. His protégé John Usher became Lieutenant Governor, and used the executive office to work for his own and Allen's interest. The inhabitants of Portsmouth finally decided to take matters into their own hands, persuading William Partridge, "a native of Portsmouth, a shipwright, of an extraordinary mechanical genius, of a politic turn of mind," to go behind Usher's back to London; in 1696 Partridge was successful in having himself named Lieutenant Governor. This mess was not resolved until the Earl of Bellomont arrived in America to take charge as governor of New York, Massachusetts, and New Hampshire.

At century's end, the inhabitants of Portsmouth lived in a town of several thousand residents that was quickly coming to be the dominant port north of Boston. A new minister, Nathaniel Rogers, watched over the parishioners of the town. Leading merchants and statesmen such as John Pickering, William Vaughan, and William Partridge worked for the people's interest against those who sought to keep New Hampshire dependent upon the lords and ladies of England. The township of Portsmouth was not so big as it was 50 years earlier as Sandy Beach, Little Harbor, and Newcastle were combined to create a separate parish. Other such changes were on the horizon. Also on the horizon was the shimmering blue-green sea at sundown, when peace reigns over the land and quiet slumber becomes the watchword for the night.

3. The Portsmouth Poor

The tallest height along the coast in the vicinity of the Piscataqua River is Mount Agamenticus, which is but a small hill, though from its peak on clear days one can see an unforgettable panorama, indeed "a most enchanting prospect." Jeremy Belknap, pastor of Dover's First Parish, frequent visitor to and occasional resident of Portsmouth, climbed Mount Agamenticus and observed the following:

> the cultivated parts of the country, especially on the south and south-west, appears as a beautiful garden, intersected by the majestic river Piscataqua, its bays and branches. The immense ranges of mountains on the north and northwest afford a sublime spectacle; and on the sea-side the various indentings of the coast from Cape Ann to Cape Elizabeth are plainly in view in a clear day; and the wide Atlantick stretches to the east as far as the power of vision extends.

This eighteenth-century description is applicable for today's adventurous mountaineer. Notwithstanding the development of almost four centuries, the Piscataqua still dominates the region. The forests still grow close to the shore and tidal currents are still quick and perplexing. From Agamenticus one sees that the seashore is altogether dramatic, a great arching bow extending from cape to cape, and the bright blue of the Atlantic reflects the sun as far as one can behold, spotted briefly by the Isles of Shoals. One can follow the river's path upstream to the west, see the great divide caused by Hilton's Point, watch as the waters of the Cocheco and Salmon Falls flow from the north, and from the south the Great Bay, Oyster, Lamprey, and Squamscot. The view inland has changed very little over the course of 300 years with the New Hampshire landscape pockmarked with hills and valleys, and further to the north great snow-covered peaks—the White Mountains—dominate the horizon.

The view from Mount Agamenticus affords a vision into the past; one sees Bloody Point on the Piscataqua, across from Dover Point, and the town of Newington. This small pastoral hamlet was once part of the township of Portsmouth until it separated to become a distinct town in 1727. South of Portsmouth, amid the deep verdure of the forest, lies Greenland, a beautiful

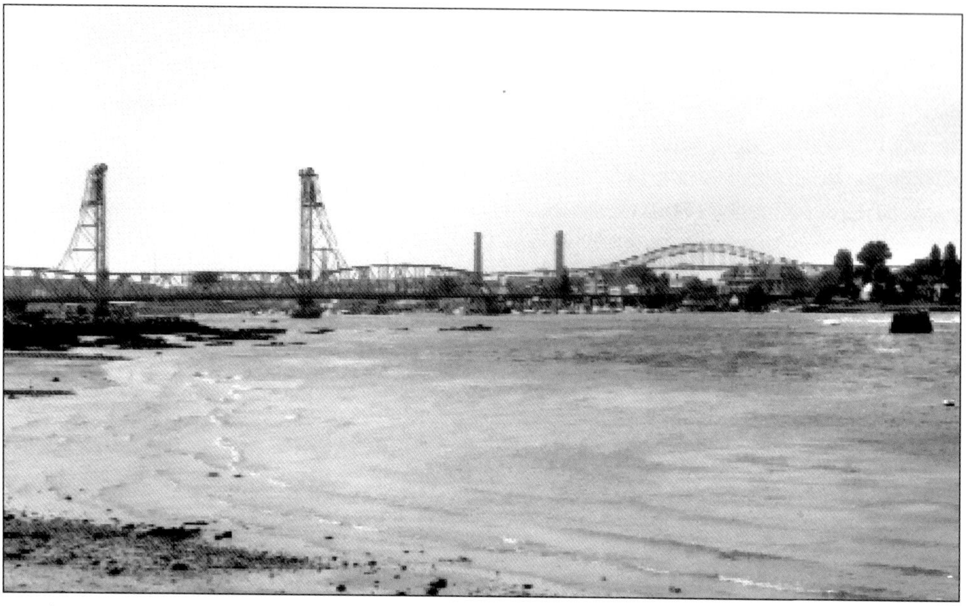

Modern steel bridges span the Piscataqua connecting Portsmouth with Kittery, Maine. The first bridges crossing the river were built of wood in the 1790s. (Photo by Benjamin Lawson.)

image of the pastoral that has been independent of Portsmouth since 1706. At the easternmost tip of Newcastle, one sees the remains of Fort Constitution, once known as Fort William and Mary. At this site, various fortifications have defended the mouth of the Piscataqua, and Portsmouth harbor, since the initial settlements of the early 1600s.

Some obstructions today, the products of modern industry, disrupt the viewer's enjoyment. Great smokestacks from factories that have long been silent rise from the towns of Dover and Newmarket. One can catch a glimpse of the gray and red buildings of the University of New Hampshire at Durham peaking behind the wall of white pines. Huge metallic extension bridges cross the Piscataqua from Portsmouth to Kittery. Tall spires climb above other buildings in these towns at the river's mouth. Several church spires point to the soul of Portsmouth, the perfect example being the steeple of the North Church, which competes with the masts of tall ships for dominance over the horizon. Located at Market Square, the North Church is today at the center of a busy movement of automobiles and people. The present structure as well as its earlier manifestation have enjoyed this preeminent position for close to 300 years, but the North Church was not the first church of colonial Portsmouth. In fact, in 1712 the North Parish was a newcomer, challenging the location and importance of the original religious community at what would in time be called the South Parish.

Joshua Moody's meetinghouse was situated south of Puddle Dock and the busy wharves of Strawbery Banke. Any pedestrian can reach the vicinity by following the narrow and winding Marcy Street, which is a delightful place to stroll in the warm afternoons of summer. The feel of the past is everywhere amid the old brightly colored houses once inhabited by fishmongers and captains. Moody's meetinghouse was just below the bridge crossing the South Mill Pond. After Moody's death, the Reverend Nathaniel Rogers accepted the call of the parish in 1697, agreeing to the terms of use of the parsonage and glebe land as well as an annual salary of £100. He was not ordained until 1699, when he was 30 years old. The Reverend William Hubbard, author of the well-known *General History of New England*, preached the ordination sermon. Nathaniel, the son of John Rogers, president of Harvard College, graduated from the school in 1687. Nathaniel and Sarah Purkiss Rogers and their two young children set up housekeeping in the old parsonage. This was apparently an old ramshackle of a house, for five years later it caught fire, destroying the house and killing Sarah's mother, the family's black servant, and their 17-month-old daughter Elizabeth. The *Boston News-Letter* (as quoted in Glen Knoblock, *Historical Burial Grounds of the New Hampshire Seacoast*, 29) published the following account of the tragic fire:

> Piscataqua, Novemb 2. On Monday the 30 [of October] about break of day, the House of the Reverend Mr. Nathaniel Rogers, Minister of Portsmouth, was burnt to the Ground in a few minutes, his youngest Child, and a Negro Woman of Mrs. Elatsons, his Mother-in-law, consumed in the Flames, nothing saved but himself, his Wife, Mother-in-Law, two Children, and the Servant-Maid, as they got out of Bed

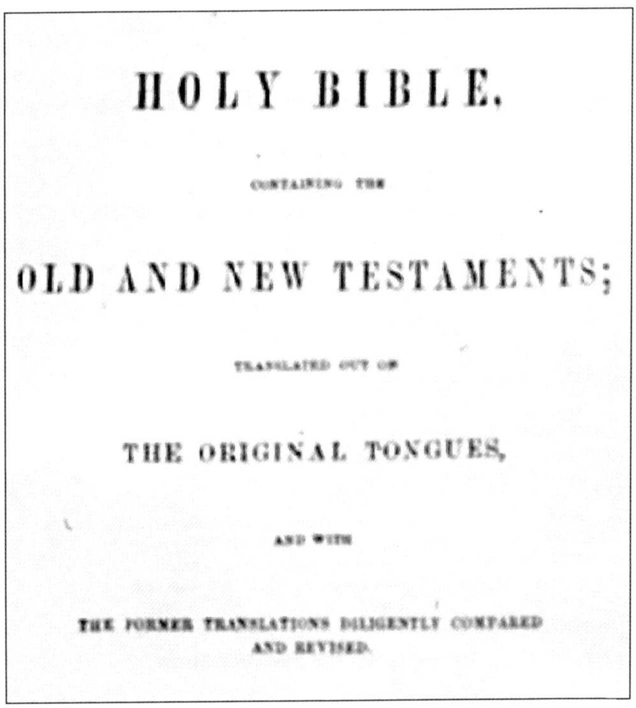
HOLY BIBLE,

CONTAINING THE

OLD AND NEW TESTAMENTS;

TRANSLATED OUT OF

THE ORIGINAL TONGUES,

AND WITH

THE FORMER TRANSLATIONS DILIGENTLY COMPARED
AND REVISED.

This Holy Bible was the book that graced Portsmouth congregational churches, published in 1862 by the American Bible Society.

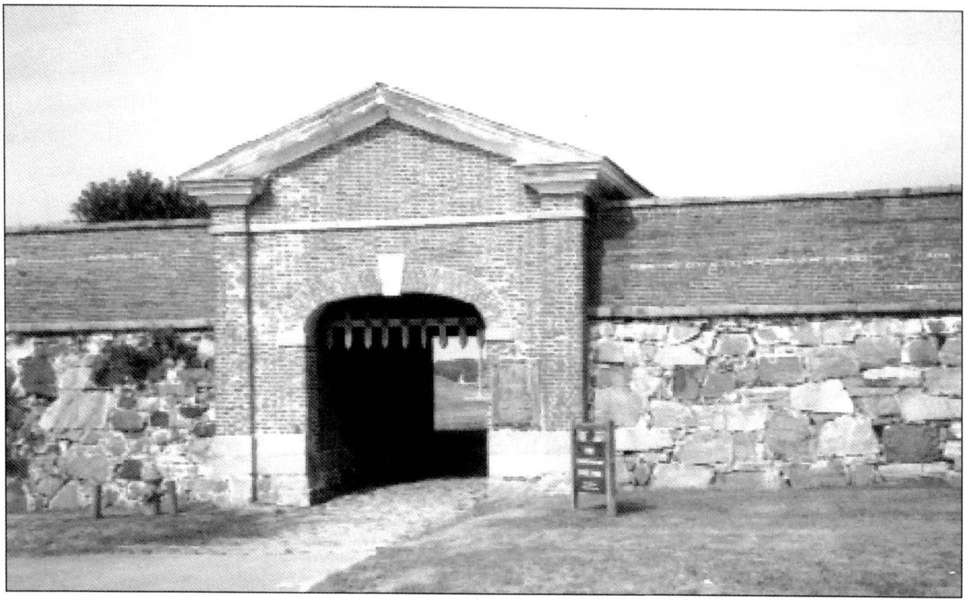

The massive front gate at Fort Constitution has a medieval look to it. The visitor today must negotiate a winding path to the fort, which is now part of a U.S. Coast Guard facility. (Photo by Benjamin Lawson.)

> without Cloaths; Mrs. Elatson saved the elder Child by throwing him out of a Chamber Window into his Fathers Arms, and immediately thereafter Mr. Rogers got a Ladder for his Mother-in-law, and so got her out of the Window, who is much burned in her Legs & Arms but think not dangerous to life. None can tell how the Fire came, most probably it began in their Kitchen; the Fire was so violent by reason of the high Wind, that had there been never so many People to quench it, and help to save the Goods, 'twere impossible to save anything.

Two of the three killed in the fire, the grandmother and the infant, were buried nearby at the Point of Graves.

The town built a new parsonage, which pastor and wife occupied in 1705. At this point in Portsmouth's development, town leaders decided to divide the acreage of the glebe land into sections that would include a new meetinghouse, a courthouse, and an "Allmes howse." The town based the latter decision on rising costs of paying residents to care for the poor and disabled. The reality of a growing population of refugees and strangers that would inevitably lead to an increasing number of dependents, young and old, converted any thoughts of benevolent community care and charity into a much more cold, administrative mentality. Young John Atkinson was one of the first to feel the impact of the town's new approach to poor relief in 1706. The infant, orphaned and unable to care for himself, was bound to Thomas Packer until he reached his majority when he turned 21. The next year, Richard

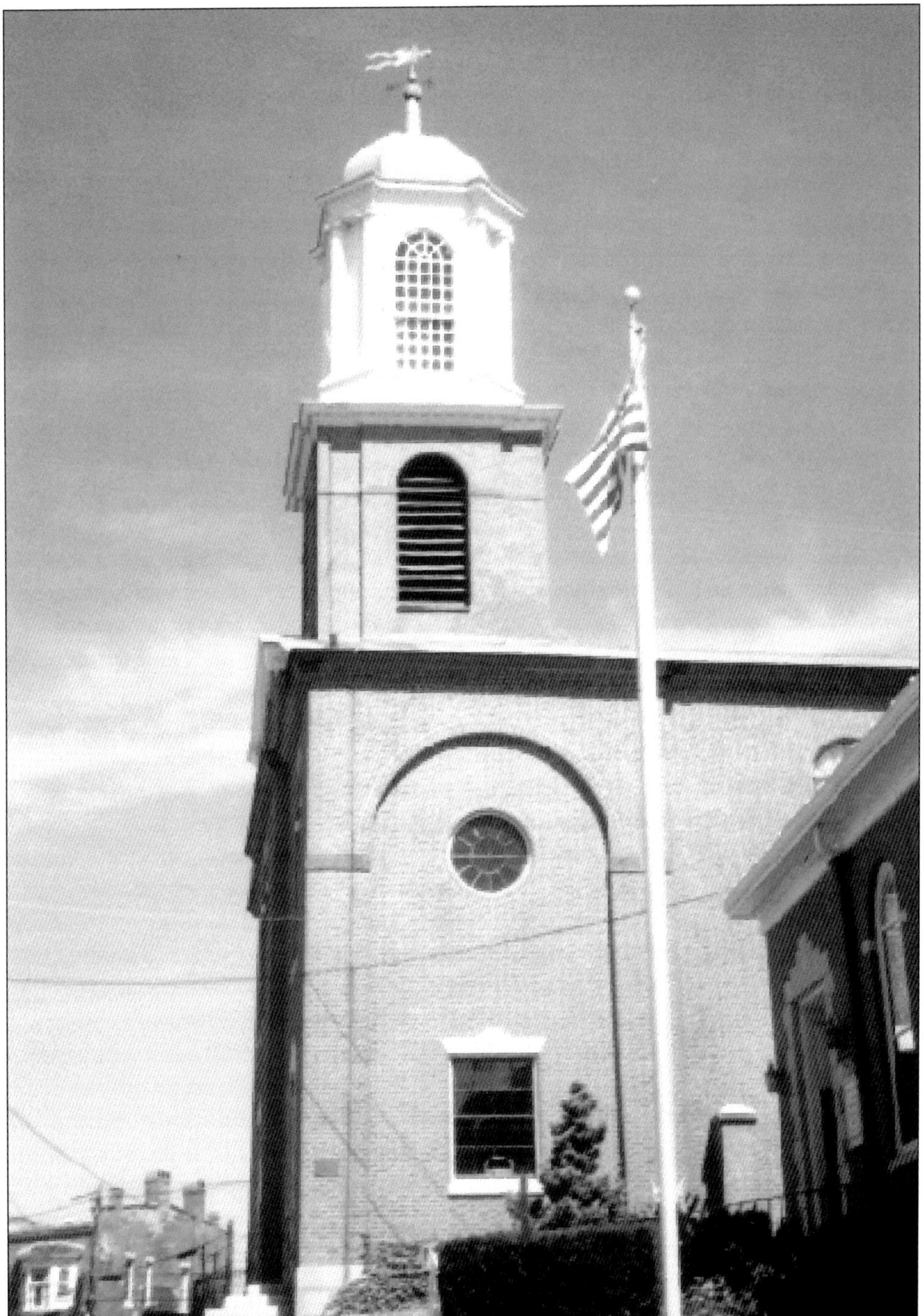

St. John's Episcopal Church sits on an eminence next to Portsmouth harbor. Its imposing steeple can be seen from many points on the New Hampshire as well as the Maine side of the Piscataqua. (Photo by Benjamin Lawson.)

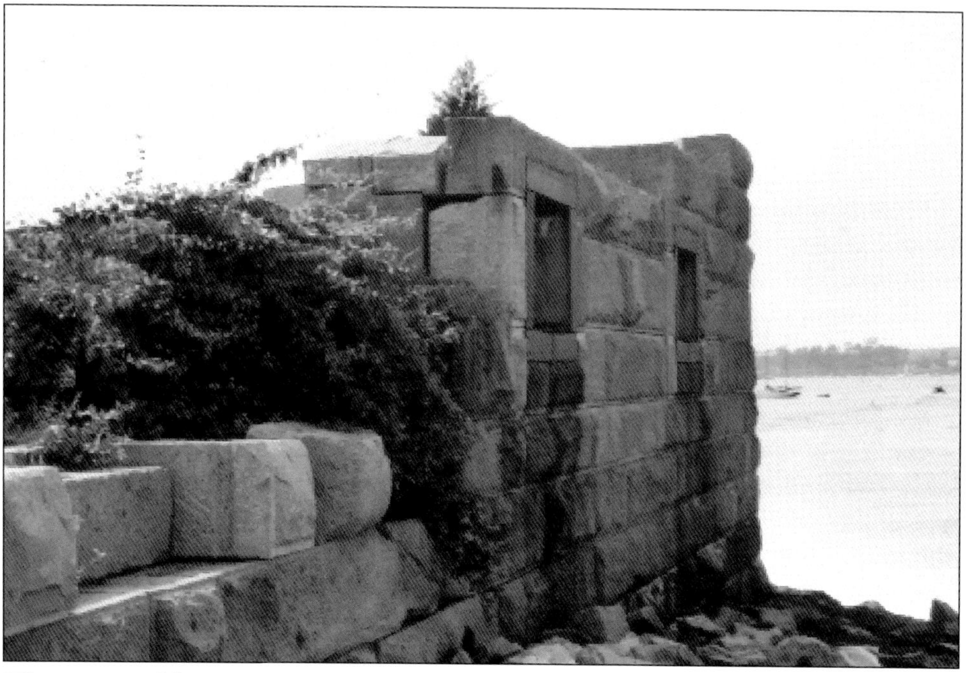

The remains of the granite outer wall at Fort Constitution reveal the age of the fort. This wall dates from the early 1800s. (Photo by Benjamin Lawson.)

Davis felt the warm hand of charity vanish during an icy town meeting. Davis and his dying wife had been granted clothing and food during her final illness, but once she died Davis was ordered to reimburse the town promptly "or to chuse his master with whome to live til such money be paid."

Caring for the poor was simply costing the town too much; for example, it was £17 annually for several years to care for Roger Andrews. Eventually in 1709, the town voted to pay £6 "to procure Andrews a passage out of the County." It is not clear from the records whether this was his desire or not. When the town ordered the selectmen to supervise the construction of an almshouse in April 1711, it was thought to be a financially responsible decision. The almshouse was an institution to bring together food, shelter, supervision, and the poor under one administrative unit.

Such an institution was consistent with English and provincial law and custom. As early as 1581, Queen Elizabeth's government established "houses of correction" to work the idle poor. King James II instructed provincial governors to advise towns to build public institutions "for the Imploying of poor and Indigent People." Boston opened its first almshouse in 1685. New Hampshire towns received instructions to levy taxes in preparation of building an almshouse and to appoint overseers of the poor to supervise relief, deciding who was in need and whether or not their poverty was due to circumstances beyond their control or their own idleness and depravity.

Puritan ministers, putting an original twist on the words of Jesus in the Gospels, declared poverty to be the product of sin and something abnormal that people should be heartily disgusted about. Cotton Mather, the great Puritan philosopher of Boston, declared that idleness was "a sin against God himself." "Our Lord Jesus Christ himself hath expressly forbidden us to countenance" idleness. Diligence was in direct contrast to indigence, the Puritans believed.

The Reverend Charles Burroughs, rector of the Episcopal St. John's Church of Portsmouth, showed in his 1835 tract, *Discourse Delivered in the Chapel of the New Almshouse, in Portsmouth New Hampshire*, that Mather's ideas expressed for generations to come the moral stance of congregational churches toward the poor. Burroughs recalled that the early settlers of Strawbery Banke desired "to secure a good state of society, encourage active employment, prevent poverty." Yet as the town grew during the seventeenth century, town leaders "began to see the importance of employing the paupers in some useful labor." New England towns assumed that every member of the community must contribute to the whole. This organic view of town life would disintegrate should any of the inhabitants become willingly dependent upon others. This idea was, once again, English in origin. Josiah Gee argued in *The Trade and Navigation of Great Britain Considered* (1729) that working the poor in "profitable works and manufactures . . . would enrich the kingdom . . . by enlarging our trade, and supplying foreign markets with our

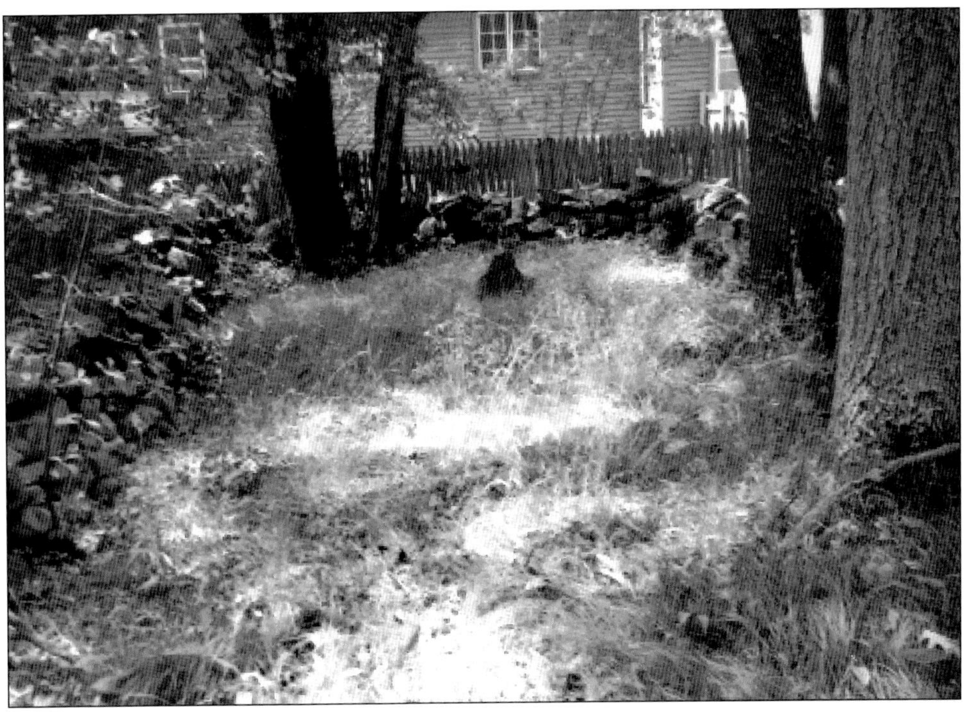

The Old Negro Burial Ground is tucked away behind the parsonage at Christ Episcopal Church. Anonymous headstones mark about a half dozen graves. (Photo by author.)

woolen goods and other products of the nation." "One who indulges himself in idleness and play," Reverend Jeremy Belknap preached, "is stigmatised according to his demerit."

Poverty in colonial New England was considered not only morally wrong, but also at times a criminal action deserving imprisonment. In 1679, the New Hampshire provincial assembly declared that those imprisoned in the provincial gaol for debt should not be allowed by the keeper "to go without the precincts of the prison." Provincial authorities typically turned a deaf ear to petitions from imprisoned debtors for relief for themselves and their families. Walter Hull in 1716, writing from the province gaol in Portsmouth, begged for the assembly's mercy. Hull had been in debtor's prison for four years, unable to work, "and not haveing one farthing In this world wherewith to pay" his debts, "nor wherewithall to Subsist my Self, my wife, and three young Children who Cry for Bread."

The almshouse, when it opened in 1716, was designed for such situations as Walter Hull's. The town showed mercy to Goodwife Hull and her children, as well as to countless other widows, orphans, destitute, ignorant, and mentally and physically disabled; there was sufficient bread in the almshouse to curb their hunger. It was the town's responsibility to care for the sick, aged, and disabled. The almshouse, it was hoped, would henceforth do so in an economical, efficient way. All able-bodied poor were to work for their food and shelter, staying true to the philosophy that the good of the town came before the needs of the individual. And only through useful employment could a person achieve what man required and God desired.

The goodmen of Portsmouth believed that employing the able-bodied poor would reduce the town's financial burden, keep the destitute busy with appropriate tasks, and reform them from their wasteful, sinful habits. The almshouse encouraged thrift in individuals and the community as a whole. Why spend time hiring individuals to care for others in their own homes when an institution existed with beds and food to house all of the poor at one time? Individual relief typically cost £10 or more and the town estimated the cost of care at the almshouse to be £8 per person. The savings derived in part from paring the number of caregivers down to one, the keeper of the almshouse. The first such keeper was Rebecca Austin, who kept the job for 34 years.

The almshouse was just down the road from the new North Parish meetinghouse built between 1712 and 1713; both structures occupied glebe land. The growth of Portsmouth's population necessitated a new meetinghouse because the limited seating at the old South Parish had resulted in disorderly town and church meetings. Established residents complained in 1706 that newcomers were proposing to relocate the meetinghouse, which was contrary "to all reson Justis and Equitey In the world." The number of people living at the North End of town near the North Mill Pond were slowly eclipsing those at the South End. Captain John Pickering, the recognized leader of the south-enders, took charge as moderator of the town meeting on September 9, 1713. "A great tumult" ensued when Pickering pushed through certain measures:

> such as, that the old meeting house shall continue town meeting house forever, and, when too much decayed with age to be repaired, that a new one shall be erected in its place; that the glebe land formerly given by the town for the use of the ministry shall wholly remain to the benefit of the minister, who shall officiate in said house; that a committee shall wait upon Mr. Rogers to see if it be his pleasure to continue preaching at the old meeting house, during his abode in the town, if not, that the said committee shall provide an able minister, for the said place of worship, and agree with him for his salary, which agreement, so made, shall be ratified and fulfilled by the town.

The split and subsequent bad feelings continued. While Reverend Rogers became pastor of the new meetinghouse at what is today Market Square, the angry south-enders called upon the Reverend John Emerson, former pastor of the parish at Newcastle. Emerson was installed at the South Parish in 1715 over the objections of the selectmen and the north-enders. Reverend Rogers was, like Emerson, a graduate of Harvard College (1689), and was a native of Ipswich, Massachusetts. He served as pastor of the South Parish until his death in 1731. He was especially successful at gaining new converts in October 1727 during a time of anxiety caused by a violent earthquake that shook the earth on the evening of October 29. Residents recalled later:

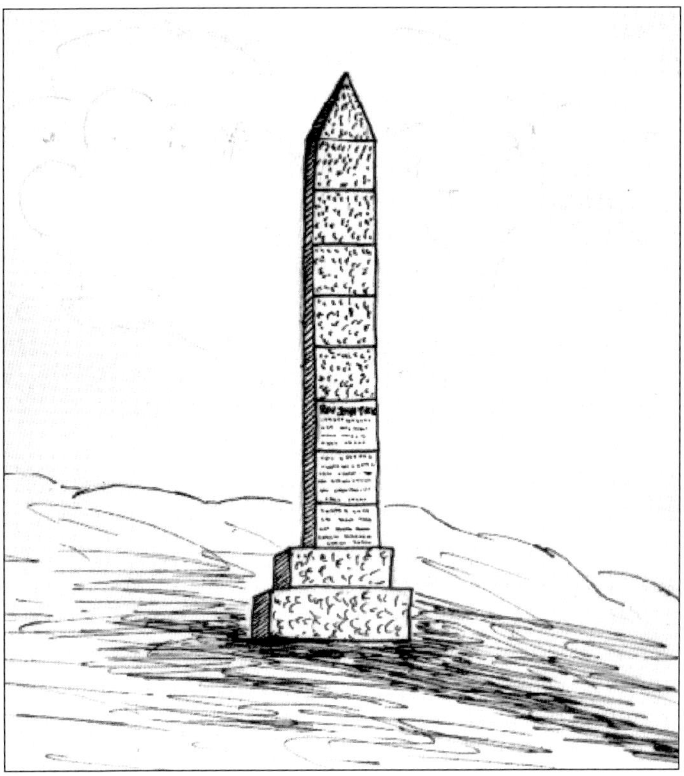

This stone obelisk was erected in 1914 on Star Island, Isles of Shoals, in honor of the Reverend John Tucke. Reverend Tucke served as pastor of the Gosport parish from 1732 to 1773. (Sketch by Benjamin Lawson.)

> it was preceded by considerable noise, resembling distant thunder. Some persons perceived flashes of light at the moment the trembling commenced. The sea was affected as well as the land, and roared in an unusual manner.

After Reverend Emerson's death, a new South Parish meetinghouse was built up the road along Marcy Street on a small rise looking down upon the Point of Graves. This building, since known as the Old South Meetinghouse, is today the Portsmouth Children's Museum. Over a century ago, it served as the first African-American meetinghouse in Portsmouth. In 1732, it became the parish of William Shurtleff, who replaced Reverend Emerson at Newcastle in 1712, as he did 20 years later. Shurtleff, who graduated from Harvard in 1707, served the South Parish until his death in 1747.

In 1723, on the other end, Reverend Rogers passed away and rests to this day at Point of Graves. The Reverend Jabez Fitch, native of Connecticut and graduate of Harvard, left his position at the Ipswich, Massachusetts parish because of a salary dispute, and migrated north to Portsmouth to assume the pastoral post at the North Parish. Reverend Fitch was well-educated, a thinker, and a historian. He preached a fascinating sermon at the ordination of the Reverend John Tucke at Gosport, Isles of Shoals, in 1732. Tucke was himself a historian, scientist, and in the words of Reverend Fitch, a "fisher of men." Reverend Tucke served the fishermen and fishwives of Gosport ("God's Port"), Star Island, for 40 years, but was not the first to preach at the Shoals. Theophilus Cotton was an itinerant for over 20 years there before his death in 1726. In Portsmouth, the Puritan Congregational way dominated the religious associations until 1732 when members of the Church of England, the Anglican Church, organized an Episcopal parish at Portsmouth. They chose a beautiful site next to the harbor on Bow Street; the new Queen's Chapel was constructed on a small eminence. Their first ordained vicar was the Reverend Arthur Browne, a native of Ireland, who served Portsmouth Episcopalians for 40 years.

Browne arrived at Portsmouth in 1736 at a time of sorrow when a terrible plague spread throughout New Hampshire and Maine and afflicted the most vulnerable, particularly children. Called the "throat distemper" by contemporaries, it raged for almost two years from 1735 to 1736—and made frequent reappearances in subsequent years as well. Jeremy Belknap, whose own children eventually suffered from the ailment, described it as "a swelled throat, with white or ash-colored specks, an efflorescence on the skin, great debility of the whole system, and a strong tendency to putridity." Reverend Fitch of North Parish, who kept a "bill of mortality" of the disease, catalogued 99 deaths in Portsmouth, 81 of whom were children under the age of ten. Hampton Falls to the south lost an incredible 160 children of the same age. Belknap heard stories from aged survivors a generation later:

> The most who died of this pestilence, were children; and the distress, which it occasioned, was heightened to the most poignant degree. From three to six children were lost out of some families. Several buried four in a day, and many lost their all. In some towns, one in three, and in others one in four of the sick were carried off.

The graveyard wanderer of today sees simple, sobering reminders of the pathos of this time in the history of the Piscataqua Valley. Besides the headstones and dates of births and deaths registering terribly short lives are the brevity of the epitaphs. One reads in them the hurried moments between disasters—the death of one child followed by the death of another. Mary Stephenson's stone has the full accounting of name and date, even simple decorations. But it is rustic, homemade, and quickly assembled. The same Stephenson family of Durham buried another child only a few months earlier. Thomas, the father, could only carve crude letters and numbers into the headstone—the child's initials and the simple duration of life:

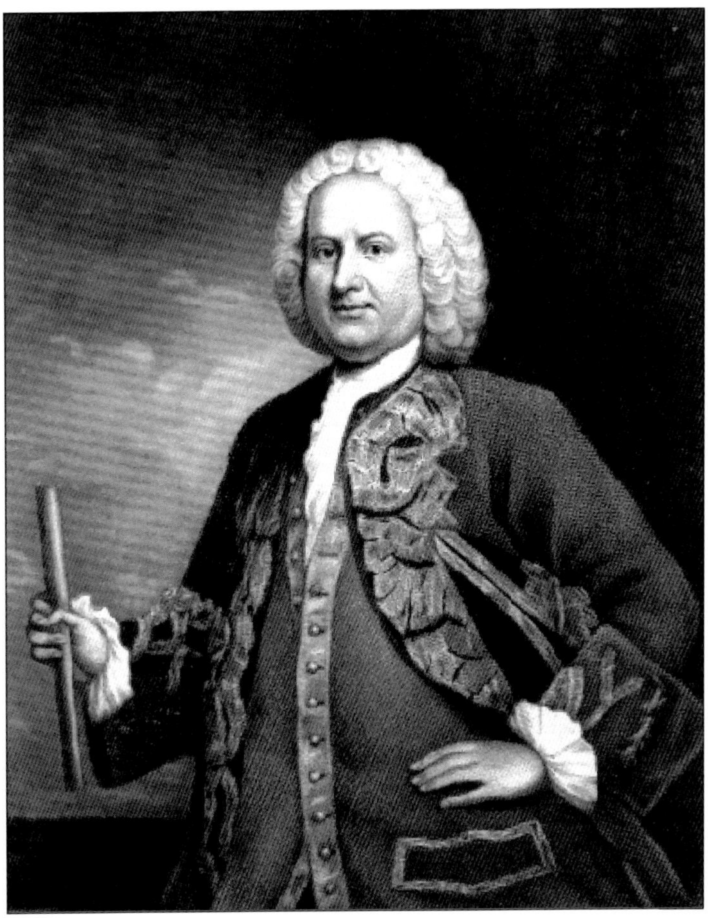

Sir William Pepperrell led New Hampshire soldiers to capture the French fortress of Louisburg during King George's War. The Treaty of Aix-la-Chapelle ending the war in 1748 returned the fortress to the French. (From Usher Parsons' Life of Sir William Pepperrell.*)*

B.S.
B: FEB: 10: 1721
D: NO: 3: 1735

Queen's Chapel hosted some of the leading eighteenth-century New Hampshire families, not the least of whom were the Wentworths. John Wentworth, a ship's captain, demanded piety and faithful religious observances from all who sailed under him. By industry and thrift, he became quite a wealthy merchant. He served Governor Joseph Dudley's council, and when Samuel Shute replaced Dudley as governor, Wentworth was elevated to lieutenant governor. Queen Anne, like her predecessor King William, appointed royal governors with authority over both Massachusetts and New Hampshire; Shute was rarely in the province, so Wentworth was the sitting chief executive of New Hampshire. His tenure (1717–1730) was a difficult one, encompassing Dummer's War—a war fought for several years on the New Hampshire and Maine frontiers against the French and their Algonquin allies—and the political machinations of jealous politicians hungering for power. Yet Portsmouth prospered under Wentworth, in part because he supported Piscataqua merchants such as Archibald MacPhaedris, William Pepperrell (of Kittery), John Rindge, and Richard Wibird. These men made fortunes trading fish, lumber, and naval stores to Spain, the Caribbean, Newfoundland, and the southern colonies, and shipping white pine masts to England. Merchants, such as William Pepperrell, owned large fleets of sloops, ketches, brigantines, and schooners—built by Piscataqua shipbuilders at Portsmouth and Kittery, but especially upriver, near the source of lumber at Dover, Durham, Newmarket, and Exeter.

The Piscataqua has long been accommodating to the dreamer, as Nathaniel Hawthorne and Thomas Bailey Aldrich discovered. Young lads envisioning themselves captaining a ship at sea spent many hours at the wharves and shipyards observing, asking questions, and imagining. Sometimes the dreams became reality, as in the case of Mathias Hains, a young teenage boy in 1729 who yearned to become a mariner. His father agreed, found John Cate to teach Mathias, and bound the boy to Cate as his apprentice until Mathias became a man. August 13, 1729 was no doubt a solemn and dramatic day for young Mathias Hains, as quoted in William Saltonstall's *Ports of Piscataqua*, 29:

> I Mathias Hains of Portsmouth in the Province of New Hampshire, by the consent of father, Hath put himself [an] apprentice to John Cate marriner . . . to learn his art trade or mystery and with him . . . after the manner of an apprentice to serve [him] for and during the term of seven years. . . . And the said master shall teach the said Apprentice to read, writ & Cypher, [and] . . . Instruct him in the Art, Trade or Calling of a marriner . . . (if the said apprentice be capable to learn) and to find [him] good and sufficient Meat, Drink, washin[g], & Lodging during the said term: and at the expiration thereof to give unto the said

apprentice two suits of apparrell ye one for Sunday and the other for working Dayes.

Apprenticeship was an important institution for educating young men to be craftsmen and tradesmen in early America. It also helped families with too many mouths to feed and not enough room to share to have a growing boy learn to become a productive member of society. Apprenticeship was one of several types of servitude in colonial America. As the Portsmouth town records reveal, before 1716 those who were able-bodied yet destitute had two choices: to move on to another town that would be as unaccommodating as Portsmouth to the wandering, "sturdy beggar"; or to bind himself out to another, a master, for a term of years of labor in return for shelter and food.

Before the Industrial Revolution of the nineteenth century, wage-earning was sufficiently rare that the colonial American (and English) economy tended to be oriented around individual entrepreneurship and proprietorship—independent businessmen who owned their own shops, stores, boats, or typically farms. The

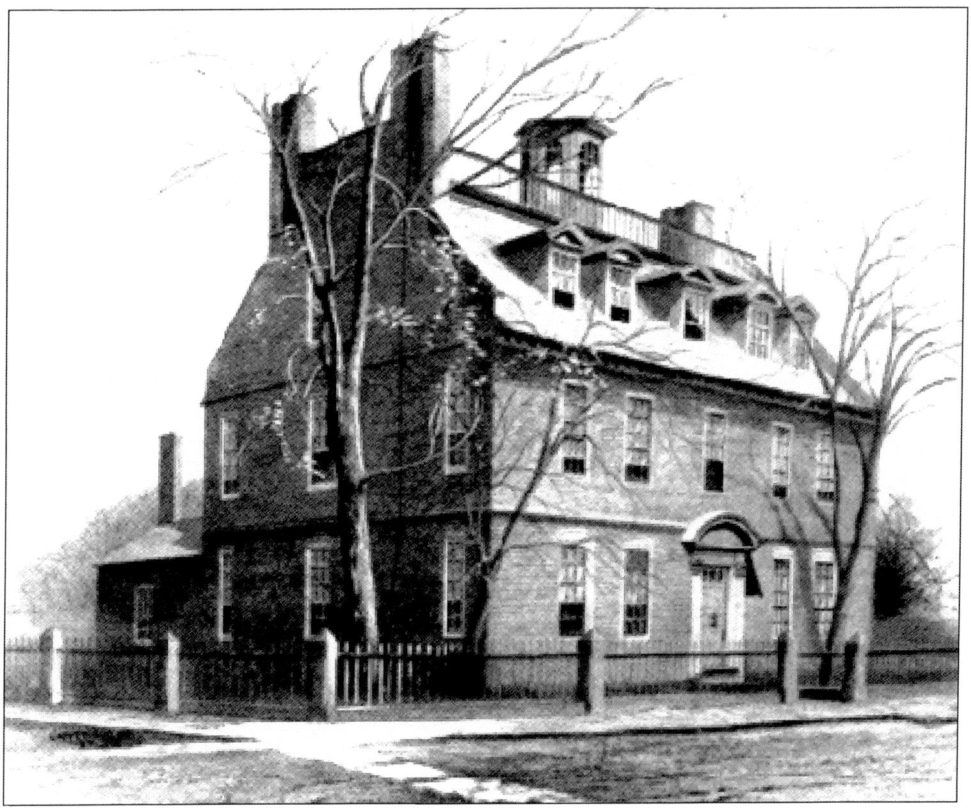

The Warner House was built by Captain Archibald Macphaedris from 1718 to 1723. His daughter married Colonel Jonathan Warner, for whom the house is named. (From Vignettes of Portsmouth.*)*

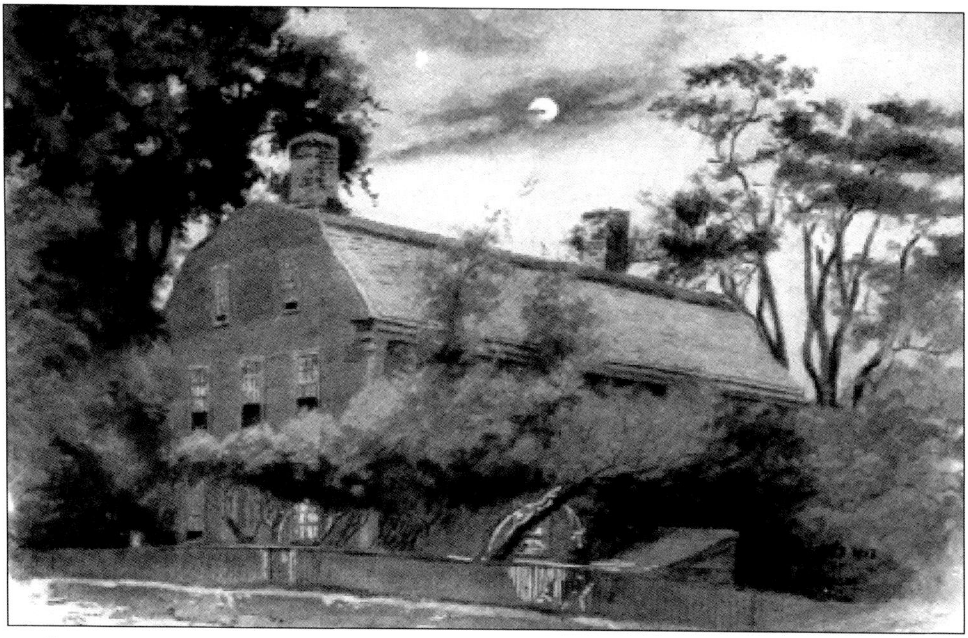

William Pepperrell of Kittery was honored by King George II with the title of baronet. Sir William Pepperrell required a mansion worthy of an English country gentleman. (From Vignettes of Portsmouth.*)*

13 British-American colonies developed a middle-class ideal that continued to influence political philosophers and statesmen for years to come. Laborers and those without property were looked down upon. Destitute members of the lower class were allowed few rights, could neither vote nor serve in political office, and were often bound to years of service of hard labor to a master; for African Americans, the years of service only ended with death.

The philosophy of labor then was essentially what it is today—each member of the community must contribute to the good of the whole; dependence upon the community is the result of age, illness, or physical and mental incapacity; and for the able-bodied, work is the means by which one simultaneously fulfills oneself and one's obligation to the community. Such was the importance of the doctrine of work in early America that it seemed highly unusual, even criminal, for a person who was healthy and able to work to avoid it, for it meant avoiding contribution to the community. The Portsmouth town fathers, like those of other towns up and down the Atlantic coast in the eighteenth century, had the answer. If one could work but refused to, the town committed such a person, male or female, young or old, to an institution to force what was at the same time a responsibility and a gift from God: work.

The Portsmouth almshouse was as important an institution to Portsmouth as was the meetinghouse, courthouse, market, and gaol. Indeed the gaol and almshouse were often indistinguishable, as many of the "sturdy poor" committed to the almshouse were ne'er-do-wells who shared living quarters with those, especially young boys and girls, who were honest and innocent. This did not make sense of course, but economic demands and town finances overwhelmed moral considerations. Even before the almshouse was built, the town had set up a system of low cost public education, and likewise young almshouse inmates were blessed with the chance to learn. In 1728, the selectmen hired William Howlett to run the almshouse school, for which he was paid £60 annually. Perhaps Rebecca Austin, the keeper, insisted as well that the boys and girls under her charge study their psalter similar to those children living in proper families. Psalms and other religious teachings would often be the only solace for the long winter days in the drafty building with rows upon rows of bunks, the stench of human filth, the woeful cries of the insane and the dying, and the grumbling of the resentful.

The province established rules for the proper operation of the almshouse and the effective utilization of inmates' energy. The 1718 "Act for Suppressing and Punishing of Rogues, Vagabonds, Common Beggars, and other Lewd, Idle, and Disorderly Persons, and also for setting the Poor to Work," borrowed liberally from the Elizabethan Act of 1597, calling upon towns to elect "overseers of the poor" to collect the tax and regulate the finances and operation of the almshouse.

Justices of the peace determined the criminals and unfortunate others who should be committed to the almshouse, such as fortune-tellers, jugglers, gamesmen, drunkards, brawlers, fiddlers, runaway servants, and other refuse from a better sort of society. A 1714 law required overseers to commit "idiots" to the almshouse to keep them off the streets and engage them in useful

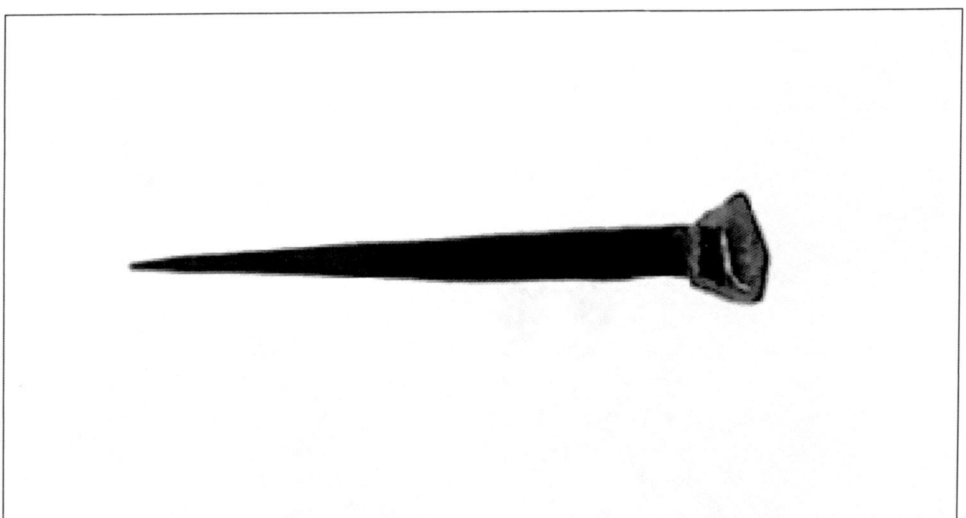

Portsmouth almshouse inmates worked at various tasks producing items for sale or use by the town. Manufactured items included iron nails, the product of the blacksmith's forge. (Photo by Benjamin Lawson.)

employment, if possible. The town was also careful not to provide assistance for a bastard if the father could be identified and held responsible. The overseer was given the power to work all inmates, whether sane or not, and to whip the recalcitrant and shackle them to the wall. Ten stripes on the bare back was the official limit; the law implied that overseers could have all newcomers whipped just to let them know the rules. A 1719 law set forth similar conditions, and added the duty of overseers to keep an eye on disorderly youth loitering and causing trouble on the streets and back-alleys of towns. Such ruffians were to show proof that they were to "be brought up or imployed in Some honest Calling which may be profitable to themselves and the Publick." Otherwise, the overseers were empowered to commit them to the almshouse, give them 10 lashes to the bare back, and employ them at "hard Labour" until discharged by the justice of the peace.

The almshouse appeared sufficiently successful to town leaders who thus delayed electing particular overseers of the poor. In 1733, the town voted that the almshouse alone would care for the poor, that out-relief, care by private individuals, would cease except for special exceptions. Yet the town in 1736 exempted Jerry Miller, who was "Bereaved of his reason," from the almshouse on the pledge of his father to care for him. The town helped out Benjamin Miller by remitting his taxes and granting him £10; two years later the town granted the Millers £20. Such special cases grew rather than diminished, making the town's vote of support for the almshouse a bit hollow. Indeed, the rising numbers and costs of the poor finally necessitated that the town elect annual overseers of the poor.

These people were wealthy and experienced town leaders who committed themselves to the most difficult office of eighteenth-century Portsmouth. The first overseers, as recorded in the town records for 1739, were Theodore Atkinson, Esq., Dr. Peirce, and Henry Sherburne, Jr., Esq. All three men came from leading Portsmouth families. Atkinson, for example, graduated from Harvard College and practiced law in Portsmouth. During his long life he served the town and province in numerous offices. In 1739, he was a provincial counselor, a commander in the militia, and an Episcopalian who at times felt obligated to share his vast riches with the destitute. He was a natural choice for the office of overseer of the poor because of his wealth and charity, both of which would be called upon with increasing frequency in the coming years.

The first task was to see that the almshouse pay for itself by employing the poor in tasks that would encourage the institution's self-sufficiency. The town ordered the selectmen to raise £100 for the overseers to purchase "Stock to keep Said Poor to work." The overseers must manage "the poor that are able to work Constantly Imployed." What "Stock" means is not clear from the town records. Rebecca Austin was in charge of the daily routine of the almshouse. She would assign specific tasks to individuals, young and old, according to their strength and energy. One would be charged with purchasing wood or, better, gathering wood chips and discarded boards by the shipyards; another would have the daily job of supplying the institution with water; some would be in charge of helping prepare the meager food of boiled fish and potatoes. Once the basic necessities were covered, other inmates who were healthy and able to work would have the task of producing items to exchange for needed supplies. Women and girls, who made up the majority of the inmates, would spend their days darning, spinning, and sewing for the needs of the inmates and to produce cloth items for sale. Those few men who were sturdy and strong would be set to tasks requiring physical labor; some would be bound out as servants to shipwrights or shopkeepers. Others would assist skilled workers, operating the bellows for the blacksmith making iron nails.

During the decade of the 1740s, overseers of the poor tended to be the same three men, Richard Wibird, Esq., Dr. Nathaniel Rogers, Esq., and John Cutt, Esq.; their job was unenviable. The almshouse, more than 20 years old, was in need of constant repair and Rebecca Austin aged as her job grew and demanded more energy. The population of Portsmouth continued to advance, and so did the numbers of the poor. The facilities of the almshouse grew insufficient to house all of the destitute on a yearly basis.

A significant group of new inmates during the 1740s were veterans wounded during King George's War, called the Cape Breton War by New Hampshirans. It formed the next to the last chapter in the long drama of conflict between the English and French for control of North America. The cast of characters on

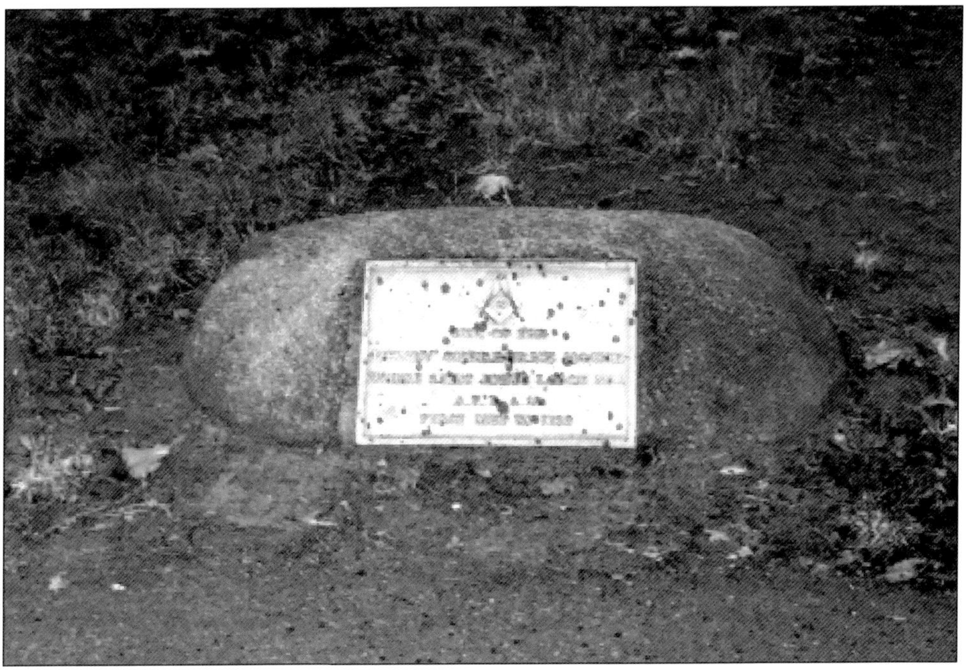

The Sherburne family of merchants and captains were important leaders of early Portsmouth. This marker commemorates the site of the Henry Sherburne House (at Prescott Park). (Photo by Benjamin Lawson.)

the British-American side included Massachusetts Governor William Shirley, Piscataqua merchant William Pepperrell, and Benning Wentworth, a Portsmouth merchant, governor of New Hampshire, and frequent scoundrel. The son of former Lieutenant Governor John Wentworth, Benning Wentworth grew to be an ambitious man intent on wealth and power. He constantly sought property and remunerative offices that would help offset his lavish tastes and multiplying debts. His high living resulted in obesity and frequent bouts of gout. His role in the Cape Breton War was minor compared to William Shirley, who administered the plans to attack the French fortress of Louisburg, and William Pepperrell, who led the attack.

Pepperrell's objective was the island of Cape Breton off the coast of Nova Scotia and the fortress that guarded French interests in the region. England had been forced by the Treaty of Utrecht ending Queen Anne's War to cede the island to the French, although Britain maintained control of Nova Scotia. All loyal Englishmen hungered to recapture Cape Breton. Louisburg was thought to be practically impregnable, which made the decision by the Massachusetts and New Hampshire governments to attempt capture appear foolhardy. William Pepperrell was rich and well-respected, but not a hardened veteran of combat. He led 500 New Hampshire militiamen north in the dead of winter. They battled against cold, fatigue, hunger, disease, and fear before they battled against the French. Thanks to the subterfuge and energy of William Vaughan, Jr., a Portsmouth merchant, a breach in the fortress was achieved and Louisburg fell to the British. Vaughan died a year later in London, whence he journeyed to receive recognition and a title for his exploits. These were denied him, given rather to Pepperrell, who became a baronet and a colonel in the British militia.

Following the unexpected capture of Louisburg, Governor Shirley and Sir William Pepperrell devised plans to defeat the whole of the French forces. Their luck did not hold, however, as misfortune and failure prevailed. The French threat of retaliation resulted in reinforcements and additional cannon at Fort William and Mary to protect the Piscataqua settlements.

Meanwhile, wounded veterans returning to Portsmouth tried to make ends meet. Benjamin Thomas, a soldier who fought at Louisburg and was wounded and "lost the use of [his] arm," which caused "great pain" and poverty, petitioned the General Assembly of New Hampshire for an allowance to defray the costs of living. He hoped not to become a "Burthen to the town"; the province granted him £20. William Rackliff of Portsmouth was captured during the Louisburg expedition where he caught smallpox and a "Violent Fever." He survived, but on his return, required compensation and back pay; the province granted him £85. Benjamin Lewis, another veteran who was ill along with his wife as they tried to feed their four children, received a grant of £4 from the province.

These weren't the only people in need of assistance, wives and widows also needed help. Fourteen Portsmouth matrons petitioned the province for help in 1745, as their husbands were fighting at Louisburg and their "familes are in Daily Want of Support & are now destitute of the help they used to have by the

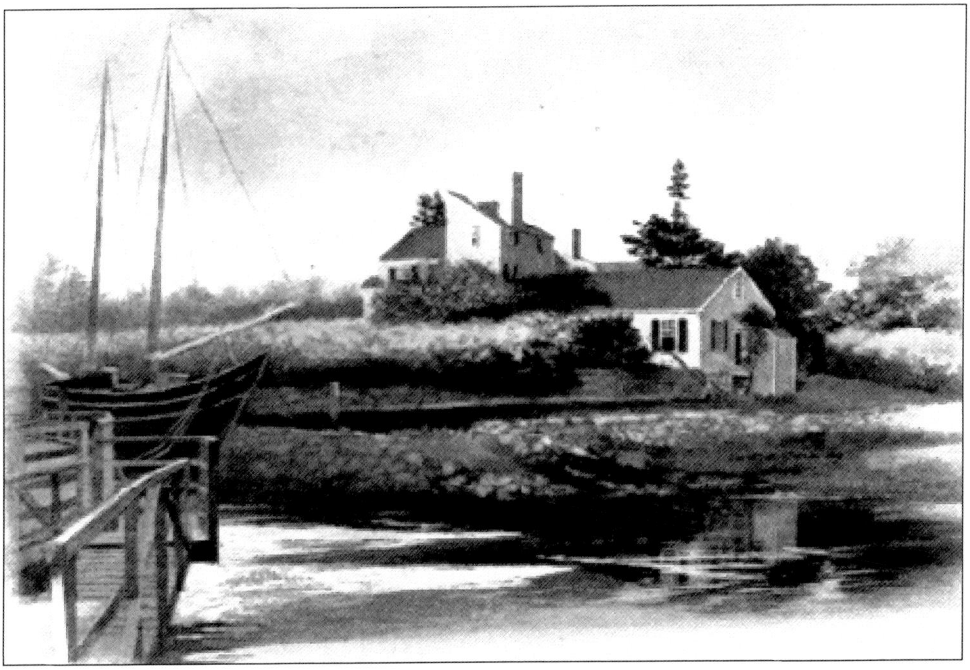

Benning Wentworth, New Hampshire governor from 1741 to 1767, built a rambling mansion on his estate east of town. The beautiful, reclusive estate overlooks the Piscataqua River. (From Vignettes of Portsmouth.*)*

Day Wages of their Husbands on which only they Depended for Subsistence." Deborah Dunn, a widow of a fallen soldier, requested and was granted £15 in July 1746. Sarah Jackson, in similar circumstances, complaining of the "Scarceness and dearness of Bread corn and firewood," was refused.

She was one of 4,000 people that inhabited Portsmouth by the 1750s and the numbers grew yearly. The amenities of town life and the opportunities to work and thrive attracted the hopeful, resolute, and the desperate. To keep up, Portsmouth built new schools "on the North Side of Islington" and at "the Rode." The town authorized the purchase of a new fire engine and necessary fire-fighting equipment, appointed five officers to organize and oversee its use when fires occurred, and created nine fire-wards.

The town established a "haymarket," and would in time build a market house to make buying and selling of farm goods more efficient. During the recent war, smallpox had been such a threat that a "Pest House" was established on Pest Island, where persons inoculated for smallpox would retreat to experience the illness, therefore acquiring immunity. A generation earlier, Reverend Cotton Mather of Boston had taken the lead in encouraging New Englanders to be inoculated for the disease. It still, in the 1750s, seemed ridiculous to many skeptics that one would voluntarily allow the blood of an infected person to be implanted into one's own blood system, knowing that the consequence would be to acquire the disease. Advocates of inoculation claimed that to introduce the blood of an infected person with a less virulent form of the disease into a healthy person would likewise engender a less virulent disease experience. Evidence had shown such individuals tended to survive and not be scarred by the pustules, then to be immune and free from fear. Yet the sick, those inoculated as well as those who were not, required quarantine from healthy inhabitants. Hence, the idea of a "pest island" for quarantine.

Other changes occurred at mid-century. Many of the established ministers of the town died within a few years of each other. Reverend Jabez Fitch, pastor of the North Parish, died in 1746, and Reverend Samuel Langdon, chaplain for New Hampshire troops during their march to Louisburg, replaced him. Reverend William Shurtleff of South Parish died and was replaced by Reverend Samuel Haven. Growth was evident by the shipyards that were busy launching ships of all sizes, particularly the *America*, a 50-gun frigate, supervised by Colonel Nathaniel Meserve. Town boosters organized a lottery to build a social library, which would be home to literate gentlemen who sought a place to read and converse. The lottery was successful enough that it led to opening the library and engendered the germ of an idea among leaders of Portsmouth to provide a solution to the ongoing financial burden of poor relief.

Town meetings were becoming more acrimonious by mid-century and the budget expanded beyond all expectations. Wealthy merchants knew how to receive large funds and expend them, and were routinely elected as selectmen and overseers of the poor. Political bickering engendered suspicion of improper use of funds, so the town elected auditors to examine the accounts of those in power. Overseers of the poor, at least, had cause to complain. The almshouse was failing, structurally, morally, and economically. It was built 35 years earlier when the town had half the population, hence half the numbers of unruly, sturdy beggars and criminals; refugees from wars; and orphans, disabled, and the elderly. The principle of working the poor to pay their keep failed and the annual cost of maintaining the almshouse was such a financial burden that often the overseers of the poor had to dip into their own pockets to pay the balance of debt. As early as 1747, the town called for a new institution to be built, a "workhouse." The name of the workhouse implied its function—to have the indigent work to defray costs of poor relief. It would be larger, more efficient, better operated than past efforts, but first it had to be built.

Townsmen saw the success of the social library lottery and petitioned the provincial assembly for permission to establish a lottery to build a workhouse. At the town meeting of May 1750, the town voted that "the overseers of the Poor [must] Provide for them in the best manner they Can at the Towns Charge till further Orders." This sounded too much like a request that the overseers use their own resources to support the almshouse while the town figured out what to do. The three elected overseers, John Shackford, George Huntress, and John Griffith, quit, and Thomas Wibird, Daniel Jackson, and Thomas Peirce, three town leaders and men with sufficient means, filled in. They agreed to serve in

1751 as well, when the town asked that they build additions to the almshouse and "make it more Convenient than it now is & make a fence if needed Round Said House."

Meanwhile, the town was feverishly trying to raise money to build the new workhouse. Besides the lottery, the town called on the selectmen to collect all "outstanding Debts" due to the town. Plans were also made to try to sell the old structure to make way for the new. In 1754, the town decided to build the workhouse on a portion of the glebe land hitherto controlled by the North Parish, and in August the town selected a committee to supervise the building of the workhouse. Three members of the social library, Theodore Atkinson, Mark Hunking Wentworth, and Henry Sherburne, Jr., were commissioned "to have the Care and Oversight" of the workhouse, ensuring that it be built "in the Best and most Convenient manner to answer the End and Design of Such an House."

The town, while discussions of construction were going on, decided upon new leadership for the almshouse. William Hooker, a worthy townsman, replaced Rebecca Austin as keeper of the poor. Hooker had served the town previously as a "tythingman" and constable, positions that required a forceful personality. A joiner by trade, Hooker had acquired considerable wealth and

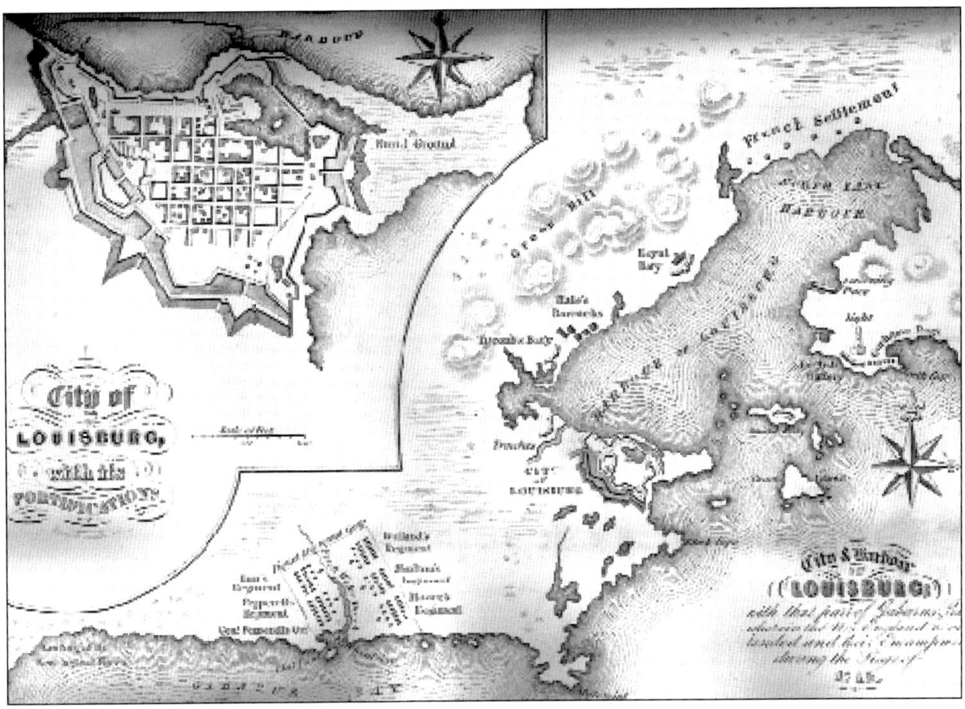

This map shows the city, harbor, and fortifications of Louisburg at Cape Breton Island. New Hampshire troops led by William Pepperrell captured the fort in 1745. (From Usher Parsons's Life of Sir William Pepperrell.*)*

could afford spending his time serving the town by working the poor and punishing the derelict.

Upon completion of the workhouse in 1756, Clement March took over the duties of keeper. March was a large, imposing man who carried a cane about him to intimidate the timid and create second thoughts in the minds of the more aggressive. He was 50 years old, wealthy, and experienced, and his accomplishments included serving Portsmouth as a constable, tax collector, and moderator of town meetings. He represented the town of Greenland in the general assembly and served the province as a judge and an officer in the militia. Notwithstanding his wealth, March preferred to live at the workhouse to supervise the less fortunate more effectively. The workhouse, a large structure that faced Broad (now State) Street, had two stories. March's job responsibilities as keeper were spelled out in the town meeting of March 1756. He was to engage in "Such Business & Service as Shall be Necessary in Order to the Looking After the People that are or Shall Live there & to Send all Such to Live there as Shall apply . . . for Support."

Numbers of the poor continued to increase during Clement March's reign, partly because of the growing population of this most prosperous seaport, as well as another war that engaged the services of many young New Hampshirans. Colonel Nathaniel Meserve, a veteran of King George's War, a shipbuilder of note, recent widower (his wife Jane having died in 1747), and a man of considerable property, led New Hampshire soldiers in the French-Indian War. Meserve joined Major Robert Rogers and Lieutenant John Stark in attacks on French forts, supply lines, and Native American allies in and about Lake Champlain and north into Canada.

In 1758, he led New Hampshirans in another attack on the fortress at Louisburg. The British-American army, however, was overtaken by smallpox and Meserve, as well as his son and most of his men, died. Louisburg was eventually captured, as was Ticonderoga and Crown Point; Quebec fell to the British in 1759. Portsmouth shipping had declined during the war because of French and Spanish aggression, but once the war ended, the city celebrated:

> On October 18, there was public rejoicing on account of Quebec's reduction, and other successes of the British arms. Thanks were given to Almighty God for the remarkable interposition of his providence in these great events, and discourses suitable to the occasion were delivered at the respective places of public worship. After which the bells rang, and cannons were discharged from various parts of town from midnight until evening, and at noon from the ships in the harbour. At 1 p.m., a grand procession made its way through town, under a standard, representing a city besieged, with the motto *Nil desperandum Christo duce* [*with Christ leading do not despair*]. The evening brought a very large bonfire up on Wind-mill Hill, where the French flag was consumed and the British preserved from the flames. There was an extraordinary display of fire-

works that illuminated the town. Over the front door of the state-house hung a representation of the city of Quebec in ruin after surrender, with General Wolfe ascending by chariot after achieving victory as ships below and above the city and the English encampments at Point Levi encompassed a backdrop of bombs and cannon playing on. The French flag flying below the English banner symbolized defeat, and the King's arms were wrapped over the whole. Joy appeared in every expression, and every heart was warmed with patriotic ardor.

4. They That Go Down To the Sea in Ships

Portsmouth owes its existence to the sea. The native Algonquians fished and canoed Atlantic coastal waters. The first English explorers and adventurers came by sea, sailing up the Piscataqua in barks, pinnaces, and other small sailing craft. The first inhabitants at Strawbery Banke made their living from the ocean, and traveled by water in canoe, rowboat, ketch, or pink. Fishing dominated the economy of the seventeenth-century Piscataqua Valley as most inhabitants before 1700 were islanders, living at the Isles of Shoals or Great Island. Shipbuilding increasingly flourished during this century as shipyards constructing commercial and private boats dotted the islands of the Piscataqua, Portsmouth, Kittery, and the towns upriver in and about the Great Bay. After the first war for empire, King William's War, and thereafter throughout the eighteenth century, sloops, brigantines, and frigates were built for war against the French, and eventually against the English.

The islanders, sailors, and fishermen of the Piscataqua Valley knew a hard life. Existence was often brutal, and frequently cut short by the dangers of the deep. One pious seaman, awed by the power of the sea and the power of God, wrote:

> They that go down to the Sea in Ships, that do Business in great Waters; these see the Works of God, and his Wonders in the Deep. For he commandeth, and raiseth the stormy Wind, which lifteth up the Waves thereof. They mount up to the Heaven, they go down again to the Depth, their Soul is melted because of Trouble. They reel to and fro, and stagger like a drunken Man, and are at their Wits End. Then they cry unto the Lord in their Trouble, and he bringeth from out of their Distresses. Oh that Man would praise the Lord for his Goodness, and for his wonderful Works to the Children of Men! (Quoted in Saltonstall, *Ports of Piscataqua*, 70-1)

Shipwreck was a constant threat and a frequent reality. Many goodwives, watching the remains of their husbands and sons, cast up from the sea, being lowered into their final resting places, recalled with comfort the words: *The Lord giveth and the Lord taketh. Blessed be the name of the Lord.* Neither the Isles of Shoals, the islands of Portsmouth harbor, nor the bluffs of Pannaway and shores of Kittery, had a lighthouse to guide incoming ships. Sometimes a lantern would be waved from the fort at Great Island, but this was hardly effective. It was not until 1771, after many wrecks and lives were lost, that the combined efforts of Governor Benning Wentworth, John Langdon of Portsmouth, and the members of the provincial assembly resulted in the first lighthouse, built at Great Island, shining out upon the mouth of the Piscataqua and the sea.

Portsmouth sea captain Nathanael Peirce knew shipwreck first hand. He was master of the *Portsmouth*, which shipped out in November 1752 heavily laden with a variety of foodstuffs for trade in French Canada. Sailing north, the ship faced contrary winds that forced the *Portsmouth* to turn south, running with the wind. Captain Peirce hoped to cruise to the Caribbean and there dispose of his cargo. Unfortunately for captain and crew, the brigantine again came upon a heavy squall, which battered the ship so that it took on too much water, and threatened to sink. As the water rose and filled the lower decks, the crew in desperation cut away some masts and sails, hoping to prevent the ship from turning on its side. The pounding waves drove everything from the

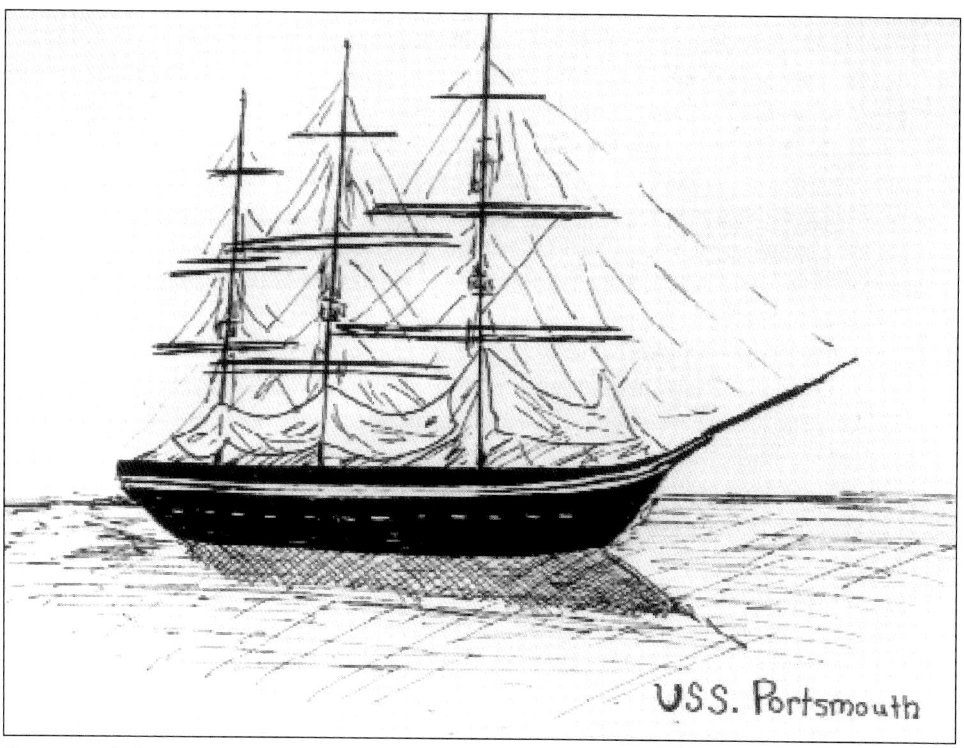

Portsmouth has given its name to many boats over the years. This drawing (by Benjamin Lawson) is of the U.S.S. Portsmouth, *a mid-nineteenth century 24-gun sloop.*

deck, including one Langford, an African-American sailor who was swept away during the night of December 6.

The crew was wet, cold, and hungry. They were able to salvage some apples and cheese, contrive a sail to hang rather like a hammock for rest, and collect drinking water by holding some article of clothing away from the sea and toward the sky during a rainstorm, then wringing the soaked cloth allowing sustenance to spill into their mouths. A large and hungry shark came upon the swamped deck and tormented them until the captain chased him away with blows from a loose board. On December 9, the ship turned on its side. Two men, William Langdon of Portsmouth and a "Dutchman," were lost. The ship righted again but the main mast stood as a continual threat that the ship could again turn on its side.

As the days passed several men, including David Brown and Nathaniel Barns, both of Portsmouth, became "delirious" and met their end. The captain devised a plan to dive into the hold to find some tools; he discovered an ax-head, which he fitted to a stave to form an axe, with which he cut away the main mast. Somehow the remaining men stayed alive for another week, their bodies swollen from the saltwater, yet growing weak from lack of food.

On December 18, Timothy Cotton of Portsmouth went mad, dove into the sea, and drowned. Eventually, the other two seamen on board were washed away, leaving Captain Peirce alone, expecting to take his last breath at any moment. He recalled,

> I was alone from the Nineteenth to Christmass Eve . . . expecting to starve to Death, and at the same Time earnestly begging God's Mercy in the Forgiveness of my Sins, and a Preservation of my Senses until my Time should come.

Soon a "Monument of his Mercy" arrived in the person of Captain Martin from Halifax, who was on his way to Portugal. The good captain and crew rescued Peirce, fed and clothed him, nursed him back to health, and he finally returned to Portsmouth on July 15, 1753. Eventually the captain decided to tell his story, and one of the few surviving versions is found in Saltonstall's *Ports of Piscataqua* (71-84).

The example of Captain Peirce explains why the seamen of Portsmouth were devout and pious Christians. Many a sermon was preached and poems sung about the vastness and sublimity of the sea, and man's utter dependence upon God.

Widows and orphans left alone and destitute as a consequence of the sea's whims often found themselves inmates of the town's new workhouse. Yet they and the other inmates, as well as the selectmen and overseers, and all the inhabitants of Portsmouth, would discover the truth of the words of the English writer Richard Burn, who in *The History of the Poor Laws* (1764) noted that, "almost every proposal which has been made for the reformation of the poor laws, has been tried in former ages, and found ineffectual."

In 1760, the Portsmouth workhouse was still new with only four years of service. Clement March, like past keepers William Hooker and Rebecca Austin, fed and housed the poor and tried to earn a profit from his position by conservative

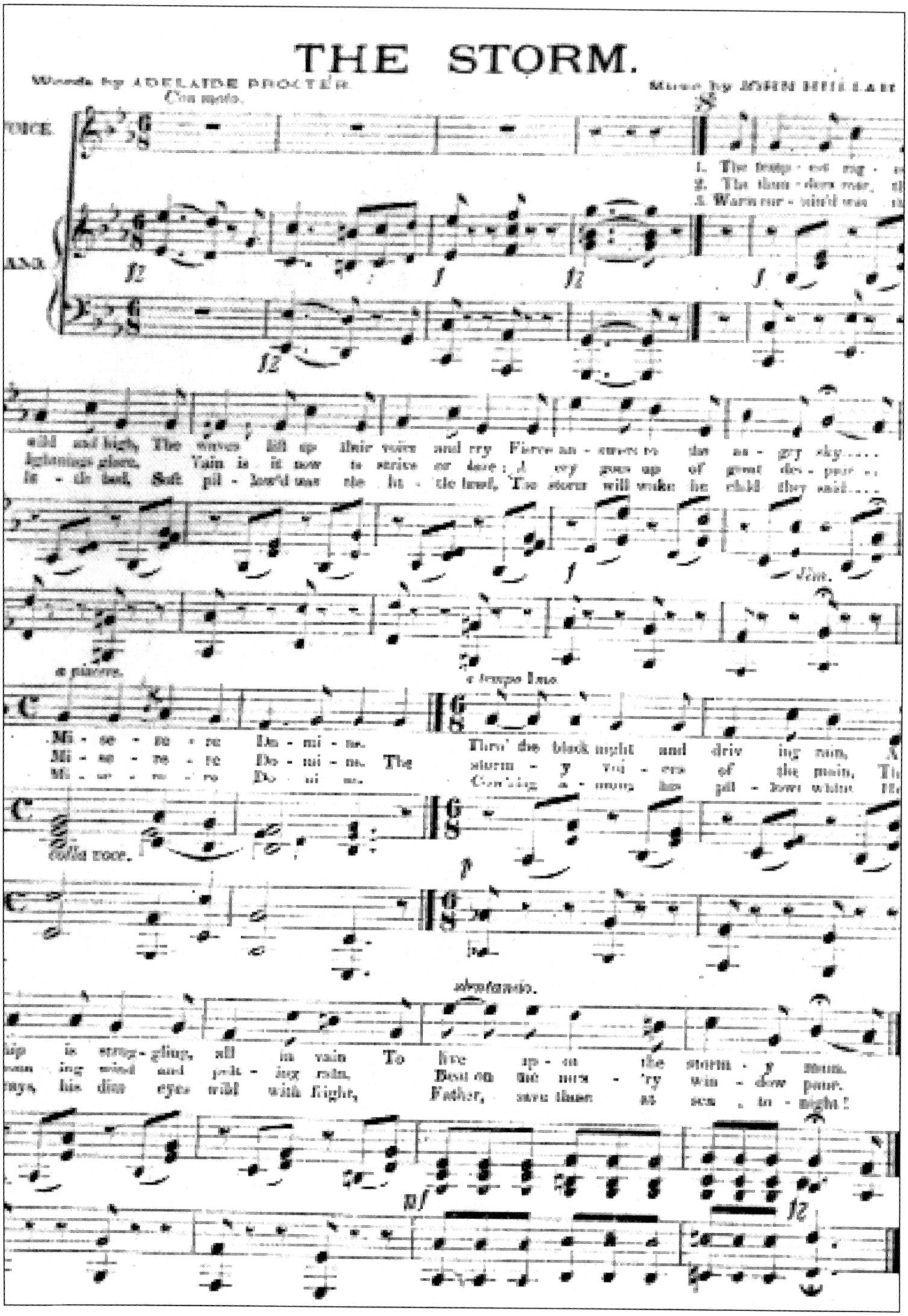

The lyrics of this song, "The Storm," were all too familiar to Portsmouth residents. Mothers, wives, and daughters frequently had occasion to pray, "Father, save those at sea to-night!" (From The Musical Treasure.*)*

management of the funds granted by the town. He was paid £27 yearly to care for Widow Hull and her family, yet Jackson hoped to spend just a little over £20, earning a profit of perhaps £6. It was also in his best interest to keep the poor at work producing material items (such as cloth, clothes, nails) for sale. The workhouse was large, with many apartments, and the deserving poor lived in different quarters from the idle poor and criminal types; the mentally disturbed were separated from all others. March also had an apartment in the workhouse and overseers of the poor, as the occasion arose, stayed there as well. It also served the community in general as it was big enough to house the growing town library and host town meetings in its spacious Union Hall. The North Parish had hitherto served as host, but now refused to accomodate the noise and volatility of town meetings.

Town historians later recalled that Clement March was tall, imposing, and sometimes violent; able paupers were more apt to work than not when they saw his shadow approach. Legend has it that March haunted the darkened halls of the workhouse, repaying any disrespect or laziness with his cane, the symbol of his authority. In Clement March's defense, the decade of the 1760s was an increasingly chaotic time. The Treaty of Paris that ended the French-Indian War brought an end to battle, but not an end to conflict and perplexity. The leaders of Portsmouth were conservative and not accustomed to stirring up trouble. Yet the conflict that exploded after 1763 between the British government and the 13 colonies was inexorable and not easily ignored.

The Treaty of Paris in 1763 that ended the French–Indian War and gave Canada to the British brought peace to the New Hampshire frontier and freedom from fear of invasion. War's end, however, brought increasing poverty to many Portsmouth residents. Contrary to expectations, the workhouse was not working so well. Townsmen complained to the provincial assembly in 1763 that a law was needed to more effectively:

> take care that poor Vagrant Persons whether Children or Adults Such as common Beggars & have no visible means of a Livelyhood . . . be Properly employed that such Children be Obliged to be Sent to Some of the Publick Schools or be Bound Out to Such Buissness as may be most Likely to make them useful to Society and to themSelves.

While the passage of the Sugar Act in 1764 irritated merchants because it imposed new regulations on trade, and Parliament's decision to impose the Stamp Act angered many inhabitants, for others the years 1764 and 1765 were times of searching for the bare necessities of life. Controversy with Britain led to instability and rising prices, particularly of bread. The inflated price was "to the Great Detriment of the Inhabitants of Portsmouth Especially the Poor," which led to the town's request that the selectmen try to regulate prices.

The conflict with England, and the growing threat of a violent split of colonies with mother country, cast a shadow over the daily activities of town life, thrusting a burden on rich and poor alike. In Portsmouth, for example, there was a crisis in leadership as the wealthy merchants who normally exercised control over economic and political affairs found events at home and abroad simply overwhelming. After serving in the capacity of overseers of the poor for four years, the town in 1766 voted to replace Captain James Stoodly, Mr. Jacob Sheafe, and Mr. John Penhallow after checking over their accounts and discovering quite a significant deficit. The town empowered the selectmen to supply the new overseers, Captain Daniel Rindge, Mr. John Griffith, and Mr. John Elliot, with £100 "to purchase Necessaries for the Support of the poor & Purchasing Stock at the Whole Sale and Cheapest Rate to Employ any Poor Person Either in the Work

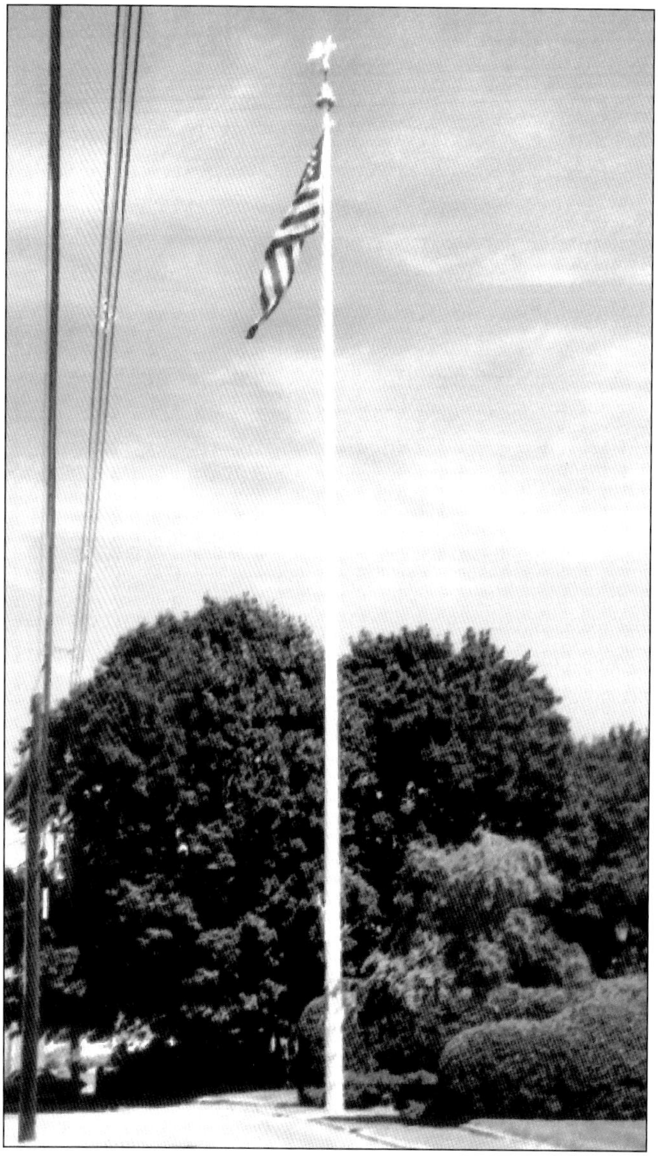

The Liberty Pole at Prescott Park was erected in 1824 on the site of the first Liberty Pole commemorating the opposition of Portsmouth patriots to the Stamp Act of 1765. The pole stands directly across Marcy Street from Strawbery Banke. (Photo by Benjamin Lawson.)

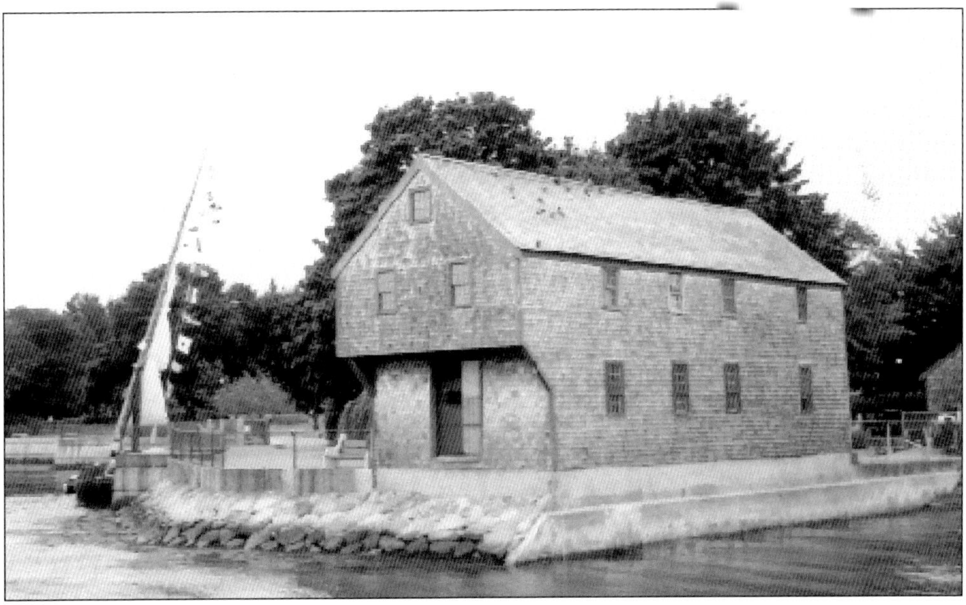

Jacob Sheafe built the warehouse that bears his name about 1700. The Portsmouth Gundalow *is moored nearby. (Photo by Benjamin Lawson.)*

House or Elsewhere in the Town." This seemed a daunting prospect to overseers and selectmen alike and all refused to serve.

Benjamin Akerman and Captain Samuel Dalling volunteered to serve as overseers and they were joined the following year by John Eliot, Samuel Griffith, Samuel Moffatt, and Captain John Parker. Again, in 1768, the town questioned the accounts of the overseers and complained of the "Numbers of poor Idle Persons that are now a burden to the public," who need to "be properly Employed and Become Examples of Industry and Good Morals as they are now Shameful Examples of Idleness & Vice." The town refused to reelect the overseers, selecting two replacements, who refused to serve.

Five of the most stalwart citizens of Portsmouth, Honorable Jonathan Warner, Esq., Honorable Daniel Rindge, Esq., John Sherburne, Esq., Captain John Parker, and Dr. Joshua Brackett, stepped in to prevent a complete failure of the poor relief system. The five demanded and received £500 to purchase supplies for the workhouse, especially "Stock to Imploy the poor in the said house or any Others that Shall be put there by the Overseers." The elected selectmen thought this was too much, so they refused their positions. Some townsmen questioned whether or not it would be advisable to return to the private system of the previous century. At a town meeting a petition to this end was proposed, which the town refused to consider. They noted that the problem derived not from the actions of the overseers, nor from the institution of the workhouse, but rather from the poor themselves, who were increasingly giving great "injury" to the overseers with abuse and a lack of respect.

In 1768, Portsmouth was a city of over 4,000 people, many of whom were loiterers or poor. Taverns were plentiful and rum all too common, disorder from abroad along with financial and moral chaos threatened the town. During assembly in March, the town voted "to Prevent any Disorders and Tumults" that might occur because of celebrations on days of "hilarity" such as Christmas or "Riots . . . and Unlawful Assemblys" due to opposition to British policies.

Impending revolution was already being felt at home as the conservative, upright, and wealthy found themselves increasingly taunted and abused verbally. Add the accumulated impact of the cost of providing for the poor, the condescension of overseers and resentment of the paupers, and the forced work and veritable imprisonment of the poor in the workhouse, and the threat of disorder and riot were at the surface. This caused such tumult that the town decided to act in 1771, voting to petition the governor, council, and assembly to proclaim "An Act to invest the Overseers of the Poor with Power more effectually to employ" the poor. The *New Hampshire Gazette* reported a vote of the town to set off a part of the workhouse to create a "house of Correction" where "idle and disorderly persons . . . should be confined to hard labour." A gaol already existed to house debtors until they could pay their creditors, and to hold hardened criminals. The house of correction was a more permanent establishment designed to imprison and punish malefactors—which to the eighteenth-century mind was synonymous with the poor—until they reformed themselves to become useful citizens.

Implementing the house of correction did the trick. With ruffians and ne'er-do-wells segregated from the rest of the poor, there were fewer problems, less disorderly conduct, and more honest labor in the workhouse. If a crisis in town affairs had been averted in 1771, the same was not true in provincial affairs. In that year, George Meserve was the Collector of Customs, charged with approving inbound and outbound traffic, enforcing British trade law and tariffs, and preventing smuggling. Meserve came from a respected Portsmouth family; his father was Colonel Nathaniel Meserve. He fell out of favor with the town in 1765 by becoming a Stamp Act officer. After threats and being burned in effigy, he wisely declined the office, yet still carried the aura of being too close a supporter of Parliament. In October 1771, he impounded the ship *Resolution* for smuggling molasses. A party of Portsmouth patriots boarded the ship and unloaded it for safekeeping. The "Portsmouth molasses party" anticipated the Boston Tea Party by two years.

The Boston Tea Party was in response to the Tea Act of 1773, which created a monopoly for the British East India Company on tea sold in America. Portsmouth patriots responded with the Portsmouth Tea Resolves, declaring their resolution to prevent said tea to be sold in Portsmouth. Governor John Wentworth, nephew of Benning Wentworth, opposed such lawlessness, and there were quite a few Piscataqua merchants, clergymen, and other conservatives who supported him. Yet the tide of events swept over Wentworth and the Loyalists.

The Boston Port Bill, which closed Boston harbor and suspended government in Massachusetts while declaring martial law in the colony, inspired liberals such as John Langdon of Portsmouth to meet and decide on a response. Langdon, a Portsmouth merchant, joined the Portsmouth Committee of Correspondence, charged with communicating with other such committees all over New England. He also attended a colonial convention that sent Nathaniel Folsom and John Sullivan to the First Continental Congress at Philadelphia.

Such actions solicited the interest of the British authorities, who decided to reinforce the small contingent of British soldiers stationed at Fort William and Mary, which guarded the mouth of the Piscataqua. The Piscataqua patriots, who caught wind of the impending visit of the British warship *Scarborough*, went by day and then cover of night to Newcastle, arresting the small garrison and carrying off the powder, shot, and small cannon. Such treason was not to be tolerated by the British government and Governor John Wentworth's proclamation, printed in Belknap's *History of New-Hampshire*, stated:

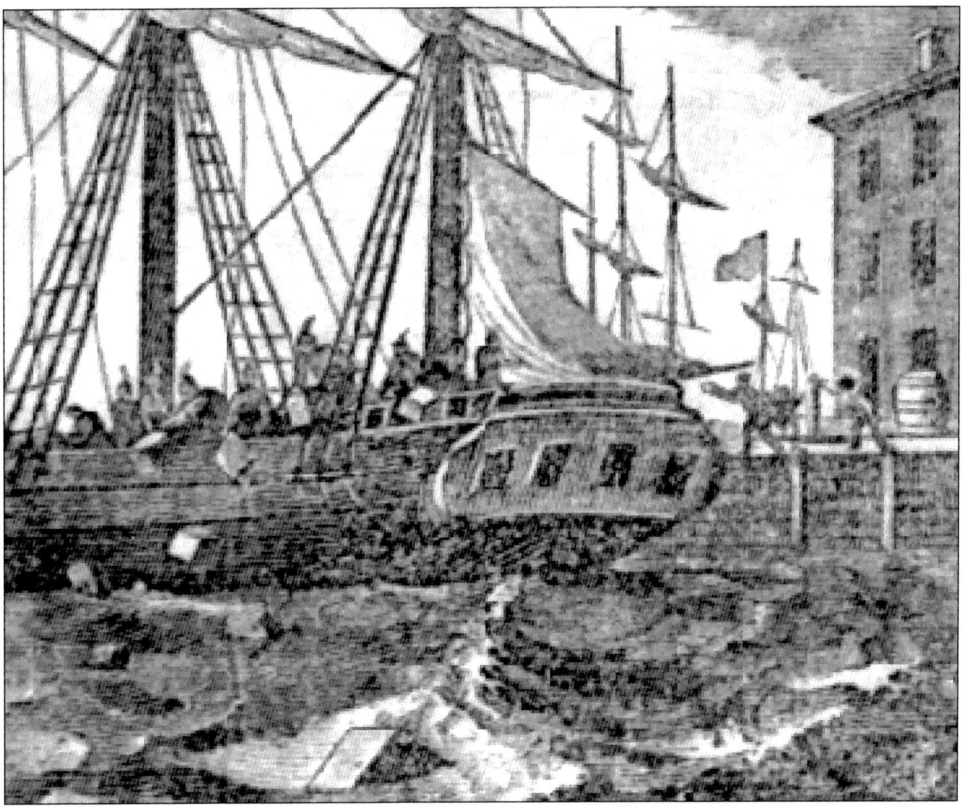

The Boston Tea Party reflected the political attitudes of Portsmouth patriots. The men of Portsmouth in 1771 anticipated the Boston Tea Party when they boarded an impounded ship and dumped hogsheads of molasses into Portsmouth harbor. (From Goodrich's History of the United States of America.*)*

> Whereas, several bodies of men did, in the day time of the 14th, and in the night of the 15th of this instant December, in the most daring and rebellious manner invest, attack, and forcibly enter into his majesty's castle William and Mary in this province, and overpowering and confining the captain and garrison, did, besides committing many treasonable insults and outrages, break open the magazine of said castle and plunder it of above one hundred barrels of gunpowder, with upwards of sixty stand of small arms, and did also force from the ramparts of said castle and carry off sixteen pieces of cannon, and other military stores, in open hostility and direct oppugnation of his majesty's government, and in the most atrocious contempt of his crown and dignity;—
>
> I do, by advice and consent of his majesty's council, issue this proclamation ordering and requiring, in his majesty's name, all magistrates and other officers, whether civil or military, as they regard their duty to the king and the tenor of the oaths they have solemnly taken and subscribed, to exert themselves in detecting and securing in some of his majesty's gaols in this province the said offenders, in order to their being brought to condign punishment . . .

John Wentworth was not governor of New Hampshire for much longer after this statement. After the battles of Lexington and Concord inaugurated the war in April 1775, and after an unlawful assembly met and passed laws and resolutions, the governor left Portsmouth for good and retired to Fort William and Mary. On August 24, "his Majesty's Ships Scarborough & Canso sailed from this Harbour 'tis said for Boston with Governor Wentworth & his Family on board." The ships also carried away the remaining cannon of the fort.

Coinciding with the decline in influence of the Wentworth family was the rise to power of John Langdon. The Langdon family owned land at Sagamore Creek near Little Harbor and were wealthy slave-owners. John, born in 1741, received a classical education at Samuel Hale's school before going to sea. Samuel Hale was a Harvard College graduate who had served the province during King George's War, after which he opened a Latin grammar school. John and his brother Woodbury both attended the school, receiving a classical education. By 1770, the two brothers were established merchants becoming more discontented with British trade policies and taxes. Besides his involvement in the attack on Fort William and Mary, John Langdon served as delegate to the Second Continental Congress that met at Philadelphia in 1775. However, upon the destruction of Falmouth (Portland) Maine in October 1775, and the continued presence of the *Scarborough* at the river's mouth, he returned to Portsmouth to supervise the construction of a 32-gun frigate commissioned by Congress. This ship, the *Raleigh*, was launched in the early spring of 1776, but did not go to war for months, as she awaited the 32 guns! By the time the *Raleigh* was armed, the sloop *Ranger* had been built and launched under Langdon's supervision. Langdon also busied himself in

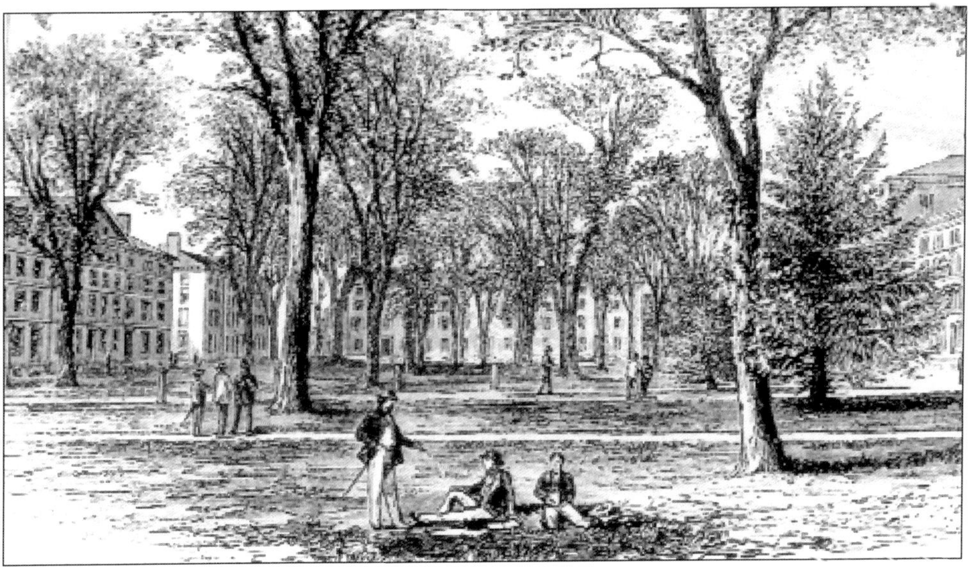

Many early Portsmouth leaders and clergy earned degrees at Harvard College. This image of the college green was drawn during the nineteenth century. (From Boston Illustrated.)

privateering, not that he went aboard these private vessels intent on capturing British ships and splitting the profits of the prize. Rather, he invested in the outfitting of almost a dozen ships, brigs, and sloops. He also served as the congressional agent overseeing maritime affairs, including judging incoming prizes and distributing prize money.

Indeed, John Langdon of Portsmouth was instrumental in the development of the United States Navy. He sat on the Naval Committee of the Second Continental Congress. By early 1776, the committee had outfitted three ships, three brigs, three sloops, and two schooners. Ships such as the *Alfred* had over 20 guns, carried about 220 men, and before the *America* was built at Portsmouth in 1780, were the largest naval frigates of the United States Navy. Brigs were slightly smaller, with fewer guns, about 15, and manned by a smaller crew. The schooners were the smallest boats with the fewest guns, less than 10. The guns were iron cannon that shot six- or nine-pound balls broadside into the opponent to take out guns, men, and masts; or grapeshot and the like to cause terror and rip sails, disabling a ship. Mid-sized sloops of war, small and quick, could carry up to 18 guns. The two most famous sloops of the war were the *Providence* and *Ranger*, both commanded by John Paul Jones.

Jones arrived at Portsmouth in March 1777 to join the crew of the French ship *Amphitrite*. The captain of the *Amphitrite*, Monsieur Fautrel, was not particularly accommodating of the young and brash Scotsman, even if the French decided to cast their lot with the Americans against the English. It was of little consequence though, for Jones soon received word that the sloop of war being built at Badger Island, under John Langdon's supervision, would be under his command. The

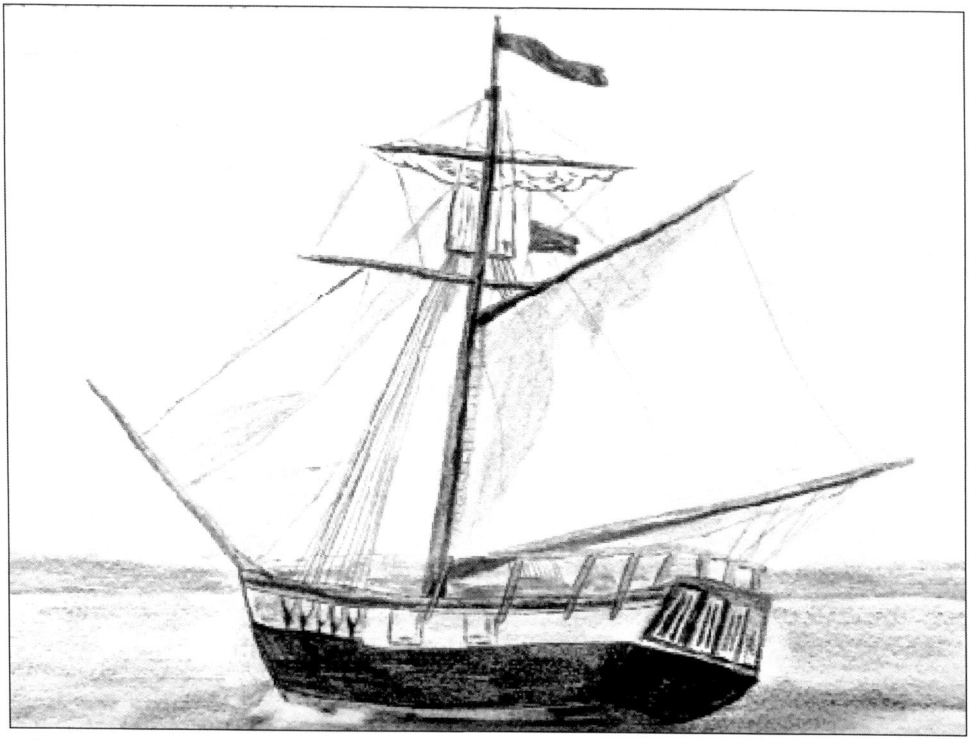

The Providence, *sloop of war, was a light, fast ship, especially under the command of John Paul Jones. A recreation of the* Providence *occasionally visits Portsmouth harbor (as in July 2002) to the delight of residents and tourists. (Sketch by Benjamin Lawson.)*

boat, called the *Hampshire*, would be renamed after New Hampshire's favorite sons of the previous war, especially the once husband of Elizabeth Brown (daughter of the Reverend Arthur Browne), Major Robert Rogers, the leader of the Rangers during the French-Indian War. Soon the construction of the *Ranger* was complete, though the guns, sails, cordage, crew, and necessary supplies such as sailor's slops and rum were not yet on hand. While he spent anxious months preparing the sloop for sea, Captain John Paul Jones lodged at the home of the Widow Purcell on State Street.

Congress ordered the *Ranger* to cruise to France, taking dispatches to American representative Benjamin Franklin, then to proceed north seeking to raid England's coast and capture enemy freighters and warships. The sloop was built for speed, and had a crew of 150. Leaders of Portsmouth, John Langdon and William Whipple, appointed the officers who would serve under Captain Jones, which included relatives and friends, experienced merchants such as Elijah Hall, sailors such as Thomas Simpson, and surgeon Dr. Ezra Green of Dover, a Harvard graduate.

Captain Jones assembled the crew in part by advertising with handbills that proclaimed the "Great Encouragement for Seamen," to sail in the "Ship RANGER" for the "GLORIOUS CAUSE" of American freedom. Candidates should "repair to the ship," where Jones promised that "they will be kindly entertained, and receive the greatest Encouragement." Any gentlemen interested in taking "an agreable Voyage in this pleasant Season of the Year, may, by entering on board the . . . Ship RANGER, meet with every Civility they can possibly expect." Hopefully such men realized that the *Ranger* was not hosting a party, rather it was a warship intent on capturing prizes and engaging in battle on the high seas.

Nevertheless, Captain Jones, known for his romantic intrigues and gentlemanly behavior, was willing to use the *Ranger* to bring back from France some expensive clothes and gloves for Mrs. William Whipple. For a Boston friend with expensive tastes, Jones was intent on returning with "Exceeding Good Boardeaux Claret," as well as the china and goodies that would round out the intended feast. (Quotes from Samuel Eliot Morison, *John Paul Jones*, 109ff)

Jones was, beyond all else, a daring commander who showed little fear at sea. The voyage to France was uneventful save the capture of several unarmed "prizes" with their holds filled with fresh fruit for London markets. After departing France in early 1778, the *Ranger* sailed north, capturing and sinking British ships, taking prisoners, and attacking port cities. Jones and his men raided Whitehaven and Saint Mary's Isle on the Irish Sea, and captured an armed British sloop, the *Drake*.

The Piscataqua hosted or produced quite a few heroes of the Revolutionary War. Besides Jones, there were the signers of the *Declaration of Independence*, William Whipple and John Langdon, Revolutionary general John Sullivan of Durham, and militia colonel Joseph Whipple. Joseph, whose remains like his brother William's rest at the North Burying Ground, was a merchant, overseer of the poor, and customs official. He had gone to sea a young man before settling in Portsmouth, where he continued his maritime connection as a ship-owner.

Whipple was the typical Portsmouth speculator. In 1773, he became a proprietor for lands north of the White Mountains where he set up a plantation worked by "servants" who were promised the opportunity to buy their own lot from the master. This fledgling town of Dartmouth (Jefferson) was on a crossroads of travel dating back centuries. Whipple kept a tavern for travelers and owned a large house that was rather like a fortress; indeed the enemy occasionally attacked his house. On one occasion Whipple was briefly held as a prisoner, though he escaped to lead the New Hampshire militia against Indian raiders in 1782. Upon conclusion of the war, Colonel Whipple journeyed north annually to work his plantation.

During one trip in the summer of 1784, accompanied by a dozen adventurers, guides, scientists, and clergymen, Whipple ascended Mount Washington. This expedition has become well known in New Hampshire history, and its participants have rightly gained fame. Joining Whipple in this the first scientific expedition to climb the tallest mountain of the northeast were Jeremy Belknap, Daniel Little, Manasseh Cutler, John Evans, and Joshua Fisher. Unfortunately, one of the participants was ignored by those who told the story—Whipple's slave. Brought along to serve the master, this man carried baggage, prepared the meals, and mended clothes. While the explorers climbed Mount Washington, the slave remained at camp, alone.

The slave's surname was no doubt Whipple, since Portsmouth masters usually gave their servants the family surname. To distinguish their servile status, the master chose a distinct classical first name, such as Scipio, Cato, Caesar, or Prince. Indeed, Joseph's brother William, the man who put his name to the endearing phrase, "that all men are created equal," owned slaves, one of whom was named Prince. Prince Whipple, unlike most of Portsmouth's slaves, earned the right to be buried near his master in the North Burial Ground. Contemporaries thought he had earned it by standing up to General William Whipple at the Battle of Saratoga and demanding his freedom as a consequence of the American fight for freedom. Whipple freed Prince, and eventually other members of Prince's family.

Few if any Portsmouth merchants engaged in the slave trade, so Portsmouth's slaves were imported directly from other countries or colonies. Some Portsmouth merchants held auctions to sell unwanted slaves, and with this practice of humans being bought and sold, families were torn apart. William Whipple bought Prince when he was a child in 1766. When he grew to become a tall, well-built man, he married Dinah Chase, slave to the Reverend Chase of Newcastle. They set up housekeeping after both were freed during the Revolution, and lived moderately

This simple headstone at the North Burial Ground marks the grave of Joseph Whipple. A merchant, landowner, and customs official, Whipple was one of the leaders of Revolutionary Portsmouth. (Photo by Benjamin Lawson.)

happy lives at their home on High Street, near the Whipple mansion. Cuffee Whipple (formerly Cuffee Chase), Dinah's brother, lived with them. Dinah became a member of the North Parish, and eventually opened, in 1785, the Ladies' Charitable African School in her home.

Portsmouth did not have many slaves, approximately 140 on the eve of the Revolution. The peculiar institution began as early as 1645, but did not thrive until after 1700; even then there was little economic demand to support a huge degree of slavery. There were enough slaves in Portsmouth to form a distinctive community of their own, which became in time the nucleus of the community of free African Americans. This community had a symbolic government with limited power, and clearly Portsmouth slaves and freedmen thought of self-government. In time they grew bold enough to petition the legislature for a general declaration of emancipation. New Hampshire never officially declared emancipation, but after 1810 there were no longer slaves in the state. After the war, such free blacks had limited rights: they could not vote, nor hold office, though they could own property and testify in court. They worked as farmers, carpenters, and sailors, but overall there was little economic opportunity for a freedman, and most migrated elsewhere. There were only a handful of African Americans living in Portsmouth by the mid-nineteenth century.

Slavery before the Revolutionary War was a mark of wealth. Merchants traded in slaves and owned man-servants, nurses, and other domestics. Even ministers such as the Reverend Joseph Stevens owned slaves. The printer Daniel Fowle, who published the *New Hampshire Gazette* for many years, had as his pressman his slave Prime Fowle. John Stavers's slave helped protect his master, a known Tory and owner of the William Pitt Tavern on Court Street, by attacking a band of threatening patriots—the Sons of Liberty. John Langdon owned several slaves, the most famous of whom was Cyrus Bruce, his waiter. According to the antiquarian Charles Brewster:

> there could scarcely be found in Portsmouth, not excepting the Governor [Langdon] himself, one who dressed more elegantly or exhibited a more gentlemanly appearance. His heavy gold chain and seals, his fine black or blue broadcloth coat and small clothes, his silk stockings and silver-buckled shoes, his ruffled and carefully plaited linen, are well remembered.

Other Portsmouth slaves were remembered as well, though the circumstances were quite different. The *New Hampshire Gazette* reported in August 1757 that James Dwyer's servant was missing. Dwyer described the slave, Scipio, as 35 years old:

> well sett, and of a yellowish Complexion; had on one of his Hands a Scar. Said Negro was born and brought up among the English; he understands Husbandry, mows well, and affects to be thought a Man of Sense. He had on, and carried with him when he Run away, a Saxon

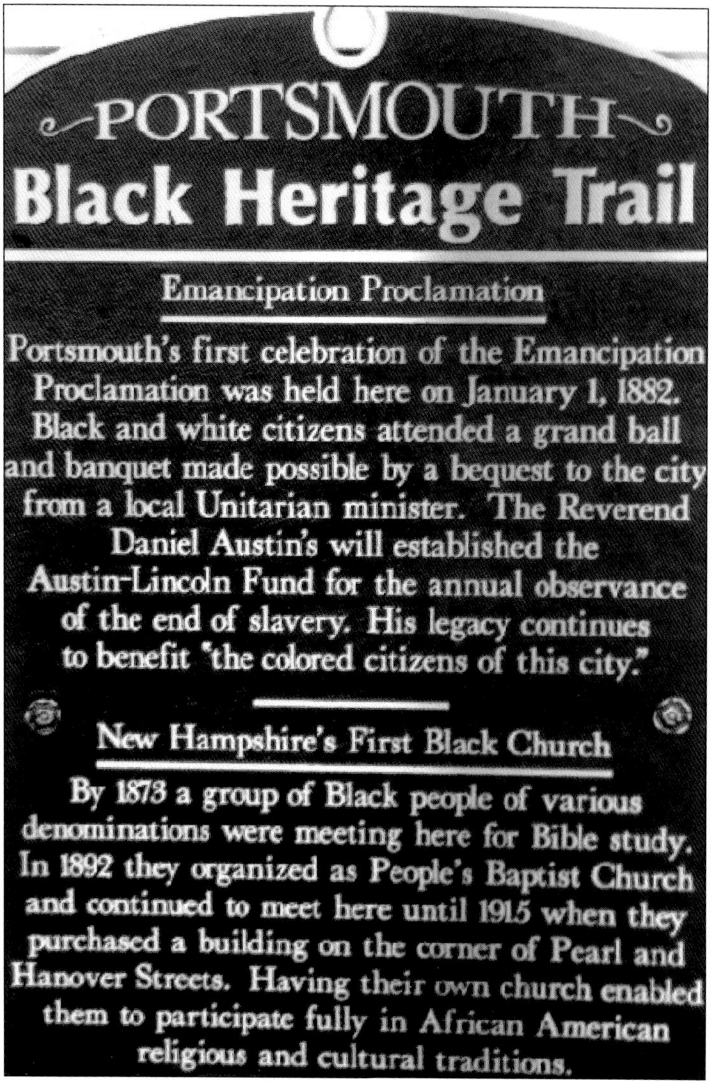

This plaque commemorates the African-American experience in Portsmouth. It is posted at the Portsmouth Children's Museum (former Old South Parish). (Photo by Benjamin Lawson.)

> blue Frize Jacket with small Metal Buttons, Slash sleves . . . , a brown Fustin Under Jacket without Sleves, scarlet Everlasting Breeches, . . . one Wollen Check Shirt, and an odd Hat and Cap.

The advertisement in the *New Hampshire Gazette* went on to say that "whoever shall apprehend said Runaway, or bring him to his said Master in Portsmouth, aforesaid, or secure him so that he many have him again, shall have TEN DOLLARS Reward, and all necessary Charges paid by *James Dwyer*." However, he added, "If the said Scipio will of his own Accord (without putting me to the Charge of the Above Reward) return home, he shall be kindly received, and have his Absconding forgiven." Like many men of the revolutionary period, Scipio used reason, and was self-reliant and courageous. He sought to protect his liberty—the only problem was that he never had it in the first place.

No one knows the ending of Scipio's story, perhaps he was captured, returned, and punished; maybe he escaped and created a whole new life for himself. Could he have been the Scipio Africanus who, along with another free African American, sailed on the *Ranger* with John Paul Jones in 1777? Clearly some African Americans rose above the condition of inequality, for not all whites supported slavery. Those who opposed the institution worked to assist slaves, freedmen, and women to help them achieve normal lives.

The Piscataqua minister, Jeremy Belknap, wrote an angry letter in November 1772 to the *Boston Evening Post* in response to the oft-used argument that the Bible justifies slavery. Africans are not cursed by God, the pastor wrote, "We have no more right to make slaves of the Africans than they have to make slaves of us." Mrs. Isabella Tappon of Portsmouth dedicated her life to helping the poor and destitute, no matter the background or color. She opened the first female asylum

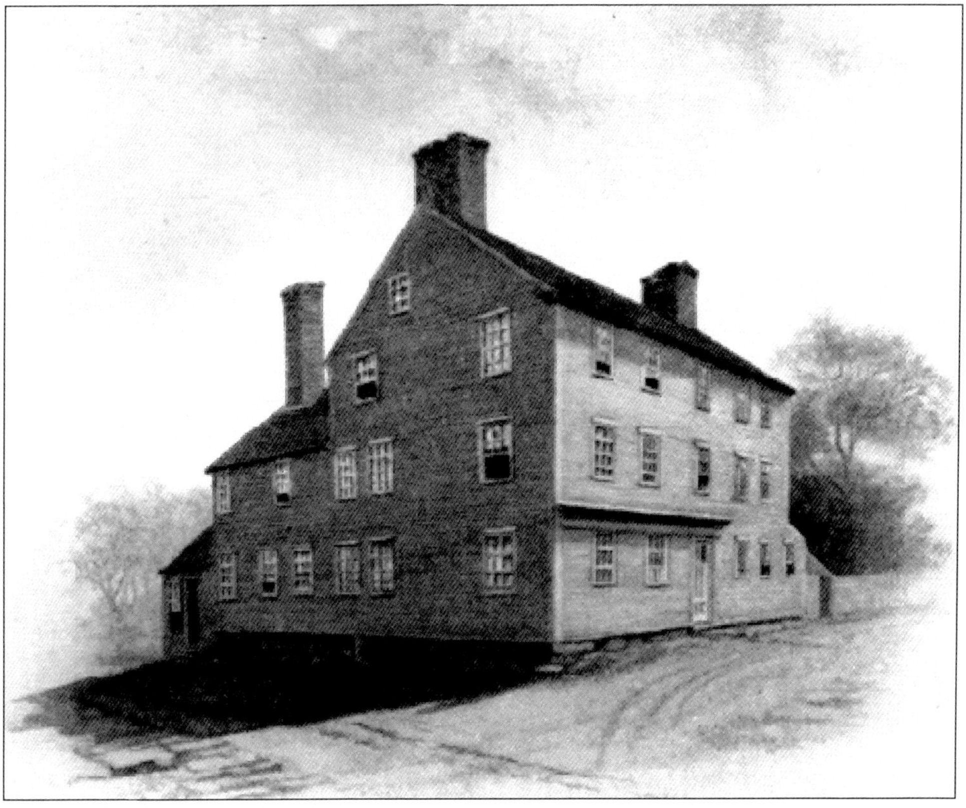

Stavers' Tavern was also known as the Earl of Halifax and the William Pitt Tavern. This tavern hosted many meetings of Patriots during the Revolutionary War. (From Vignettes of Portsmouth.*)*

for poor children, and began a Sunday School in her own home. On Sabbath days she welcomed African-American children to her home for "religious instruction" and lessons in "sewing, knitting, and reading."

Mrs. Tappan received encouragement and assistance from her husband Amos, a grammar school teacher, and her brother, the Reverend Joseph Buckminster. A native of Rutland, Vermont and a graduate of Yale College, Buckminster came to Portsmouth in 1779. In becoming pastor of the North Church, he replaced the venerable Reverend Samuel Langdon and his temporary replacement, the Reverend Ezra Stiles, soon to be president of Yale College. Buckminster was a conservative Calvinist who believed fully in providence and God's sole discretion in determining who is saved and who is damned. He could not escape the usual anxiety that accompanies rumination upon John Calvin's theory of predestination, suffering frequent bouts of depression. These were temporarily removed (though later accentuated) by his courtship and marriage to the beautiful and popular Sarah Stevens, the daughter and only child of the Reverend Benjamin Stevens. Quite a few gallants sought her hand in marriage; one of the most eligible suitors was Ebenezer Hazard.

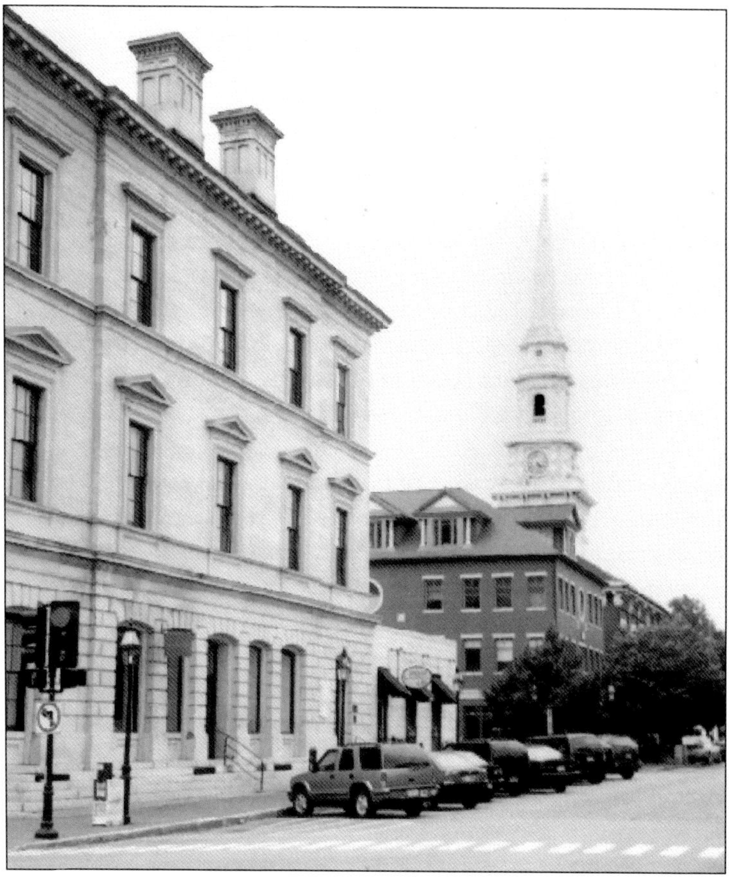

Market Square continues to be the center of Portsmouth. This photograph (by Benjamin Lawson) shows the North Church with the old Custom House in the foreground.

Hazard was a native of Pennsylvania and a graduate of Princeton College; he frequently passed through Portsmouth and Kittery during the war on official business with the U.S. government. He was the Surveyor of Post Roads, charged by Congress with the task of laying out and maintaining postal routes and hiring and supervising local postmasters.

The Piscataqua postmaster was Jeremiah Libbey, a benevolent shopkeeper, overseer of the poor, and founder of Portsmouth's first Universalist religious association. In 1781, Hazard made many excuses to be on the road north of Boston, journeying to Portsmouth then on to Falmouth, Maine, for reasons he kept to himself; he always stopped at Kittery to see Miss Stevens. Jeremy Belknap of Dover, who was good friends with Hazard, suspected something was up, and asked the bachelor Hazard if the "new business" he had complained about was in fact Miss Stevens. Hazard was reluctant to respond, but when Belknap broke the news of Buckminster's engagement to Sarah Stevens, Hazard admitted that she had been the object of his attention. Hazard wrote that he had wondered why Miss Stevens's attention had been so firmly fixed on Portsmouth. "No other damage will arise from" his courtship of Miss Stevens "than a small derangement of my plan of operations," which meant matrimony. "In matters of this nature, circumstances must and will govern." A few weeks later, Hazard confided to Belknap that he wished the couple well, but "am not sure I shall not break the tenth commandment."

Belknap, who engaged in witty writing yet was cautious about being too explicit in his letters, enjoyed designating mutual acquaintances with pseudonyms. Buckminster, since he lived in Portsmouth, the big city compared to Belknap's town of Dover, earned the title of *Metropolitan*. Hazard wrote in the spring of 1782 complaining that Belknap had failed to inform him of Buckminster's marriage to his former amour. "Why did you not inform me that the Metropolitan was married?" Hazard wrote. "I have had a most rapturous letter from him upon the subject, which, were I as intimate with him as with you, would probably produce some laughable speculations." Belknap responded that on a visit by the man:

> the Metropolitan's raptures had so taken hold of my imagination . . . that I could not help complimenting him upon the subject, withal adding that he had a reason to be in raptures. I hope I have not transgressed the bounds of friendship in so doing. They seem at present to be very pleased with each other.

In August 1782, Hazard wrote Belknap that "the Metropolitan's raptures still continue. I expect he will claim the flitch of bacon," a prediction soon fulfilled.

Hazard informed his friend in December that "the Metropolitan's lady advances fast toward blessing him with a boy!" Yet it was not to be, for Sarah Buckminster's pregnancy miscarried, which filled her apprehensive husband with anxiety. During her second pregnancy he was "gloomy" with prognostications of doom. Sarah was weakened by the first, and the second was a severe physical trial, and Belknap himself feared for the happiness of the couple. He wrote Hazard:

> I am seriously afraid that, after the effect of her present pregnancy shall have appeared, her nature will be too feeble to support a third. Her mother died young! Her father [Reverend Stevens], talks of journeying to the southward, and I wish he may put his design into execution. It will agreeably relieve him from the dull business of preaching to a few sleepy fishermen [at Kittery] and paddling up and down to Portsmouth every week, which is all his amusement.

During these anxious times, Joseph Buckminster did his best to find mental distractions. Upon hearing about the successful launchings of hot-air balloons, first in France and then in Philadelphia, Buckminster worked out a plan whereby a smaller version of such a balloon could be fixed to a horse-drawn carriage, which:

> would so counteract the force of gravity as to abate the friction of the wheels and axis, by which means a less power might be sufficient to move it. A carriage going up an hill might be as light to the horse as on plain ground, and one on the plain ground as light as on a declivity.

Science was a favorite subject of Deists, those who denied the Trinity, and believed God to be a passive though a benevolent creator. Buckminster constantly sought ways to counteract their philosophical assumptions and supposed logic. He was delighted to receive from Belknap an anti-Deist pamphlet to give the Portsmouth Deists a "bone to pick," for Buckminster was "much worried" that a litter of such "puppies" was "under his nose."

Whether Deist or Christian, everyone in Portsmouth had a difficult time explaining what happened to young Mehetable Widdon, a Portsmouth 18-year-old, in June 1783. She claimed to have been "struck blind with lightning" though:

> there was no stroke of lightning on or near the house. She had just been stooping to a cradle, and was raising herself up with her face towards a west window, and not nearer to it than five or six feet, the sash being down, when a sharp flash of lightning met her eye, which, as she says, caused the sensation of heat in her face, and immediately deprived her of sight. She remained so three weeks, but was not all the time so totally blind but that she could discern night from day, and in one or two instances the colour of people's clothes who were near her. Blisters and cold baths were applied to no purpose. On Wednesday the 9th of July, she dreamed that she should recover her sight on the following Friday, which accordingly happened. When she awoke on Friday morning, the 11th, she found that she could open her eyes, but with pain; and by little

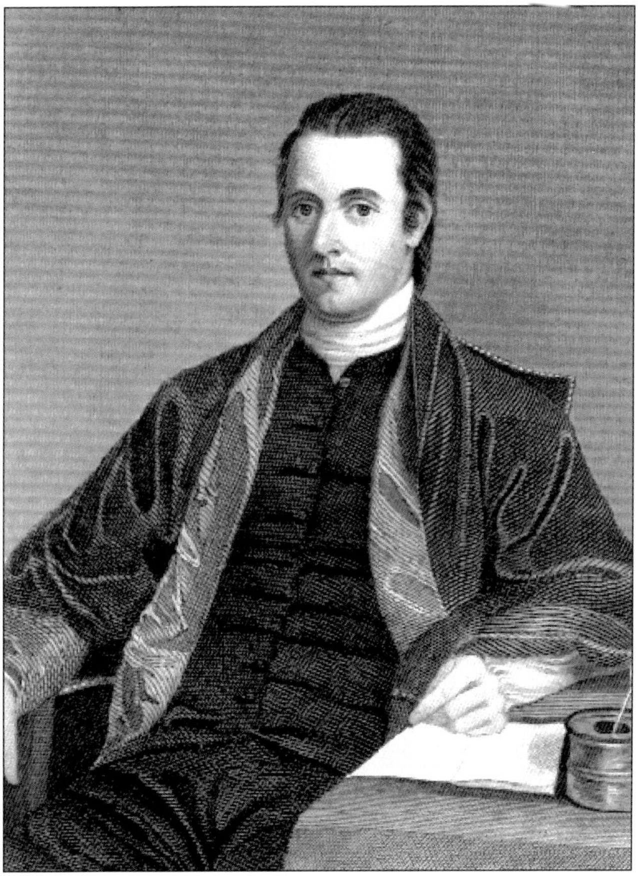

The Reverend Joseph Buckminster was pastor of the North Church from 1779 to 1812. From the pulpit Reverend Buckminster preached a traditional Calvinist theology. (From Memoirs of Rev. Joseph Buckminster, D.D.*)*

> and little, in the course of the forenoon, she got them completely open, and could see clearly. For several days afterward . . . she was obliged to open her eyes gradually in the morning, and this was attended with pain. She cannot bear a strong light, but sees clearly and distinctly within doors, or in a cloudy weather. She seems to be a modest, sensible girl, and has a grateful sense of the Divine goodness in her recovery.

Had Mehetable not recovered, there were numerous excellent physicians in Portsmouth, as well as a new hospital. Ammi Cutter, Hall Jackson, and Joshua Brackett were town leaders and benevolent physicians who were instrumental in opening the hospital in 1782 on Henzell's Island after a failed attempt to open one in 1778. Generally speaking, the hospital existed to inoculate citizens for smallpox, followed by three weeks of quarantine. Each physician received $8 for his trouble; paupers admitted to the hospital were inoculated gratis.

Disease follows close upon the heals of war. A smallpox outbreak was always a threat, indeed more fearsome than British Regulars. The war brought to a head the debate about smallpox prevention that had been occupying physicians and interested others even after Cotton Mather pushed for inoculation in the early years of the eighteenth century.

Some Portsmouth residents believed that inoculation was a justifiable risk to take, even though it involved purposefully "having the Small pox" by introducing the diseased blood into a healthy person (as depicted in the last chapter). Yet during this era, other Portsmouth residents believed that it was best to let Nature or God's will be done to allow smallpox to "spread the Natural Way." A document that survives from the beginning of the war in 1776 (quoted by Nathaniel Adams, *Annals of Portsmouth*) expresses the belief of Selectman Samuel Cutts "that 3/4 of the people think it much less resque" to take their chances with smallpox—that in fact inoculation was misguided, as it tended to spread the disease among the otherwise healthy inhabitants. So town leaders came up with a proposal:

> following Method Established for ye present—viz
> 1 to have the pest House used for a Hospital for inoculation—
> 2d that a Committee of 5 respectable persons be Appointed to regulate the pest House & Establish the following Rules
> 3d That a Doctor of fidelity be Appointed, who must reside at [Shapley's] Island during the pleasure of the Committee—
> 4th That two or three persons be chosen and Sworn to conform to the directions of the Committee, to Attend upon ye order of the House—
> 5th that no person be Admitted upon the Island without Written leave from the Committee—
> 6th That if any person Clandistantly goes upon the Island in order to have the Small pox, shall be Subject to a penalty of 30£ Lawfull money—
> 7th That any & Every person that chooses to go down to the Pest House to be inoculated, must Apply to the Committee, & pay them . . . Lawful money for the Charge, & then obtain a certificate from said Committee to the Doct[r] of his having Agreed to the Terms of inoculating.

War brought other headaches from which the town selectmen, committee of safety, and provincial government could find little relief. One was expressed by the committee of safety in November 1775, as recorded by Nathaniel Adams. In the opinion of Generals Washington and Sullivan, "a thousand Men were requisite" to defend Portsmouth harbor from enemy attacks. Yet the town already had hundreds of men serving in the militia elsewhere and could only field 500 to defend the harbor. The committee informed the province:

> If so small a Number as 500 are posted there, the Enemy, from whose late behavior, we can expect nothing but Treachery, and Surprize, in case they can obtain by such means, either of the ports, will make use of those very works to dispossess us of the rest, which as they have a plenty of Ammunition, of which We are Short, We fear they may too easily

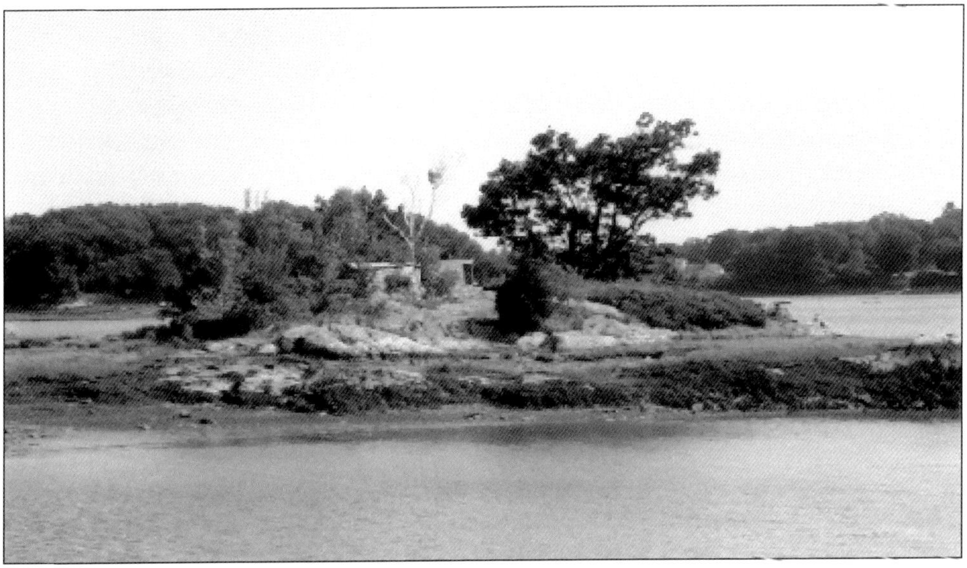

The lonely island in the river is caught, as it were, between Portsmouth and Newcastle. Dozens of such islands pose an ongoing challenge to navigators of the Piscataqua. (Photo by Benjamin Lawson.)

> do—That the Harbour of Boston being liable to freeze, which is not the case with this, an Acquisition of this kind would be of vast importance to the Enemy, while it would strike a general Damp on the inhabitants of this Colony, an Event carefully to be guarded against at this critical Season of the War.

Another headache that the town assembly addressed in 1776 was the profiteering going on by merchants and others at the expense of other citizens, particularly the poor:

> We are concern'd to see Monopolies Extortion & Oppression so predominant in Town & Country by which the Poor, the Widow, the Orphan the Fatherless & many other Classes of People are suffering under every discouragement, & is more Instrumental of Proselyting many to the side of our Enemies, than even the most open Bribery & Corruption for while we are Complaining of Oppression from the British Government & flying from the Effects of such Oppression, we are made doubly miserable under the disguise of Friendship.

The growing numbers of the poor continued to stretch Portsmouth's resources to the limit. Shipping dropped from 12,000 tons in 1774 to 500 tons by 1780. The "Mechanic & Laborer" of Portsmouth lost their jobs and were uncertain of the future. "Multitudes are reduced from easy Circumstances, to want & beggary, and half the Inhabitants at least have frequently been without Bread or Fuel." Many of the poor came from the Isles of Shoals and the Portsmouth Committee of Safety, the quasi-legal revolutionary committee of the town, had feared at the beginning of the war that Shoalers were exporting fish to enemy ports. Shortly thereafter "a resolve passed the General-Court of this State, order[g] the Inhabitants of the Isle of Shoals to remove from thence, to prevent any Intelligence which might otherwise be given to the Enemy."

As a consequence, the inhabitants of the Isles of Shoals abandoned their homes and fled to towns on the mainland. Portsmouth inhabitants thought "the poorer Sort of them" fled to their town, where they became part of the growing burden on local resources. The scarcity of coin, curtailed trade, and astonishing rate of inflation meant that what money people had, now became quickly worthless. Poor relief by 1780 cost the town an incredible £80,000 in inflated currency.

Elizabeth Lewis was one of the many distraught and impoverished inhabitants of Portsmouth who petitioned the town, as well as the General Court of the state, for aid. Although she could not write, Mrs. Lewis nevertheless allowed her political sympathies and fiery independence to be known as she begged the state for support:

> To the Honourable the Councile and the House of Representatives for the Sate of New Hampshire Now Convened at Exeter for the Dispatch of Business. The Humble Pition of Elizabeth Lewis of Portsmouth, Humbly Sheweth to your honours That when it was the sovereign Pleasure of the suprem Director of all Human Events to Permit a Spirit of Timidety to Seize the Bulk of the British Nation in Suffering their Rulers to Pursue such a Systim of Policy Disgracefule to them as a Nation Inasmuch as their conduct was Unjustifiable by the Fundamentals of their own Constitution and when it Become the Indispinsible Duty of the Inhabitants of these States for the Preservation of their Own Liberty's as well to Guard the sacred Disport the Natural Rights of Posterity to embody a Number of its Freemen to Counteract the Flagitious and Sanguinary Disigns of Evil & Disingning Men—That John Lewis the only Son of your Petitioner Engaged in the Service of his country in troops Raised by this State for the Preservation of American Liberty as Early as the year 1775. That on the 6th Decbr 1776 he Inlisted into the Company of Capt Benjamin Titcomb During the Present war That on the 26th following at the battle of Trenton he served the Sacred Cause & paid the Last Trible Due to his Country by Breathing his Last in its Service.

The same year, Major Samuel Sherburne petitioned the general assembly for aid, having served under General Sullivan during the Rhode Island campaign. During the action, he "lost his left Leg by a shot from the Artillery of [the] Enemy." Two years later, soldier Richard Sherman likewise petitioned the general assembly for help. On Christmas day 1782, he claimed:

> that your petitioner enlisted in the Continental service in the year 1777—that at the retreat from [Fort] Ticonderoga he was wounded by the enemy in the hip; that afterwards, at the Capture of Burgoyne [at Saratoga] he was wounded in the arm—and lastly with Genl Sullivan, at Susquehanna, he was wounded in the body the ball passing, after entering the breast, thro' the shoulder.

While soldier Sherburne was away at war, the male citizens of Portsmouth, assembled "att a legal Town Meeting held at the West-Chamber in the State-House in Portsmo" in 1780, and agreed that the following instructions be sent to the town representatives William Whipple, John Langdon, and George Gains, who were sitting at the Continental Congress. Like all seaport towns, Portsmouth was laboring under the strain of curtailed trade, triple-digit inflation, swelling numbers of poor and disabled, and sorrow and horror over the tremendous loss of life that war brings. Many of the citizens of Portsmouth, being reluctant revolutionaries, believed that Congress mishandled the course of the war up to that point (1780). *The Instructions* to the town representatives, recorded by Nathaniel Adams, reads in part:

> At a time when our obstinate foes are pluming themselves on their skill in financing, building their fond hopes of conquest upon our

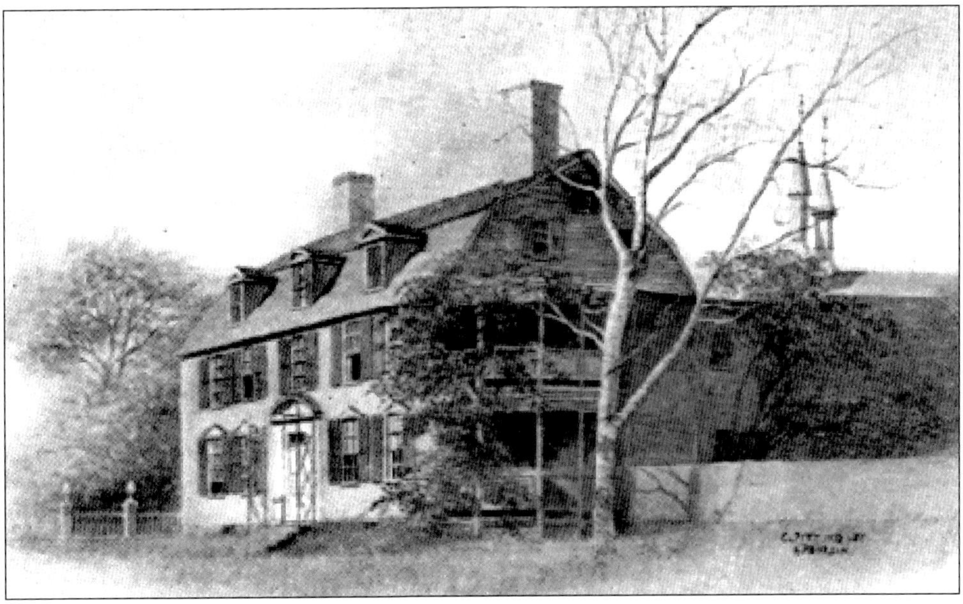

The Lord House was the temporary residence of John Paul Jones during the War for Independence. Here the gallant Jones entertained Patriots and their ladies while he awaited the outfitting of the Providence *and construction of the* America. *(From* Vignettes of Portsmouth.*)*

> want of experience in that art, and failure of our paper currency; while our agriculture, alliances and resources are increasing, with pungent sorrow, we behold our medium of trade, the nerves and sinnews of our defence labouring under the loss of public faith! Without enquiring into the policy of former administrations, or faulting them for not providing funds adequate to its support, or for taking other measures to prevent its depreciation, which have had a contrary effect; realizing that public and private credit must ever be supported by integrity and honour; we instruct you to revise all the laws now existing respecting our paper-currency, and to use your influence for the repeal of any inconsistent with those principles; and for enacting such as shall give credit and permanency to the currency, rescue the widow and orphan from the hand of oppression and injustice, and fix a lasting criterion for commutative justice between the subjects of this state, that none in future may have just cause of complaint. Convinced from reason and experience, that all embargoes and restrictions of trade between the States, are anticommercial and tend to destroy the harmony and friendly intercourse which the principles of the american constitution are calculated to encourage and cherish, we recommend it to you not to consent to any such embargoes and commercial restrictions but on the contrary that you upon all occasions strive to preserve the most intimate cordiality and friendly intercourse between these states, ever emulous, with care and caution, to nurture and bring to maturity a plant of such nice contexture.

The building of ships at Portsmouth harbor brought about some diversion during the dismal years of war. The 74-gun *America*, constructed on Langdon's (Rising Castle) Island from 1778 to 1782, was the biggest ship assembled during the war. John Paul Jones had oversight for most of this time and at one point the *America* required:

> 50 carpenters, 20 ordinary laborers, 20 caulkers, ten riggers, 10 sailors, 2 mast-builders, and an uncertain number of blacksmiths, sail-makers, coppers, plumbers, painters, glaziers, carvers, boat-builders, ship-copperers, tinners, cabinet-makers, and tanners" working on "700 tons of timbers, 100 casks of naval stores, 40 tons of iron, 1,000 water-casks, masts and spars of all sorts, sheets of lead, train oil, and oakum.

One other necessity that was needed was 1,300 gallons of rum to keep the men in good spirits (Saltonstall, *Ports of Piscataqua*, 102–3).

Captain Jones expected to take command when the ship was finished, but by then at the end of 1782, the war had drawn almost to a close, and Congress determined to present the ship to France as a gift for the years of assistance during the war. When John Paul Jones heard the news his "nose," according to Jeremy

Belknap, was seriously "out of joint." Yet in the end, he graciously helped launch the ship. Belknap was on-hand for the launching November 5, 1782. Although rumor had it that the whole thing was a disaster, Belknap reported the contrary to his friend Ebenezer Hazard:

> two attempts . . . were made before she could be got off. During the first, I was an eye-witness, being on the island, and very near the ship, the whole time. The reasons of her not going off was, in the carpenter's phrase, that she was too strait-laced. . . . They had taken so much care to keep her from falling, that she could not move but about twelve feet, and all the hawsers, tackles, and screws that could be used were ineffectual. At the second attempt she was launched, and I have been assured by those who saw it (being myself then at Boston) that she went off as easily and gently as a canoe.

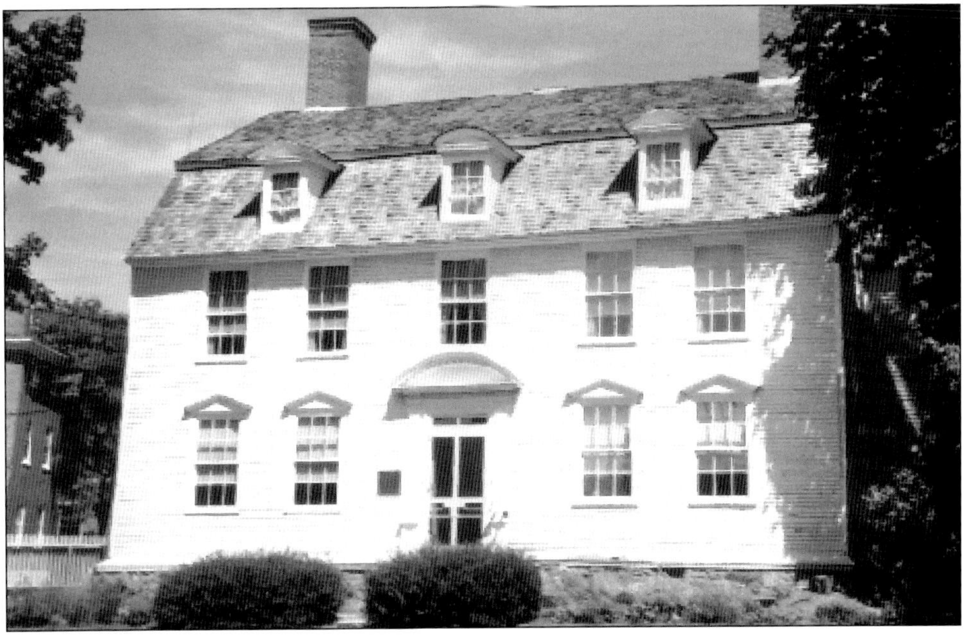

The Lord House is today better known as the John Paul Jones House. The Portsmouth Historical Society owns the house, which is open to the public. (Photo by Benjamin Lawson.)

5. Washington Comes to Portsmouth

The people of Portsmouth found much to celebrate in the immediate years after the war ended. The proclamation of peace in 1783 brought forth the town ministers to preach collective thanks to God. Church bells kept up an unending peal above the general hilarity in the streets, people congratulated each other, enemies embraced at long last, and toasts were raised to the soldiers who brought liberty to America.

The town celebrated five years later the ratification of the Constitution. The biggest parade ever seen in Portsmouth wound about the city streets. The antiquarian Nathaniel Adams, himself an observer, related that, "about 11 o'clock a large concourse of the inhabitants assembled on the parade, and moved in procession through the principal streets" in a set order according to profession. First marched farmers guiding "a plough drawn by nine yoke of oxen." Next came sowers and reapers leading "a cart for gathering in harvest." Craftsmen involved in the construction and outfitting of ships marched next. "Mathematical instrument-makers with an azimuth compass" navigated a boat under construction. Other representatives of Portsmouth's marine economy followed, such as ship-captains and harbor-pilots "with spy-glasses and charts" guiding "the ship Union completely rigged, armed and manned, under an easy sail, with colours flying, elevated on a carriage drawn by nine horses," representing the nine states that had ratified the Constitution.

As the parade wound through the streets, laborers, mechanics, butchers, bakers, barbers, masons, carpenters, leather-workers, metal-workers, watch-makers, brick-layers, and wheel-wrights were followed by "printers, preceded by two lads with open quires of printed paper, followed with cases and apparatus decorated, and compositors at work." Pressmen worked, printed, and distributed to the crowds "songs in celebration of the ratification of the Federal Constitution, by the state of New-Hampshire." And the people sang:

> A government of freemen never knows
> A tyran'ts shackles on the press t' impose.

Next came town professionals such as teachers, doctors, lawyers, sheriffs, judges, and state dignitaries such as John Langdon, "president of the state, and president of the convention," who led members of the state ratifying convention, state legislators, and soldiers in their bright uniforms. "Every profession was distinguished by some insignia or badge peculiar to it. All intended to represent that in consequence of this union, commerce, and all the arts dependent on it, would revive and flourish. During the procession several Federal songs, composed for the occasion, were sung, accompanied by the band."

The marchers enjoyed a repast of food and drink, highlighted by "nine patriotic toasts," after each of which "the artillery fired a salute." Their bosoms thus warmed with drink and patriotism, "the songs were again sung," the band again played, and "the procession formed in the same order, and was saluted by thirteen guns from the artillery"—a "Federal salute." "On their arrival at the court-house, a salute was fired from the ship, and the company dispersed. The ship fired another salute, as she passed the President's house." That evening, more toasts and music

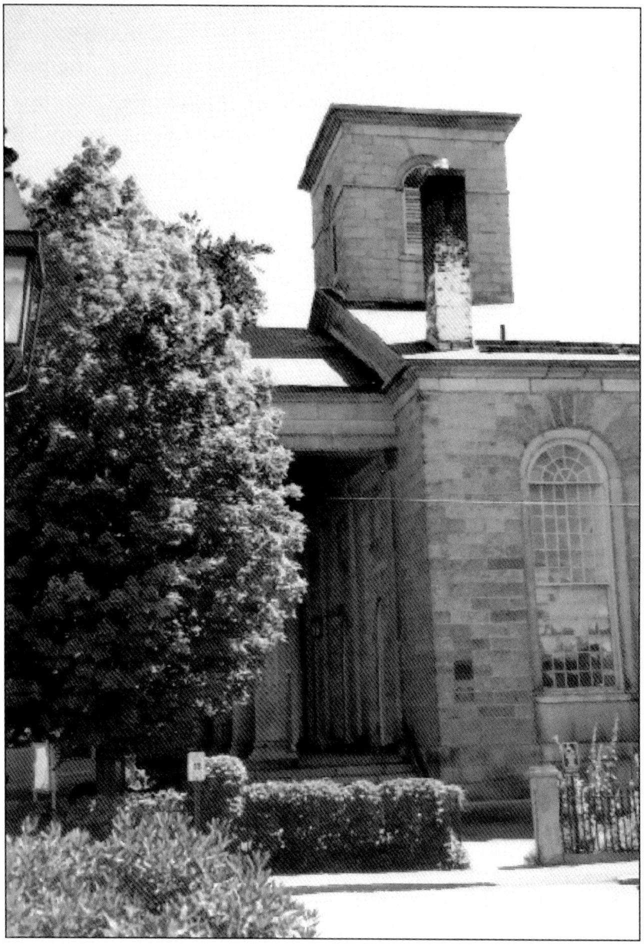

The South Church on State Street was built in the 1820s. It is the home of the Unitarian-Universalist Society. The Universalists were a growing denomination after the American Revolution. (Photo by Benjamin Lawson.)

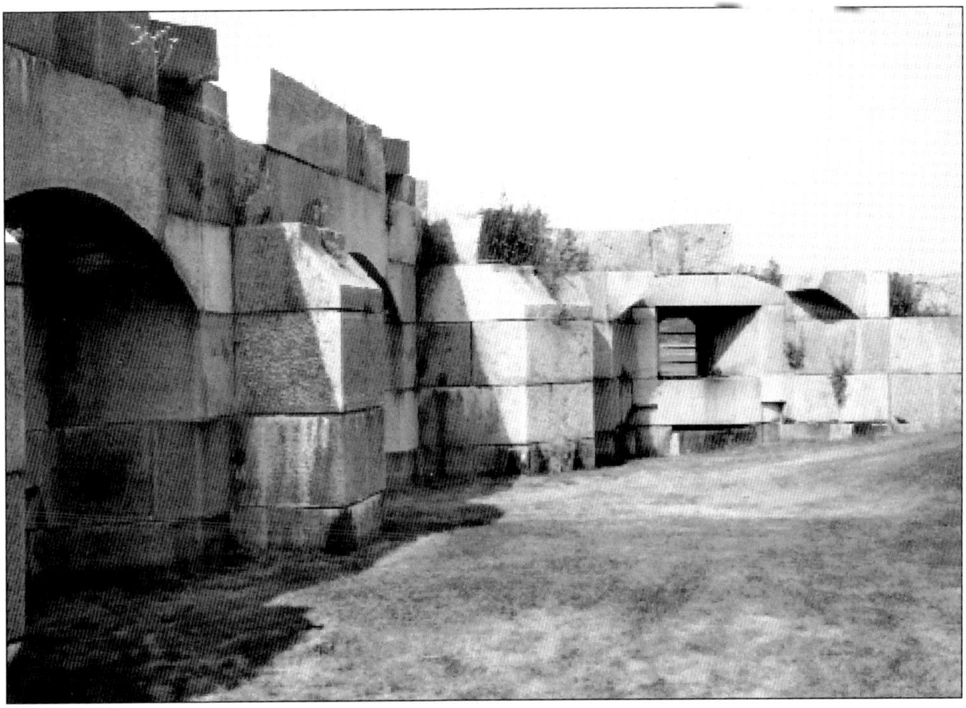

These massive granite fortifications at Fort Constitution date from the uncertain period leading up to the War of 1812. Patriots changed the name of the fort from William and Mary to Constitution around the time of George Washington's visit to the city. (Photo by Benjamin Lawson.)

ensued, and "joy sparkled in every eye, and pleasure was seated in every breast," and "all seemed to anticipate the happier days, which they were to enjoy under the Federal government."

The new Constitution inspired in the citizens of Portsmouth a desire to discard any reminders of royalty, in particular the appellations of places and institutions that seemed inconsistent with a free republic. Renaming places did not occur overnight. During 1789, and in subsequent years, Queen's Chapel turned into St. John's, King Street became State Street, and Fort William and Mary was christened as Fort Constitution. The biggest change that is closely tied to Portsmouth and its inhabitants occurred sometime around 1789. It continues to be a mystery who named the tallest mountain of the Northeast—the grandest peak of the White Mountains—Mount Washington. This imposing slope had been known to residents of the seacoast for well over 150 years and sailors at sea could often spy its white summit. Indeed, from any eminence along the seacoast the mountain could be seen on clear days.

Native Americans called the mountain Agiocochook, while white settlers and inhabitants of towns along the seacoast and of the Piscataqua Valley referred to it as the White Hill, the Mountain, the Great White Hill, the Great White Mountain, or, the Great Mountain. Yet at the same time that the new government began in

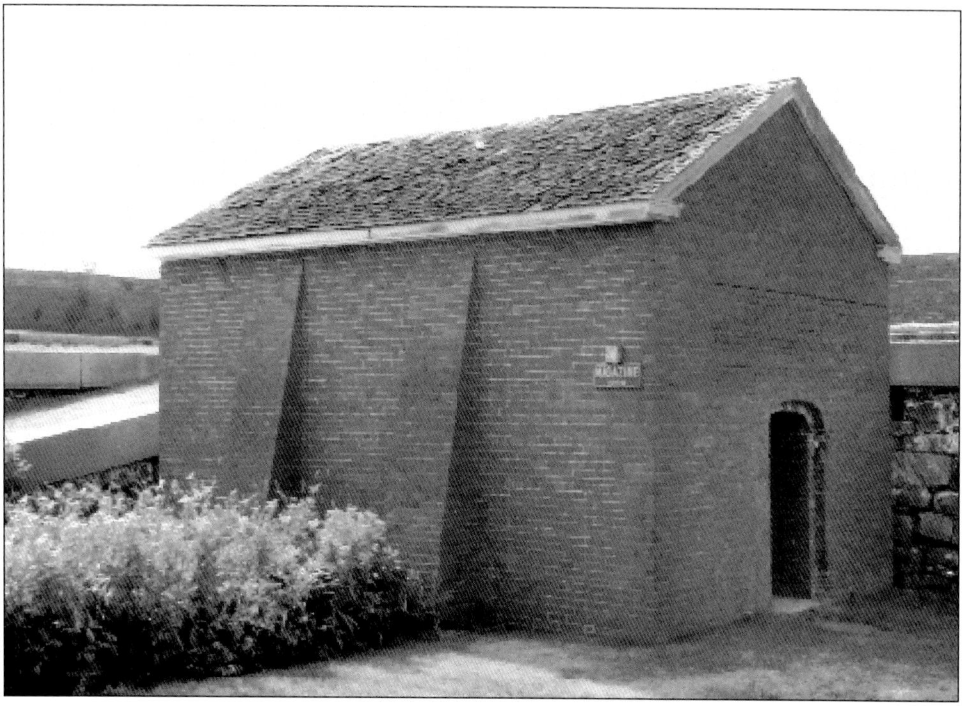

This ammunition magazine was built in 1808 at Fort Constitution at a time of great tension between the United States and Great Britain. The Embargo Act of 1808 angered the British and curtailed Portsmouth trade. (Photo by Benjamin Lawson.)

1789, and the first president took office, someone renamed the Great Mountain, Mount Washington.

One Portsmouth resident, Joseph Whipple, had climbed it and owned land just beyond in Dartmouth (Jefferson), New Hampshire. He journeyed almost yearly to his lands, passing through the Western (Crawford) Notch, hiking under the shadow of the Great Mountain. When General Washington became president, there was no one more enthusiastic about the man than Whipple. Washington rewarded his loyal supporter by bestowing the office of Collector of Customs upon him. Did Whipple in turn honor President Washington by suggesting that the most imposing, glorious mountain of America be named after the grandest patriot of America? Perhaps.

It was in 1789, then, that the new government was organized under the leadership of President George Washington, Vice-President John Adams, two senators from each state (John Langdon and Paine Wingate from New Hampshire), and congressmen (Samuel Livermore, Nicholas Gilman, and Abiel Foster of New Hampshire). Conservatives, who called themselves Federalists, led by Alexander Hamilton of New York, dominated Washington's government. Langdon was an early supporter of Hamilton's policies of national leadership controlling state finances. President Washington believed that without strong federal leadership, the finances and security of the United States of America would be at risk. Yet not everyone supported the new government. Almost half of the delegates in the 13 state ratifying conventions voted against the ratification of the Constitution. It was Washington's job to ensure that all Americans supported the federal government and his presidency. This was the germ of his idea to travel about the United States discovering the sentiments of the people and addressing their concerns.

Washington wrote in his diary that he:

> had conversed with Colonel Hamilton on the propriety of my making a tour through the Eastern states during the recess of Congress to acquire knowledge of the face of the Country the growth and Agriculture there of and the temper and disposition of the Inhabitants toward the new government.

Hamilton concurred, so Washington set out on October 15 from New York (the current center of government), stopping in various cities along the way. Expectant Bostonians declared that "a family of children cannot receive a long absent parent with more real joy than will be felt by the citizens of [Boston] on his coming." When he arrived on October 26, the *Boston Gazette* reported that the president was "attended only by his two private secretaries and servants." One of his secretaries, Tobias Lear, was a native of Portsmouth. Residents received

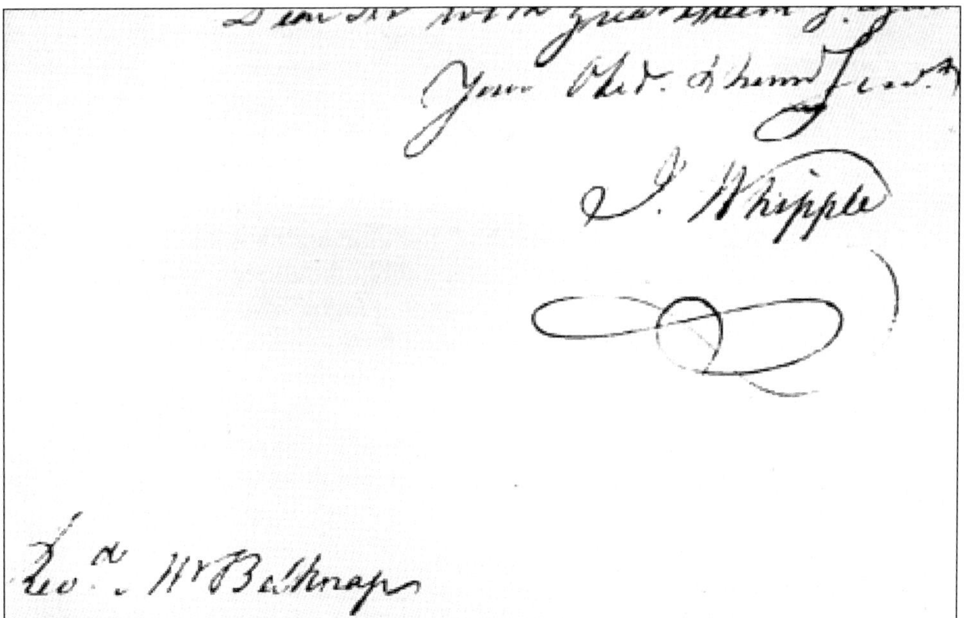

Shown is Joseph Whipple's signature to a 1789 letter written to Jeremy Belknap. Whipple was a scientist, explorer, merchant, and patriot. (Courtesy Massachusetts Historical Society.)

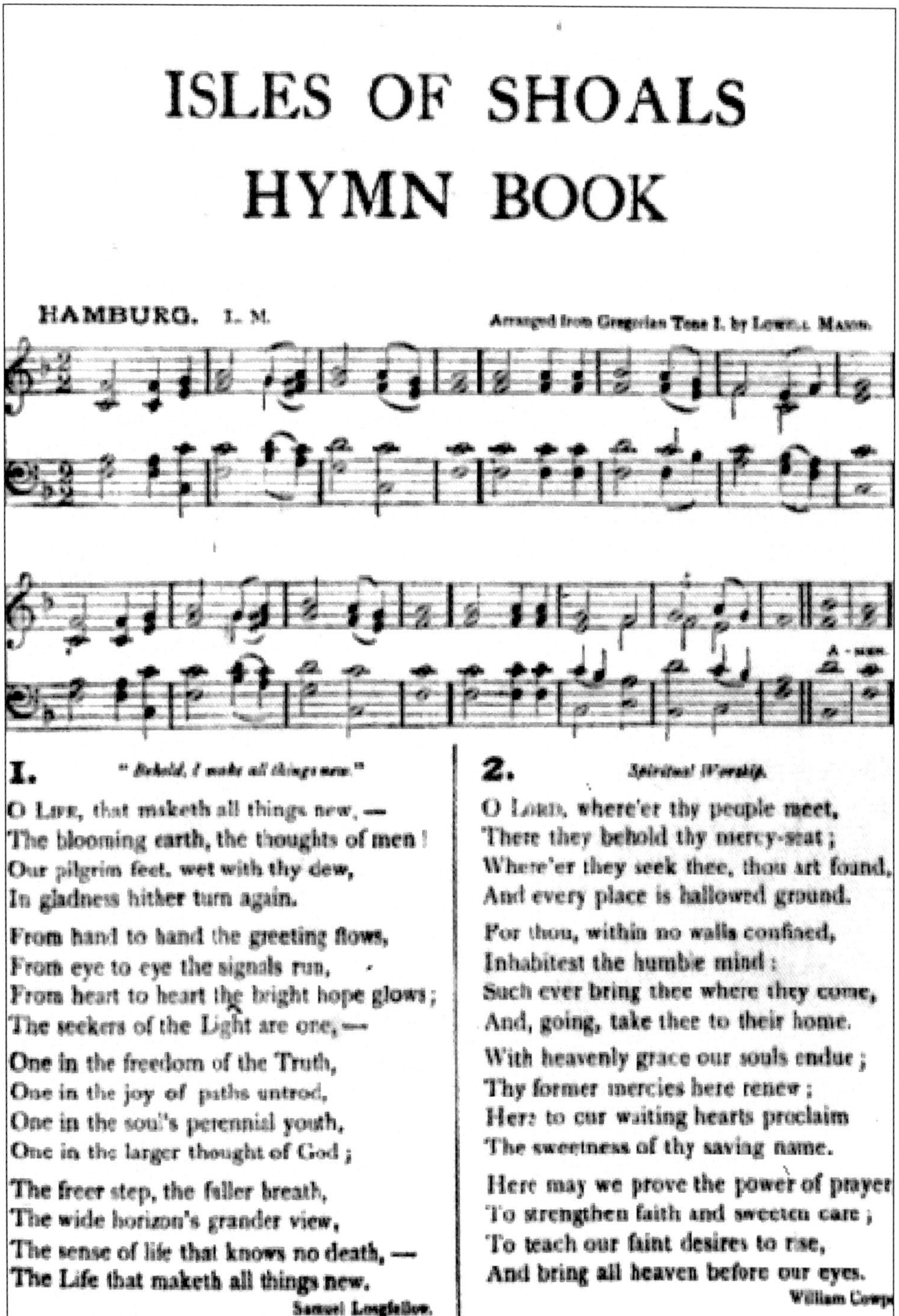

ISLES OF SHOALS HYMN BOOK

HAMBURG. L. M. Arranged from Gregorian Tone I. by LOWELL MASON.

1. *"Behold, I make all things new."*

O LIFE, that maketh all things new, —
The blooming earth, the thoughts of men!
Our pilgrim feet, wet with thy dew,
In gladness hither turn again.

From hand to hand the greeting flows,
From eye to eye the signals run,
From heart to heart the bright hope glows;
The seekers of the Light are one, —

One in the freedom of the Truth,
One in the joy of paths untrod,
One in the soul's perennial youth,
One in the larger thought of God;

The freer step, the fuller breath,
The wide horizon's grander view,
The sense of life that knows no death, —
The Life that maketh all things new.

Samuel Longfellow.

2. *Spiritual Worship.*

O LORD, where'er thy people meet,
There they behold thy mercy-seat;
Where'er they seek thee, thou art found,
And every place is hallowed ground.

For thou, within no walls confined,
Inhabitest the humble mind:
Such ever bring thee where they come,
And, going, take thee to their home.

With heavenly grace our souls endue;
Thy former mercies here renew;
Here to our waiting hearts proclaim
The sweetness of thy saving name.

Here may we prove the power of prayer
To strengthen faith and sweeten care;
To teach our faint desires to rise,
And bring all heaven before our eyes.

William Cowp

The Isles of Shoals Hymn Book was published in 1908. After years of economic and social chaos and moral dissipation, the residents of Star Island were attempting to revive culture and religion.

news of the President's tour and intended visit on October 20th. The *New Hampshire Spy* editorialized that Washington's visit would "afford the citizens . . . an opportunity of paying their respects to the man whom Heaven has selected from the millions of Americans to wield the sword of peace and war." One might think that such rhetoric was forced, but Washington's visit to Portsmouth would prove the contrary.

The President arrived at the New Hampshire border on the last day of October, 1789. He recorded in his diary that he departed Newburyport, Massachusetts, on the morning of October 31 after spending a day at receptions and watching parades. His Massachusetts entourage crossed the broad Merrimack River at Salisbury, then after 3 miles came to the New Hampshire border, where he was met by "many respectable characters." These were state dignitaries such as Senator John Langdon, General John Sullivan (president of the state), and Senator Paine Wingate. The *New Hampshire Gazette* reported that Washington, elegantly dressed in his military uniform, sat astride a striking white horse. The President "then passed the troops drawn up to receive him; who severally vied with each other, who could pay the most respect to the man whom Heaven approves, and Americans delight to honour." He was pleased with the "several troops of well clothed Horse in handsome uniforms, and many officers of the Militia also in handsome (white and red) uniforms." "The President then dismounted from his horse" and "took his carriage"; 700 horse soldiers escorted the once-general to Greenland. "The way, for the most part," was "lined with spectators of all ranks." Washington traveled north along what is today Route One. He stopped at Wells' Tavern in Hampton Falls for refreshment, sitting over his cup for a minute to greet old comrades, veterans of the Revolutionary War. He proceeded to Greenland, following what is today Post Road, to the delightful center of the town. Eventually he arrived at Portsmouth.

Washington approached the town from the south, halting briefly at the Plains to freshen up at the Globe Tavern, and to mount his steed to enter the city with dignity. "At his entrance into this town," the *New Hampshire Gazette* reported, "he was saluted by thirteen cannon," representing the 13 states, "from three companies of Artillery." The crowds of people, through which Washington's carriage and horse had passed all day, grew larger. Men and women who had only heard of Washington pointed to the dignified man in the carriage, applauding and congratulating him.

Tobias Lear, who rode in the coach while Washington was mounted, became astonished and embarrassed—but the shouts and applause were too great to correct the initial impression. Eventually, as Washington's entourage made it into the center of town, notables and dignitaries who knew the man corrected the mistake. Citizens lined the streets according to rank and profession. "The windows and doors of every house were crowded with ladies, anxious to see and bless the man whom America stands so much indebted." Church bells "rang a joyful peal, and repeated shouts from grateful thousands, hail'd their Deliverer welcome to the Metropolis of New-Hampshire." The cannon at Fort William and Mary, soon to be Fort Constitution, boomed a salute to the President and "ships in the harbour were dressed" in maritime finery. Washington, on his way to becoming the "Father of his Country," but still human, was somewhat embarrassed by the grandiose reception. He was, of course, the epitome of dignity and reserve, and he welcomed his role as the symbol of the new republic. Some extravagance was acceptable, but one bard went too far:

> Behold he comes! Columbia's pride,
> And Nature's boast—her fav'rite Son,
> Of valour wisdom—truth—well try'd—
> Hail, Matchless WASHINGTON.

The parade approached the state house in late afternoon. "Children of the schools," the *Gazette* reported, "with diamond shaped cockades on their hats from which a quill projected, were arranged near the State House. The different schools were designated by different colored cockades." Speeches were made and "odes were sung;" dinners were planned and receptions prepared. A fireworks show of 13 rockets lit up the town and revealed the smiling faces of its delighted inhabitants.

Washington himself enjoyed the fireworks from his room at Colonel Brewster's "Coffee House and Tavern" at the corner of Court and Pleasant streets, where he had retired several hours before, after first stopping at Stavers' Tavern on Court Street for drinks and then Senator Langdon's house for tea. According to the *Gazette*:

> The day concluded without any unlucky occurrence to mar the pleasure excited by so auspicious an event, everything was conducted with the greatest possible order and regularity, each countenance beamed with lively joy—sorrow was banished far away, and each heart beat grateful to the name of WASHINGTON.

The next day was a Sunday and in the morning Washington, an Anglican, attended Queen's Chapel. The Episcopal rector was Reverend John Ogden, who preached to a packed house—quite unusual for a parish that until recently was struggling to survive. Indeed, just four years before the Wardens of the church had petitioned the General Court of the state to allow the church to sell the pews of those who had once upon a time purchased them but failed to continue to make payments. Tobias Lear accompanied the President, who was elegantly dressed "in a complete suit of black silk velvet—coat, vest, and small clothes—with black silk stockings and brilliant shoe buckles," to the special pew reserved for him.

In the afternoon, Washington again attended church as was the custom in New England; this time he graced the North Parish, and listened to the Reverend Buckminster's sermon from the vantage point of the Whipple pew. William had been dead five years, but his widow still presided. Buckminster was in awe of Washington and worked himself into such a frenzy that he spent more time eulogizing Washington than praising Christ. He declaimed:

We see the MAN whom heaven designed as the principal instrument of accomplishing one of the greatest revolutions in the nations of the earth. . . . We see the MAN endued . . . with that rare assemblage of qualities which unites the jarring interests, views and affections of an extensive continent. . . . We see the GENERAL, who, with a cool, intrepid bravery, faced every danger; with unexampled firmness sustained every discouragement; and, with persevering magnanimity surmounted every obstacle of a long and unequal war; and under the auspices of an indulgent Providence, procured for us peace, liberty and independence. . . . We now see this illustrious PATRIOT, like the father of a great family, visiting the various branches, to bless and to be blessed, to start the tear of joy and awaken mutual congratulations. He comes, not attended with mercenary guards, like kings and emperors who hold their dignity by hereditary descent; who even fear where no fear is; he comes, not in the triumph of military parade, to show the spoils and laurels he hath won; but he comes triumphing in the confidence and affections of a free and

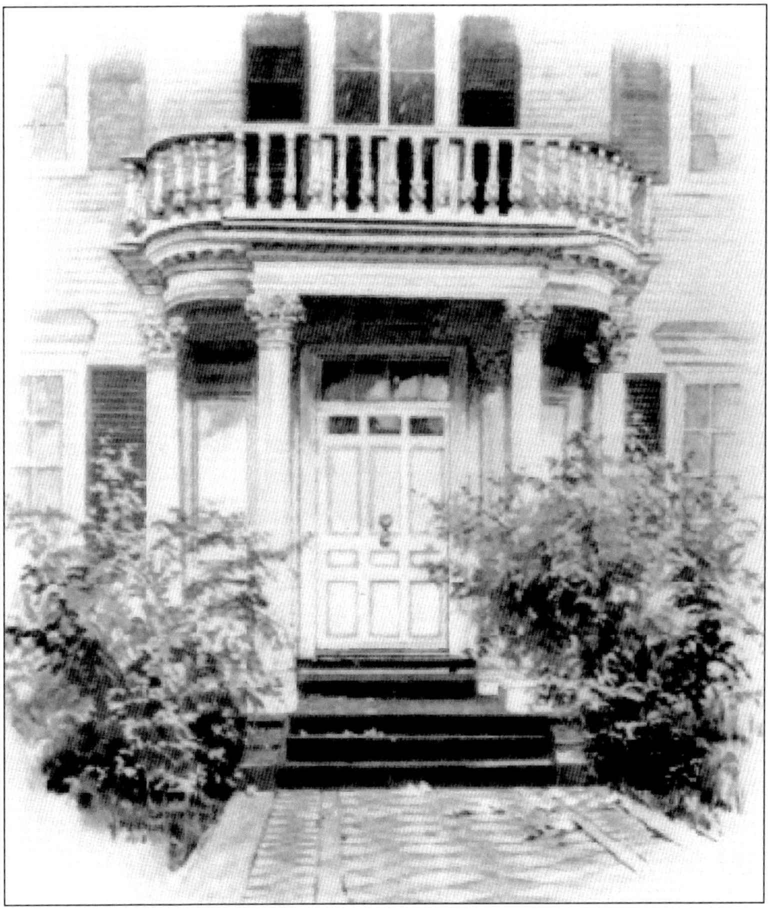

George Washington strode through the imposing entrance of the Langdon Mansion in 1789 on his visit to Portsmouth. (From Vignettes of Portsmouth.*)*

> grateful people, who, under God, hail him the deliverer of their country, and the protector of its liberties.

Monday morning, the President went on a tour of the harbor. Having tasted "dumb-fish" at Brewster's Tavern, he yearned to catch the source of this New England delicacy. But the cod would hardly cooperate with the General. Perhaps they were frightened off by the continued congratulatory commotion coming from Fort Constitution, which fired a 13 cannon salute when Washington's barge rowed by. Not to be outdone by cannon, a barge on the other side large enough to host the town band followed Washington, playing patriotic tunes for the President's (possible) enjoyment. Washington's hosts blamed the tide for the lackluster angling. Overall, the President was impressed by the harbor:

> [it] is well secured against all Winds; and from its narrow entrance from the Sea and passage up to the Town, may be perfectly guarded against any approach by water. The anchorage is also good and the Shipping may lay close to the Docks.

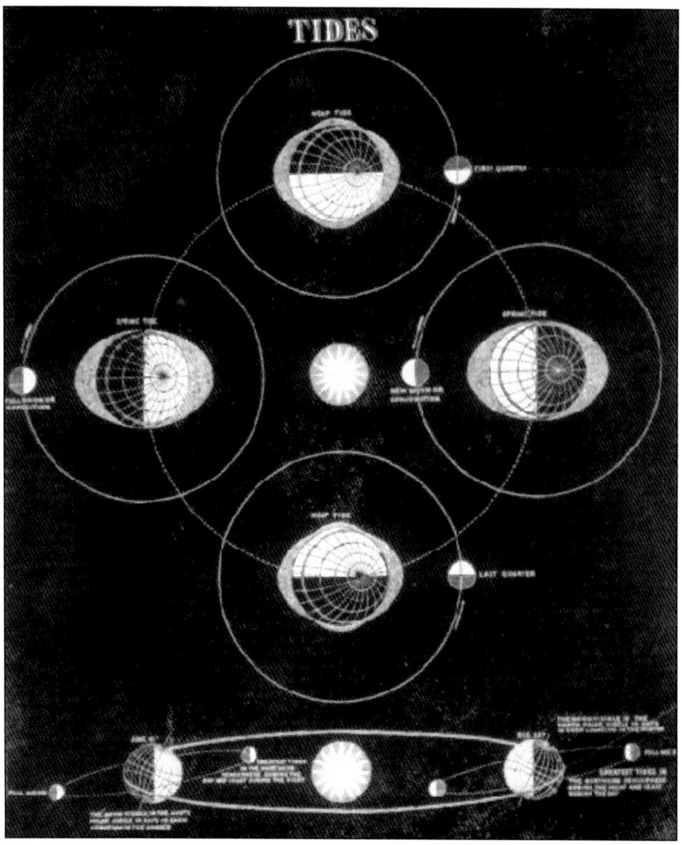

Smith's Illustrated Astronomy *was a nineteenth-century textbook frequently used in public and private schools. This diagram of tides would interest the aspiring merchants and sailors at the Portsmouth Academy.*

In the afternoon the President dined at the tavern and after the town addressed him with a profusion of thanks. The President responded in modest spirit, praising the common cause and devotion to the public good.

Tuesday morning, the President "sat two hours" for Christian Gulager, "a Painter of Boston." If the President was impatient to leave town, he does not reveal this or other emotions in the finished portrait, which hangs at the Massachusetts Historical Society. In the afternoon he made a pedestrian tour of the town, stopping off at Stavers' Tavern to visit with General Sullivan, then proceeding down by the water's edge on Hunking Lane to see the home and family of Tobias Lear. Mrs. Lear received him and offered relaxing conversation. Before dusk, the President continued his wanderings about town, visiting with the Reverend Samuel Haven, then with John Langdon at his home on Court Street. Reverend Haven, knowing Washington's love of agriculture, "presented me with an ear and part of the stock of the dyeing corn, and several small pieces of cloth which had been dyed with it, equal to any colors I had ever seen." Although the President declared most of the Portsmouth homes to be "indifferent," he lauded the Langdon mansion as "one of the best I have seen any where in the United States." Washington wondered why most of the houses were clapboard—why not brick or stone? An unnamed informant told the President that the rainy and foggy climate made the inside of brick homes cold and damp, a problem not readily found in the snug homes made of wood.

Washington's final evening in Portsmouth featured a grand ball given in his honor at the Assembly Hall on Vaughn Street. Over 100 gentlemen and ladies attended, astonishing the President with their conversation and elegance. "There were about 75 well dressed, and many of them very handsome, Ladies," the President confided to his diary; "among whom . . . were a greater proportion with much blacker hair than are usually seen in the Southern States." The ball included a series of toasts to President Washington, the King of France, the 4th of July, the new Vice-President John Adams, "the band of heroes who fought and bled in the cause of freedom," and other such sentiments, concluding with: "From the sources of American Independence may freedom be diffused through the earth." With this climatic event, Washington's visit came to an end.

The likes of such a ball, with other grand toasts, a hall filled with music and dancing, graced by beautiful ladies and their dapper escorts, would not be seen in Portsmouth for another 34 years. By then, in 1823, the compliment of wealthy denizens were the sons and daughters of the Portsmouth elite of an earlier generation, the age of the American Revolution. The festivities at Franklin Hall in 1823 commemorated the founding of Portsmouth 200 years before, in 1623. The gentlemen and their consorts danced about the hall, the walls of which "were entirely covered with portraits of eminent persons" from the Piscataqua past. Perhaps there hung a portrait of Captain John Mason, the proprietor of New Hampshire, or John Pickering, one of the wealthiest seventeenth-century leaders. Or perhaps there were images of Joshua Moody, that Portsmouth divine who dominated the First Parish, or Nathaniel Rogers, who became the first pastor of

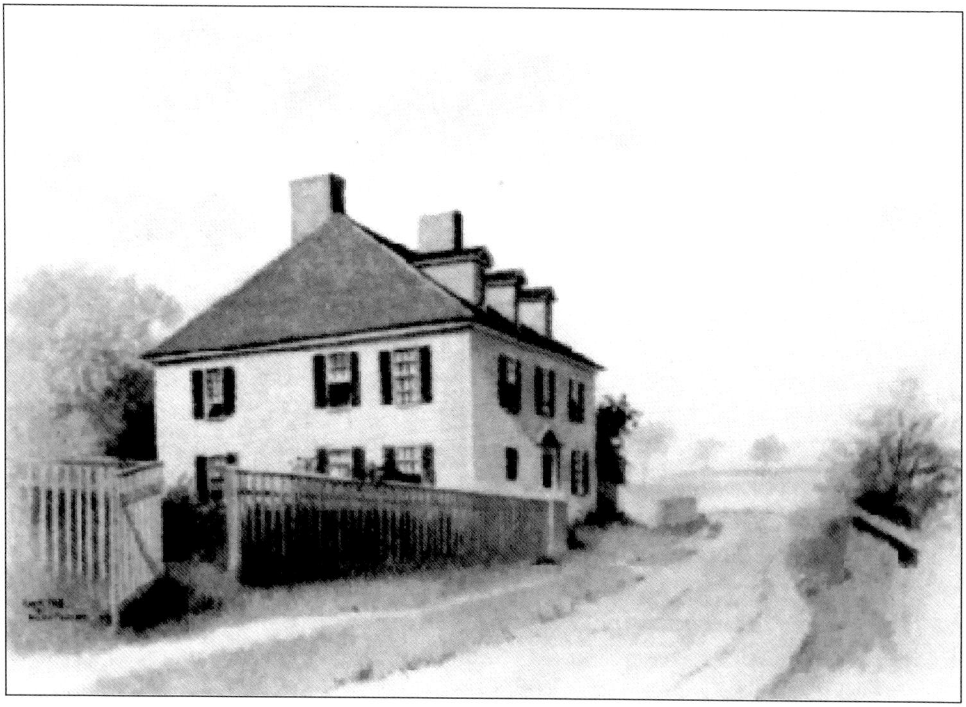

George Washington visited the Lear family homestead on his tour of Portsmouth in 1789. Tobias Lear was the President's personal secretary. (From Vignettes of Portsmouth.*)*

the North Parish. Doubtless the Wentworths shared a space on the wall, especially the controversial Governor Benning Wentworth. One would assume that Sir William Pepperrell, the hero of the capture of Louisburg during King George's War, or General John Sullivan, the hero of the War for Independence, would find their likenesses at the hall. Perhaps there were more recent funerary images of Governor John Langdon, who died in 1819, and his brother Woodbury, who died 14 years earlier; merchants such as John Sherburne and Jacob Sheafe; physicians and community leaders such as Dr. Hall Jackson, Dr. Joshua Brackett, and Dr. Ammi Cutter, all of whom received their medical training under the tutelage of Dr. Clement Jackson of Portsmouth. Portsmouth had in recent years lost eminent teachers of mind and spirit, such as Samuel Hale, the famous Latin tutor; Samuel Haven, pastor at the South Parish; Joseph Walter, of the Independent Congregational Church; and Joseph Buckminster, the somewhat melancholy voice of the North Parish.

This, then, was a night for history, for celebrating the past, to recall grand people and events. Much had happened during Portsmouth's long history, particularly during those years since Washington's visit in 1789. The population climbed year after year, which can be traced by the census reports that began in 1790 and occurred every decade thereafter. In 1790 the population was 4,720 and ten years later it was 5,339. In 1810 it was 6,934 and in 1820 it totalled 7,327.

Such growth occurred even as the Portsmouth economy went through varied twists and turns, rebounding after the dismal years of the Revolution only to plunge into the depths of slack trade, yielding greater numbers of the poor during the years of embargo in 1808 and 1809, the War of 1812, and in subsequent years. The economy and the suffering of the poor were accentuated by the plague of fires that swept through the streets of Portsmouth on three different occasions in short order: 1802, 1806, and 1813.

The 1802 fire was the worst yet, as it spread quickly from one wooden building to another, from clapboard to clapboard, and laid the town in ashes at its conclusion. The fire destroyed over $200,000 worth of property. The 1806 fire was less devastating, yet still costly, accumulating $70,000 worth of damage. However, none could eclipse the terrible fire of December 22, 1813, which cost the city $300,000. Antiquarian Charles Brewster reported that the fire followed a path "from west to east" ranging "one third of a mile" wide. It destroyed houses along Pleasant, Court, and Broad streets. Residents feared for the whole town, though the water's edge ultimately formed a barrier to prevent the fire's continued ravages. In all "there had disappeared in one short night 108 dwelling houses (occupied by 130 families), 64 stores and shops, and 100 barns, &c., making in the whole 272 buildings."

Many of Portsmouth's elite congratulated themselves on handling these catastrophes, and the resulting numbers of homeless and destitute, with dexterity and charity. After the 1802 fire "the selectmen appointed a committee of fire gentlemen to receive such donations as the charitable and benevolent may be disposed to make to those who suffered by the fire." They raised and distributed $45,000 to the poor. The same was the case in 1806 and 1813; $4,300 was raised for the former and for the latter $77,000. Some of these funds came from the charity of surrounding communities. in 1808, the Portsmouth Marine Society began to raise money for "the relief of decayed and distressed maritime members" of the community.

The same year benevolent ladies established the Portsmouth Female Asylum to help destitute girls aged three to ten. The trustees of the asylum joined by subscription. The girls were educated in sewing, cleanliness, Christianity, writing, and reading. The inmates were orphans and children of parents unable to care for them. The trustees were diligent in caring for the girls, visiting the asylum every week to inspect the girls' diet, clothing, progress in their devotions, and reading. Their governess was required to take the girls to church every Sunday, and read to them from the Bible so "to inculcate the principles of religion." "The Rules and Regulations . . . of the Portsmouth Female Asylum" required a strict daily regimen:

> From the first of May to the first of October, the children shall rise at six o'clock in the morning, say their prayers, wash themselves in cold water, and comb their heads; breakfast at eight, play until nine, attend school from this hour until twelve, dine at one, attend school from two o'clock to five, play until six, and retire for the night at eight o'clock.

During the winter, the schedule constricted to accommodate the fewer hours of daylight. Two of the leaders of the Portsmouth Female Asylum were Mrs. Daniel Webster and Mrs. Nathaniel Adams. The Websters had lost their home to the 1813 fire. In 1820, the Mechanics Association of Portsmouth established a fund to help family members of deceased members, and nine years later members of the South Parish established a charity fund to help destitute parish members.

Progress and reform were the watchwords of the American middle-class during the early nineteenth century. In Portsmouth, Nathaniel Adams was instrumental in founding the St. John's Lodge, a Masonic organization dedicated to the principles of "brotherly love, peace, and good will among mankind" as well as relief of destitute members. Masonic Lodges were especially popular in late eighteenth- and early nineteenth-century New England. At this time, traditional Christianity and organized religion were under attack by Enlightenment thinkers advocating reason and science over revelation and faith, Deist thinkers who were unclear about the role of Jesus Christ in man's redemption, Unitarians who doubted the Trinity, and Universalists who believed that all humans, Christians and non-Christians, are saved by a loving God. The group that incorporated all of these elements into their thinking was the The Masons. The St. John's Lodge petitioned the General Court for incorporation:

> on the first Wednesday of December in the year of Light 5799 . . . Humbly shew the MASTER, WARDENS and MEMBERS of *St. John's Lodge in Portsmouth*. That in pursuance of their sublime institution, which was, for the promoting brotherly love, peace, and good will among mankind, and relief of all distressed brethren; they have raised a small fund, which they are desirous of so securing, that the proceeds may be appropriated for such laudable purposes. They are also desirous of erecting a suitable building for the accommodation of said Lodge at their orderly meetings. But without the aid of this Honorable Legislature, they are unable to secure said fund, or erect such building. They therefore pray your Honors, to grant them an act of incorporation, under such restrictions and limitations as your Honors may deem expedient. They would further observe to this Honorable Legislature, that from a perfect sense of the purity of the institution, (which is well known to many of your Honors as Masons) and of their honest intentions in this application, and a firm belief in the candour, discernment, and good intentions of your Honors, they have the fullest confidence, that no unworthy prejudice can be harboured against them. They therefore now, and will ever, as is their bounden duty as Men, and Masons, to do, most humbly pray the *Grand Architect* of the Universe, that He, would take your honorable Court under his holy protection, and that finally, as a band of Brothers "made perfect" thro' the working of his divine favour, we

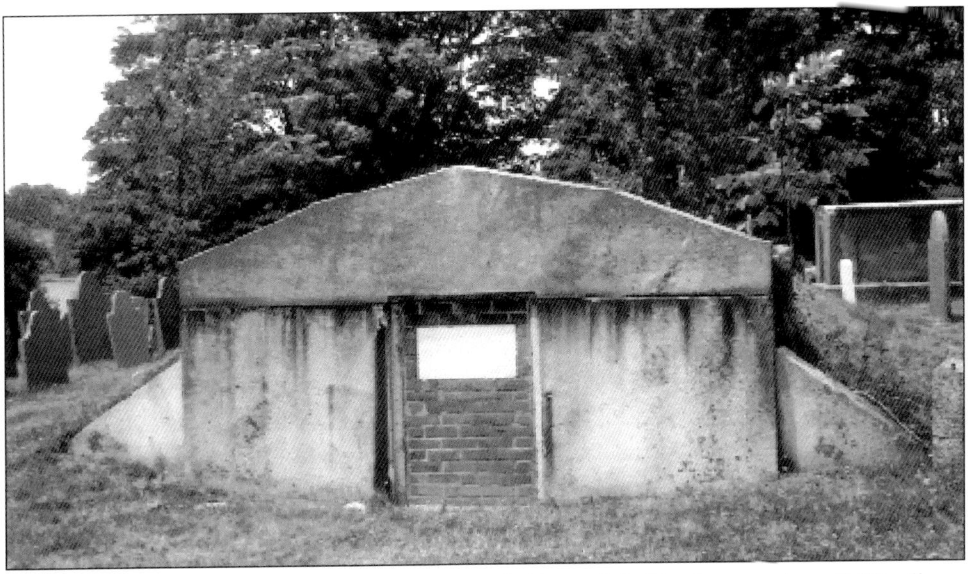

This granite and brick vault at North Burial Ground holds the remains of Woodbury Langdon. John Langdon's brother Woodbury was a leading merchant of Portsmouth. (Photo by Benjamin Lawson.)

> may all meet upon a level in the *Grand Lodge* of "perfect bliss," under the "Arch of perfect knowledge," where the "word," which was from the beginning, shall be the "Star of light," as a sign, and token, to guide us to joy forevermore.

Nathaniel Adams, the "Grand Master of Masons in New Hampshire" who along with 58 others signed the petition, was the founder of the Portsmouth Athenaeum in 1817, which was dedicated to preserving Portsmouth's past. Adams was also a proprietor of the Portsmouth Library, and in 1787 he petitioned the General Court of the state respecting duties being laid upon books bought for the library:

> The memorial of Nathaniel Adams in behalf of the Proprietors of the Portsmouth Library humbly shews that said Proprietors have at a great expence, for the purpose of promoting learning and knowledge laid the foundation of a Publick Library, to which they are continully making additions by the importation of the works of the latest and most celebrated Authors, but they find themselves subjected to the additional expense of the Impost upon all their importations, which they conclude was not the intention of the legislature to lay upon a matter so generally advantageous to the Community.

Nathaniel Adams was most aware of the significance of the bicentennial celebration of 1823. It inspired Adams to eventually pen a chronology of Portsmouth's past,

Annals of Portsmouth, published 12 years later in 1835. In the book, Adams recalled in detail Portsmouth at the time of Washington's visit, and the massive parade that celebrated the hero's coming. In the wake of Washington's visit, and during the next decade, a burst of activity and creativity reflected the optimism and confidence that New Englanders had in the new government and president.

In 1794, for example, the Piscataqua Bridge opened. It was a great wooden structure that spanned the difficult currents separating Dover Point from Bloody Point. It was a private undertaking, built with money gained through the sale of shares to fund its construction and return revenue from the eventual tolls. Unfortunately for the promoters and investors, the bridge was not profitable. A document from 1798 shows that after operating for four years the tolls had brought in $8,181.75 while the expenses of upkeep were $2,812.31, netting only a profit of $5,369.44. The problem was that the original construction of the bridge cost $65,947.34! The Treasurer of the Piscataqua Bridge, Thomas Martin, lamented that "it is now and probably will continue to be to the proprietors a very Unproductive property." Nevertheless, Martin did admit that "the Bridge is of great public utility." After 200 years of relying upon ferries, the inhabitants of the Piscataqua Valley now could travel from Dover and Rochester to Newington and Portsmouth with ease and efficiency. John Peirce, the man of energy behind

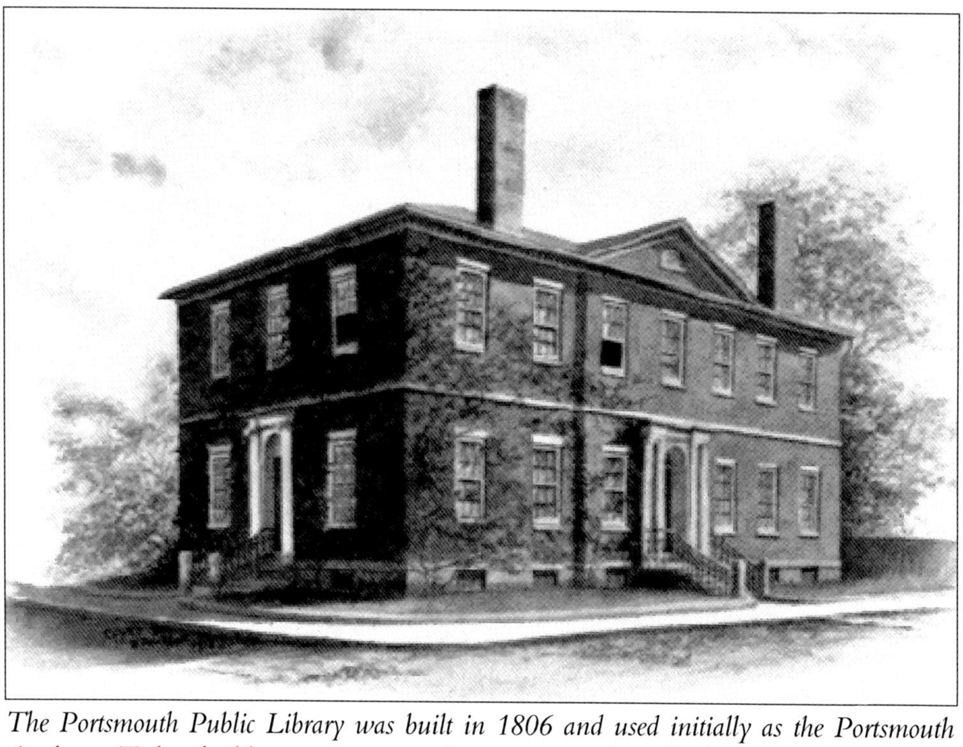

The Portsmouth Public Library was built in 1806 and used initially as the Portsmouth Academy. Today the library serves as an important repository for documents and books on Portsmouth history. (From Vignettes of Portsmouth.*)*

the undertaking, also directed a project to build a turnpike from the Piscataqua Bridge to Concord.

The attitude of improvement continued to yield results in and about Portsmouth with the turn of the century. Portsmouth entrepreneurs and inventors developed an aqueduct to bring fresh water into the city by means of wooden pipes; hot air balloons to, perhaps one day, free man from the constraints of gravity; salt-works to make salt from evaporation of sea water; and several other new bridges. In 1822, two bridges opened spanning the Piscataqua: the Portsmouth-Newcastle Bridge and the Portsmouth-Kittery Bridge. Most important, the United States Congress in 1800, recognizing the importance of the Piscataqua to the nation's trade as well as the prolific community of shipbuilders building and launching ships in the security of Portsmouth harbor, authorized the purchase of Fernald's Island upon which to base the Portsmouth Naval Shipyard.

The shipyard was the result of Joshua Humphries' efforts, who served in the Adams administration and sought a suitable, defensible place for United States warships to be built. The swift water and deep harbors of the Piscataqua convinced him to purchase the land upon which to establish the shipyard. It turned out some remarkable boats, particularly the 74-gun *Washington*, named in honor of the man who once thought so highly of the Piscataqua.

The *Washington* was built during the War of 1812, which was not a popular one in Portsmouth, and save for a few privateers, not profitable either. Most of New England opposed the war, which was brought about by constant British harassment of American shipping. Yet harassment is not war, when trade is cut off with predictable consequences for a maritime economy. British warships cruised Atlantic waters, capturing American vessels bound for distant ports, particularly Asia. The response of Piscataqua captains and sailors was the same as during the previous conflict with the English in 1776. Lacking an effective navy, merchants and speculators outfitted small "privateers" that were heavily armed, carried large crews of "marines" to board and capture enemy ships, and were rigged for daring attacks and quick escapes. The number of privateers during the War of 1812 was small compared to the Revolution, when Portsmouth outfitted 100 privateers. Yet the privateers of the War of 1812, such as the *Portsmouth Packet* and the *Fox*, ended up with hundreds of captured enemy ships that yielded wonderful profits for owners, captains, and crewmen. But this was the only bright spot during, and after, the war when Portsmouth merchants were unable to reestablish trade on a prewar footing.

Through the years there had been many parades and processions to commemorate various events. In 1799, upon news of George Washington's death, Portsmouth residents marked his passing with a solemn procession ending with eulogies recalling his greatness in war and peace. After fire destroyed St. John's Church in 1806, the parishioners and interested others marched in a parade to initiate building a new church. The parade of 1823, marking the bicentennial of Portsmouth, was the grandest since the welcoming Washington received in

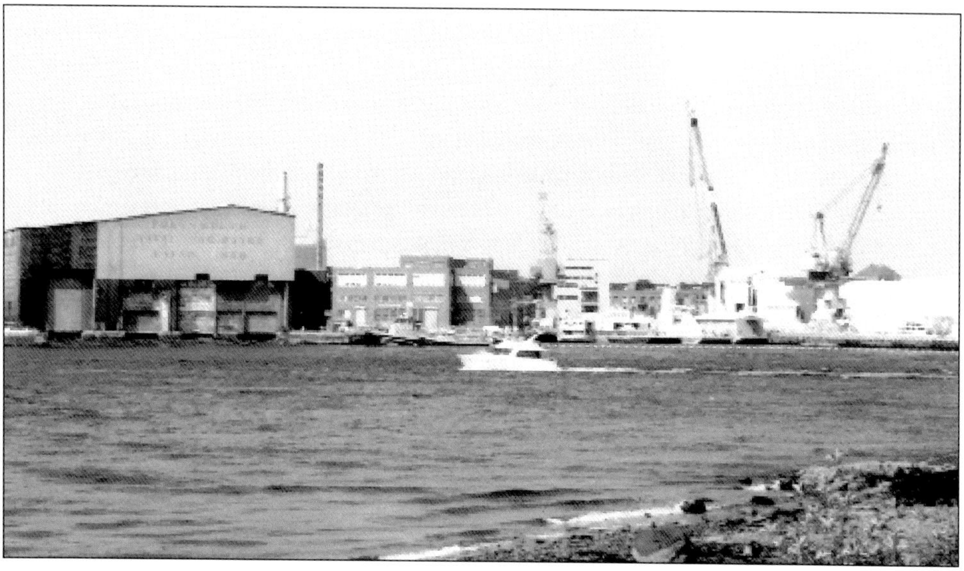

The Portsmouth Naval Shipyard was established in 1800. President Washington during his visit to Portsmouth in 1789 commented on the likely prospects of Portsmouth Harbor as a site for an important shipyard. (Photo by Benjamin Lawson.)

1789. The marchers, described by Nathaniel Adams, included soldiers, educators, professionals, craftsmen, laborers, town dignitaries, the order of Free Masons, and the "poet" and "orator" of the day. They "moved through several of the principal streets in town" winding through avenues from the South Parish to the North Parish. The mass of citizens tagged along, in varying degrees of order and decorum, marking the end of the procession.

Nathaniel Adams reported that once the parade reached the North Parish at Market Square, they filled the church to listen to the opening prayer "by the Reverend Bennet Tyler, D. D. the President of Dartmouth College":

> . . . an ingenius oration was delivered by Nathaniel A. Haven, jr. Esquire, in which he gave a sketch of the characters of the merchant adventurers, who first promoted the settlement here, delineated some of the principal traits which distinguished them, and pointed out a few, who had risen to eminence in the learned professions. A poem was delivered by Oliver William B. Peabody, Esquire, of Exeter, which discovered his knowledge of the history of the country; it was elegant and classical. Some odes, prepared for the occasion, by the Reverend Thomas C. Upham, of Rochester, were sung in the best style by the Portsmouth Handel Society.

Upon conclusion of the parade, speech, poem, and songs, "about two hundred gentlemen" retired to Jefferson Hall, where they ate and drank and "closed the day with hilarity," after which they danced with their wives and others far into the night.

Portsmouth at its bicentennial, according to Nathaniel Adams, was a compact city much smaller than the original settlement when, like most early colonial towns, the boundaries of the township were huge. Over the intervening years Rye, Newcastle, Greenland, and Newington formed separate parishes, then towns. The town of Portsmouth had expanded beyond Strawbery Banke to range between the two mill ponds, North and South, which at high tide formed the town into a distinct peninsula jutting into the Piscataqua River. The peninsula was one of small hills and narrow, haphazard lanes. Adams counted "thirty-seven streets and fifty-three lanes," eight churches, and about a dozen schools in 1823. The tendency of builders since Washington's visit was to use brick rather than wood.

The jewel in the crown was the harbor, "which is safe and commodious, sheltered from every storm; the water is sufficiently deep for the largest ships, and the anchorage good." The current of the Piscataqua at high tide was extremely rapid. The Shipyard, 23 years old, had two large shipyards worked by a number of "carpenters, smiths and labourers." All told, Portsmouth boasted "thirty-eight ships, twenty-six brigs, one hundred and five schooners, one bark and twelve sloops."

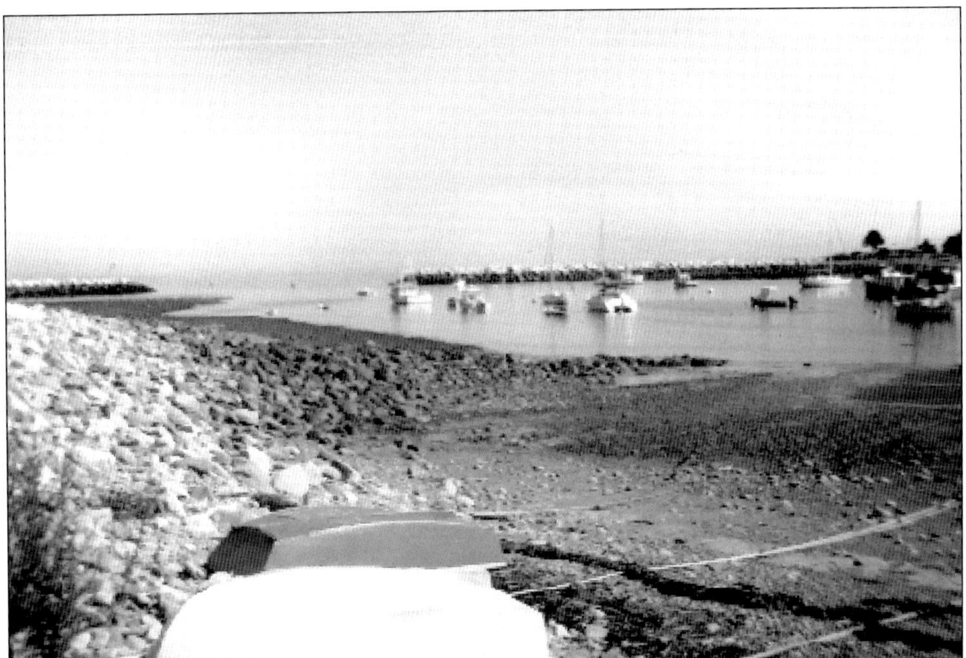

This photograph (by Benjamin Lawson) is of Rye Harbor at low tide on a sunny summer day. Rye, originally known as Sandy Beach, was part of Portsmouth until at the end of the seventeenth century it became an independent town.

At "43° 5' N. latitude, and 70° 41' west longitude" the town is perfectly situated for refreshing breezes and good general health of the inhabitants. "It is not uncommon," said Adams, "to find persons between 80 and 90 years of age; there is one woman living upwards of one hundred and four years of age, in the full enjoyment of her mental faculties, and who was able to walk the last summer between eight and ten miles in a day." Perhaps she took the same route Washington did when he came to Portsmouth in the autumn of 1789.

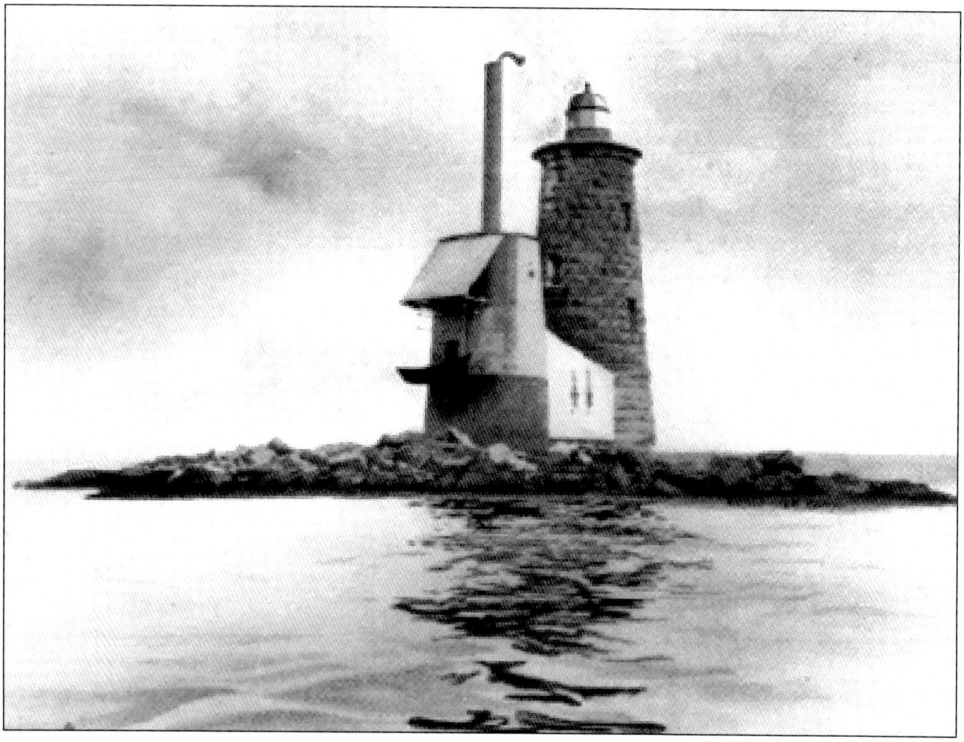

The reflection of Whaleback Lighthouse dances in the water on a cloudy day. Whaleback was built in 1872. It guards Portsmouth harbor from its location near Kittery. (From Vignettes of Portsmouth.*)*

6. An Old Town by the Sea

Charles W. Brewster once described himself as a "rambler" with a penchant for "spinning [the] street yarn." A reporter and editor with the *Portsmouth Herald* for a half-century, Brewster enjoyed tracking down a story, particularly when that story involved the Portsmouth past. He traced down historical tidbits, was an indefatigable searcher for original documents, and enjoyed interviewing the aged and recording their memories. Brewster was a true antiquarian. If one is to be an antiquarian, what better town for such an avocation than Portsmouth? The town's winding roads and narrow alleys reflect the nooks and crannies of the historical past. The survival of historical records involves more chance than purpose, as it turns up in unexpected places. Charles Brewster was hungry for knowledge of the past, and pursued this passion his whole life. The result was a series of brief articles and literary portraits of Portsmouth history, published in serial form over the years in the *Portsmouth Journal*, eventually reissued in 1859 as *Rambles About Portsmouth*.

Brewster's concluding "Ramble," number 149, was an autobiographical reminiscence of his 50 years as a newspaper man in Portsmouth. He penned it in February 1868, when the world was so very different from the beginning of his journalism career in 1818. Brewster was a methodical, patient man who found diversion in quiet walks and conversation with family and friends. He lived according to schedule, rarely varying from the day-to-day regimen of self-imposed duty. He rose early, had breakfast, walked from his home following Islington Road to Market Square to his office on Ladd Street. He worked six days and rested the seventh, declaring that the restful Sabbath invigorated him to pursue the task again on Monday.

So dedicated was he to his newspaper and profession that Brewster rarely traveled; Portsmouth was his world, its people his friends, its past shaping his sense of self, and its buildings the landmarks of reference. He felt himself extraordinarily qualified to comment on the town's changes over the 50-year period from 1818 to 1868. He thought his own growth and development mirrored the town's, even "the world's progress." Yet as Brewster carried forth this ramble in his mind, examining the present while recalling the past, he contemplated the metamorphoses of Portsmouth from a town to a city reflected in its expansion in area, industry, technology, and institutions. Was Portsmouth a better city in 1868 than it was a town in 1818?

When the young Charles Brewster arrived for work on February 16, 1818, Portsmouth was a town of 7,000 people. Brewster was a 16-year old novice beginning a job at Charles Turell's *Portsmouth Oracle*. The newspaper had been in print for 25 years, having been started by Charles Peirce. Brewster recalled the daily chore of lugging armloads of firewood up stairs to the second floor, and he was not alone in this exercise. All across America in 1818, young men were lugging loads by canoe, barge, flatboat, keel boat, gundalow, and larger craft up rivers and down, toward the Appalachian Mountains and beyond their forested slopes to the Ohio, Mississippi, and Missouri rivers. That year the United States of America was two-thirds its present size, stretching from the Atlantic coast across the Appalachians and the Midwestern plains to the Rocky Mountains, which formed a barrier to Spanish holdings on the west coast.

Although Charles Brewster would never journey beyond New England, much less to the West, the events shaping America in 1818 nevertheless had an impact on Brewster and his community. The massive Louisiana Territory, purchased from France in 1803 and explored in subsequent years, would shape American politics during Brewster's lifetime. The controversy over slavery in the western territories would bring about failed political compromises, the election of Abraham Lincoln in 1860, and the Civil War from 1861 to 1865. Brewster, a lifelong conservative, eulogized Republican and Whig politicians such as Lincoln and Daniel Webster. In 1818, perhaps the young man was sufficiently cognizant of American politics to know that the policies of James Madison and his Democrat-Republican party got

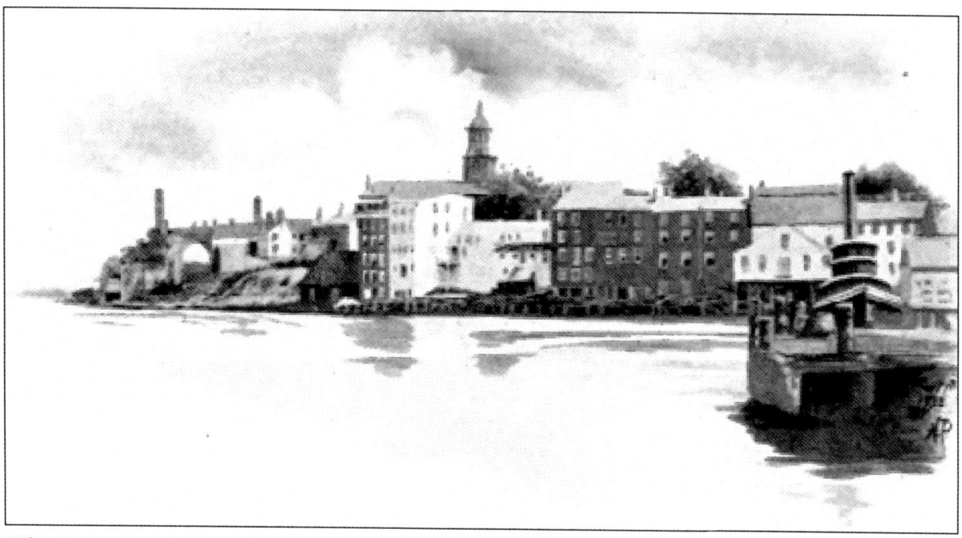

The Portsmouth waterfront has not substantially changed during the past 100 years. Today one still finds St. John's steeple off in the distance, waterfront businesses, and tugboats at their moorings. (From Vignettes of Portsmouth.*)*

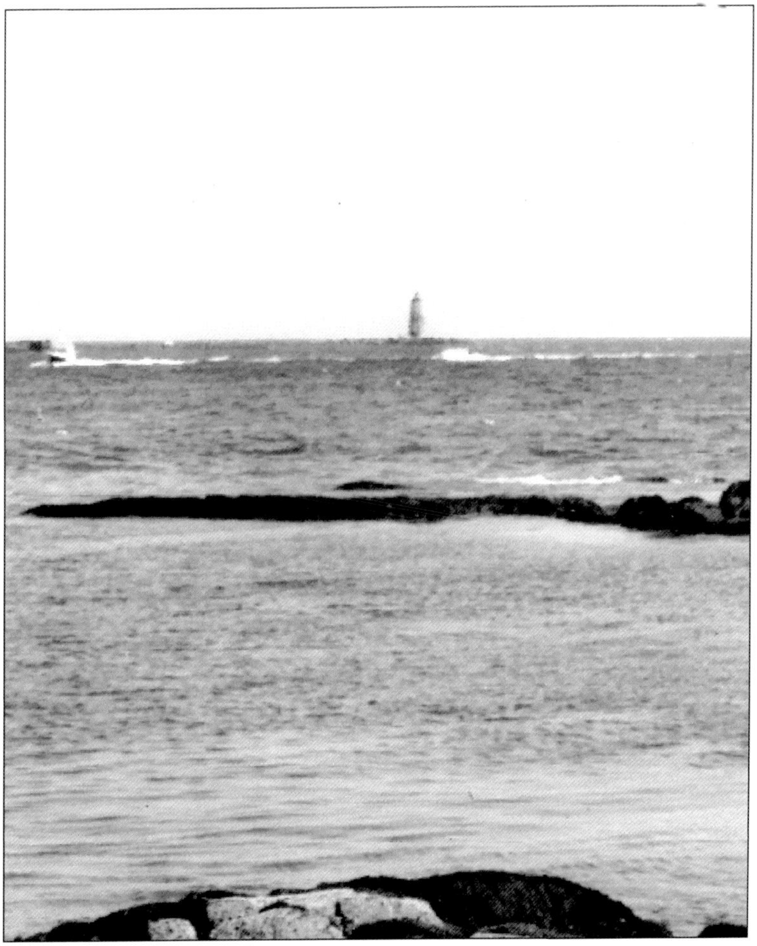

Where the Piscataqua ends and the Atlantic begins is unclear from this photograph (by Benjamin Lawson). Whaleback Lighthouse is seen in the distance.

America into the War of 1812. He was also aware that the same party continued to dominate American politics in the post war years, and that presidents such as James Monroe, then concluding his first year in office, had southern sympathies that irritated Yankees such as Charles Brewster.

One suspects Brewster had enough wit to ruminate on these matters. Clearly he was a quick learner, and ambitious. He threw his energy behind Nathaniel Haven when he bought the *Oracle* in 1821 and changed the name of the newspaper to *The Portsmouth Journal of Literature and Politics*. Haven ran the paper well, gave it a wonderful reputation, and set the stage for Brewster's success when the 23-year old bought the paper from Haven in 1825. Henceforth under his leadership the newspaper was typically known simply as the *Journal*.

Early American newspapers had more essays, stories, and recollections than news. Brewster was this type of newspaperman—in love with the remarkable and the quaint, apt to focus on the narrative rather than the chronology. When Brewster's interest peaked while considering Portsmouth's maritime environment, he was at his best. For example, Brewster combined contemporary observations with personal recollection when reporting on a ramble to the South Mill Pond, where he visited the ropewalk owned by John Handy. Brewster was amazed by the changes. He recalled when he was young seeing the same ropewalk, a long imposing building wherein cordage was spun, ablaze in fire. Forty years later, it was a factory relying on steam power; the ropewalk manufactured much more in less time.

The wonders of the modern machine could not entirely replace Brewster's pleasant memories of the past, when work as well as production was slower, yet it was human strength and skill that wound the fibers, not a machine. Brewster recalled another ropewalk near the North Mill Pond and the North Burial Ground. Here men and boys spun the cordage for the 74-gun *Washington* during the War of 1812. The long building made to manufacture rope was replaced by another, housing the people and machines of the "Great Eastern," the massive locomotive powered by steam. Brewster's love for the railroad was tempered only by his love for the past. He could not help comparing the speed and power of the modern train with comparable technology of the century before. John Stavers, owner of Stavers' Tavern, conveyed travelers to and from his establishment with "the Portsmouth Flying Stage Coach," powered by six stallions, holding up to six people. It was bumpy, dirty, hot in summer, frigid in winter, subject to the whims of horses and driver, carrying forth over muddy and rutted roads an interminable amount of time. Thank God for the Great Eastern!

Such were the hazards and delays of stage travel, that some Portsmouth inhabitants opted for different means of conveyance. The baker Robert Metlin, who was born during the reign of Charles II and died the year Washington took office, used to walk to Boston to get his flour. He would begin early in the morning and keep a brisk pace the entire way, arriving late at night. The next day he purchased the flour. The third day he returned home to Portsmouth, pulling a small wagon loaded with the means of his trade.

From his office on Ladd Street overlooking Market Square and the harbor, Brewster observed the movements of his fellow citizens, interviewed the survivors of a past time, and recorded their perceptions of the changes in the town. "At the present day," he wrote in Ramble #134:

> we do not see the busy wharves, the fleets of West Indiamen, the great piles of bags of coffee, and the acres of hogsheads of molasses which we used to see; nor do we see Water street crowded with sailors, and the piles of lumber and cases of fish going on board the West Indiamen for uses in the Tropics. But if that day is gone by, we have other occupations, and the old town seems as bright and handsome as ever.

The structure of Portsmouth mirrored these changes. The Court House, once the pride of Portsmouth and graced by the "spirits of the past," was taken down in 1836. The large imposing structure, built in the best tradition of the eighteenth

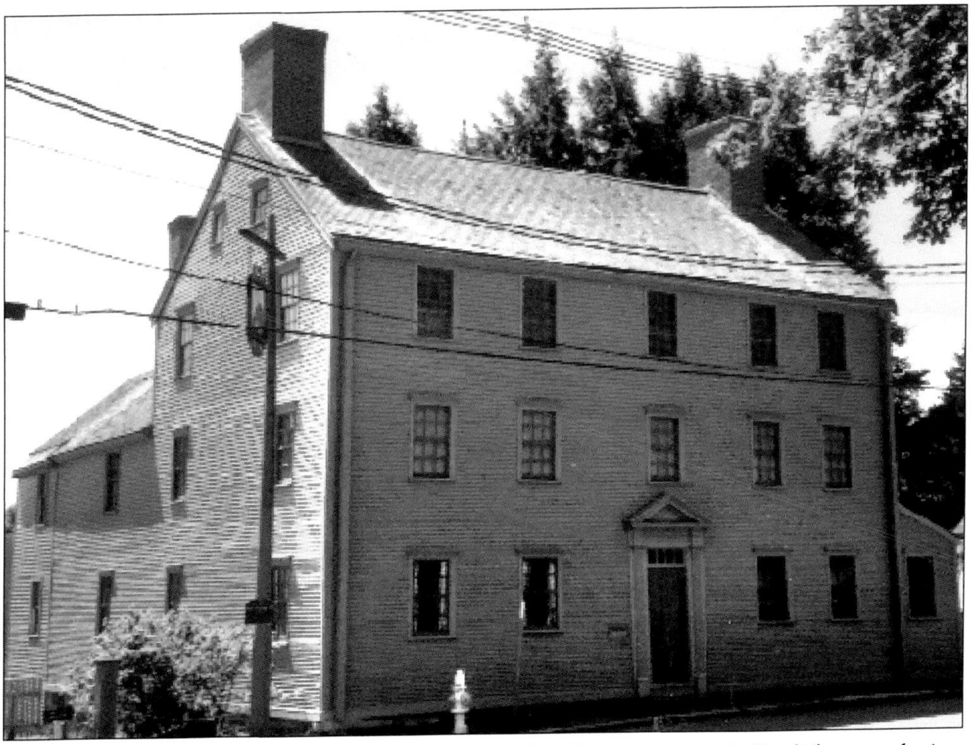

Stavers' Tavern was owned and operated by John Stavers, a loyal Englishman, during the Revolutionary period. After being strongly encouraged to pledge allegiance to the United States, he changed the name of the tavern from the "Earl of Halifax" to the "William Pitt." (Photo by Benjamin Lawson.)

century, recalled great patriots and glorious revolution. Next to the Court House was the North Parish, where Buckminster preached orthodox Puritanism even into the early 1800s. This building fell victim to progress in 1854. In Ramble #70, Brewster lamented such a material revolution in the city:

> When the old North church was built in 1712, it was symmetrical in form, the steeple being in the centre of the front. An enlargement on the west side was afterwards made. The Vane bore the date of 1732, when it was put up. It was not gilded until 1796. When destined to come down in 1854, the Vane is thus personified, to enable it to tell its story. Hardened by long exposure, tenacious of life to the last, the man of the spire whirls around with every breeze. He sees in the garden a few rods to the north-west, an aged oak of two centuries, which is the only visible object older than himself. Listen to his appeal.

The Old North, like the Old South on Marcy Street, was breezy in summer but bitterly cold in winter. The religious could not quite justify the use of fuel during the two Sunday services, so they sat in their cold pews trying to listen to the Word of the Lord. Attendance was sparse from Christmas to Easter. None of the Congregational, Baptist, or other societies owned an organ at the time of the War of 1812—only St. John's Episcopal graced the lyrics of Watts and Doddridge with the pious tune of the organ. Queen's Chapel changed its name to St. John's in 1791 after petitioning the General Court of the state for incorporation.

The destructive force, "the desolating fires of 1802, 1806 and 1813," became an unwitting ally for Portsmouth change and progress. Fire vanquished the old northern part of town: Market Square, the regions of Daniel Street, Penhallow Street, Bow Street, St. John's Church, and the North Parish. Market Square became an open crossroads of movement and interchange of products and ideas. The Custom House, Rockingham Bank, and Piscataqua Exchange Bank were built in the same area as the North Parish. Market Square was not only the financial center of Portsmouth, but the cultural center as well. The Portsmouth Athenaeum began in 1817, taking rooms in the same building on Congress Street that still

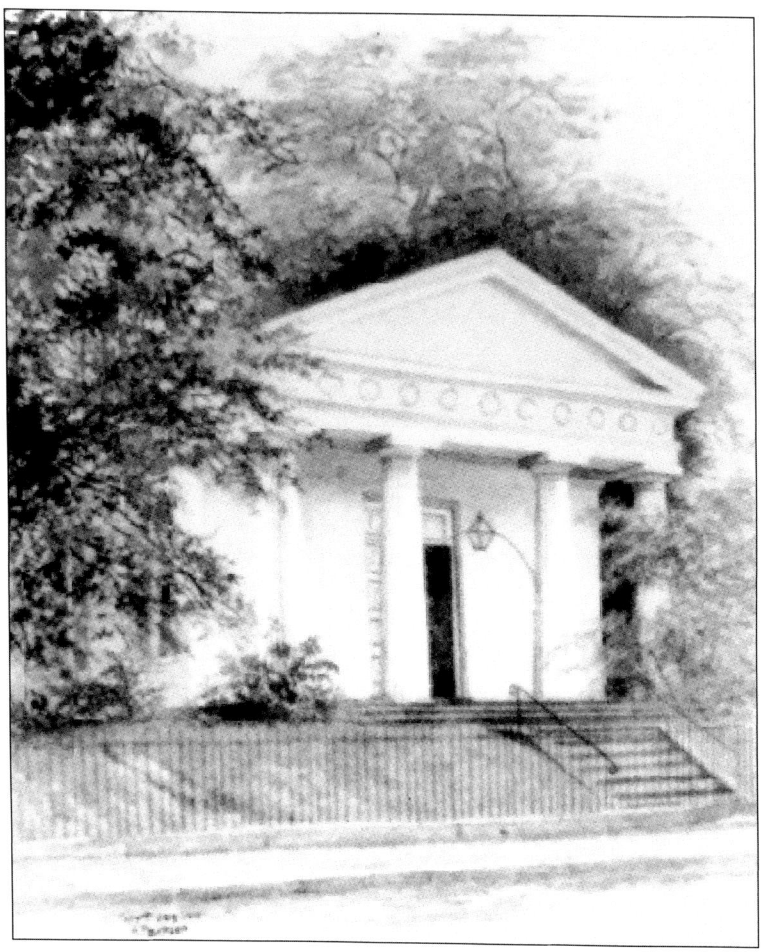

St. John's Chapel on State Street was built in 1832. Helen Pearson's drawing recalls the building in 1913; it has since been demolished. (From Vignettes of Portsmouth.*)*

contain its massive collection of local history and literature. St. John's Masonic Society, which was led by the Athenaeum's Nathaniel Adams, used rooms in the same building.

Construction leading to a new bridge built across the North Mill Pond also altered the old town, restricting the inflow of water from the river, particularly at high tide. Likewise, the town constructed a new bridge over the South Mill Pond, also altering the fluid dynamics of pond and river. According to Brewster, before the construction of these bridges, at high tide Portsmouth could become almost an island, as the waters of the two mill ponds at times threatened to meet. With Puddle Dock also being similarly bloated by the tide, the old town could look like a series of islands in a great blue sea.

During Brewster's time the workhouse on Court Street continued to feed, house, and work those individuals who had not the benefit of relief from private organizations. After Clement March's tenure as keeper, Deacon John Noble was "Superintendent" from 1790 to 1801, then William Vaughan from 1801 to 1825, followed by his daughter's husband, John Grant, from 1825 to 1830, then Captain Robert Neal to 1834. By that time the wooden building had grown old from too many years caring for, working, and punishing the poor. A building can withstand only so much human suffering.

In 1834, a new almshouse was built at the "town farm" northwest of the North Mill Pond, on the outskirts of the city. Brewster referred to the almshouse as a "noble brick edifice." It would serve the town for decades until a county facility, located at Barrington, was built in the 1880s to house the indigent, orphaned, disabled, and insane. The town jail (the old gaol) was on Congress Street, where it had been since its construction in 1782. Fortunately most malefactors served their sentences in "our State Prison," which implemented modern ideas of incarceration sans corporeal punishment.

Portsmouth's old "Stone Jail" was slowly being retired. Brewster recalled many prisoners whose wrists were shackled in irons being whipped on the "bare back" with "the cat-o-nine tails, every blow leaving a ridge, while the cries for mercy rent the air." He clearly remembered "the branding process, when the horse thief was pinioned down on the broad stone at the west door of the jail, and with a cork filled with needles, India ink was pricked in over his forehead and down his nose, to form the letter T."

Other "barbarities" coming to an end included imprisonment for debt. In 1827, the state decided to allow debtors release from jail as long as they did not leave town. In 1840, the New Hampshire legislature discontinued any form of imprisonment for debt.

Brewster noted happily other improvements that occurred during his time from 1818 to 1868. Of special note was the Portsmouth Aqueduct. Most families dug wells in and about their property, some even on public roads. The aqueduct, on the other hand, which brought spring water into Portsmouth from freshwater springs several miles outside of town, was the brainchild of the Exeter native Eliphalet Ladd. Colonel Ladd was an engineer, architect, and entrepreneur who served in

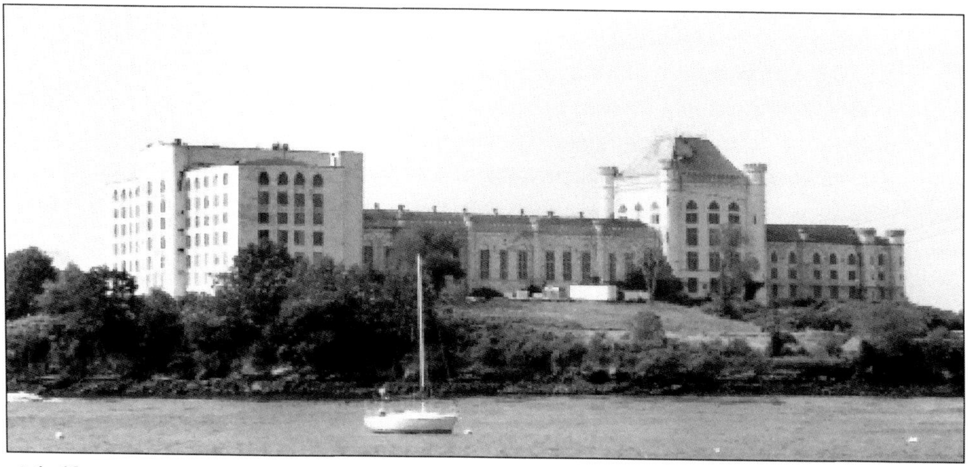

A half century ago imprisoned sailors had a wonderful view of Portsmouth harbor. The old naval prison, although closed, is still an imposing sight. (Photo by Benjamin Lawson.)

the French-Indian War and American Revolution. He was a shipbuilder of note and responsible for erecting the buildings on Ladd Street and off Market Square, where Charles Brewster produced his newspaper. Ladd surveyed the route of the wooden aqueduct and joined with 17 others, including Joseph Whipple, Collector of Customs, and Dr. Joshua Brackett to petition the General Court of the state for incorporation. The petition, dated November 27, 1797, reads:

> The Petitioners, Inhabitants of said Portsmouth, Humbly shew:—
>
> That they conceive an Aqueduct for the purpose of watering said Town might be a lasting conveniency to the Inhabitants, and in case of fires would prove a great public benefit; And that the only water that could be applied to that purpose is more than two & one half Miles distant, and that from the Nature of the Ground through which the Aqueduct must pass, being a considerable part of it low marsh & Rockey or Ledge Land, it would necessarily be attended with great expence; They therefore pray that they & such others as may hereafter be interested in it may be incorporated with the exclusive Right and full powers to Effect the purposes aforesaid, & to continue in succession, to them & their heirs and Assigns forever,—and they as in duty bound shall ever pray.—

Upon approval by the state legislature, the petitioners formed the "Portsmouth Aqueduct Company" in December 1797 to implement the plan. The scheme worked wonderfully well, to Eliphalet Ladd's and Charles Brewster's incomparable delight. Brewster exuded thanks and praise for his fresh spring water in Ramble #49:

> But it is the real benefit of the public generally, more than the pecuniary benefit to the aqueduct proprietors, that we take into view, when we bring into remembrance those who have bestowed upon Portsmouth blessings which are now many leagues in length, and flow in upon a thousand households every hour. The springs (which from their flowing in winter bore the name of the "warm springs" more than a century before an aqueduct was extended from them) are inexhaustible—they have never diminished in the least in the greatest drought. An analysis of the water shows it of unsurpassed purity. Who can duly estimate the blessing!

Other engineering marvels were the many bridges that spanned the Piscataqua that improved trade, eliminated the exclusive use of ferries, and connected Portsmouth to points north, east, and west. Of particular note was the Piscataqua Bridge, built in 1794, which spanned the churning water of the "horse races" formed by the narrow strait between Bloody Point and Dover Point. Brewster, being not much of a traveler, was more excited by the bridges constructed to connect Portsmouth with Kittery. He well remembered the constant reliance on ferries for those who did not own a rowboat or canoe, or did not choose to brave the currents in such small craft. In Ramble #132 Brewster well recalled:

> fifty years ago, the canoe was the boat used almost exclusively by our market folks on the river. On a Saturday morning in summer, as well as on other days, might be seen what was called the Kittery fleet, consisting of some twenty canoes, deeply laden with provisions of all kinds, mostly rowed by women, coming down the river, or up, as the tide served.

The Portsmouth Bridge now made such efforts generally superfluous. Brewster wrote in Ramble #83,

> In passing over Portsmouth bridge those who know the depth of water and the strength of the current, cannot but admire the skill by which it has been constructed over the Piscataqua, at a place where it is more than a fourth of a mile in width. After nearly forty years' use, rendered by recent improvements stronger than ever, it may now be regarded as permanent. How would the head swim, in looking down the dizzy distance, were all the water to be removed, leaving the traveller elevated between sixty and seventy feet above the ground! Yet he goes over without fear, and without danger, while the great iron horse by his side drags his long train after him, as easily and as safely as the eel glides through the water.

One reason for the bridge was to connect Portsmouth to the Portsmouth Naval Shipyard. Brewster had taken the road to the shipyard and found it delightful:

> From the elevation a few rods from the road, just before entering upon the Point bridge, is presented the grandest a panorama in the vicinity: on the east the winding and green banks of Spruce Creek are traced to a considerable extent; further in the distance [Mount] Agamenticus stands out with scarcely less importance than the more distant mountains of our own State. As we turn around, Portsmouth, the Navy Yard, the various islands in the harbor, forts Sullivan and Washington, Newcastle, fort Constitution, the several light houses, the Shoals, and the white sails bending to the breeze, sprinkled over the vast blue ocean—altogether present a scene which invites you to look about again and again.

Residents of Portsmouth were not always as infatuated about bridges as was Brewster. The leaders of Portsmouth in 1757 actually opposed building a bridge, proposed by the town of Newcastle, to link the Great Island with Little Harbor. Petitioners addressed the Provincial Assembly with their concerns, arguing that the town of Newcastle had no authority to build the bridge unless the assembly gave their permission. The Portsmouth petitioners believed that sailors had a "Natural Right" of "a free unmolested, unimbarrass'd Passage." The only way they could countenance such a proposal would be if the Newcastle bridge builders planned "to build an Arch from Shore to Shore, & of such Diameter as will admit any Vessel that can come into that Harbour to pass under it."

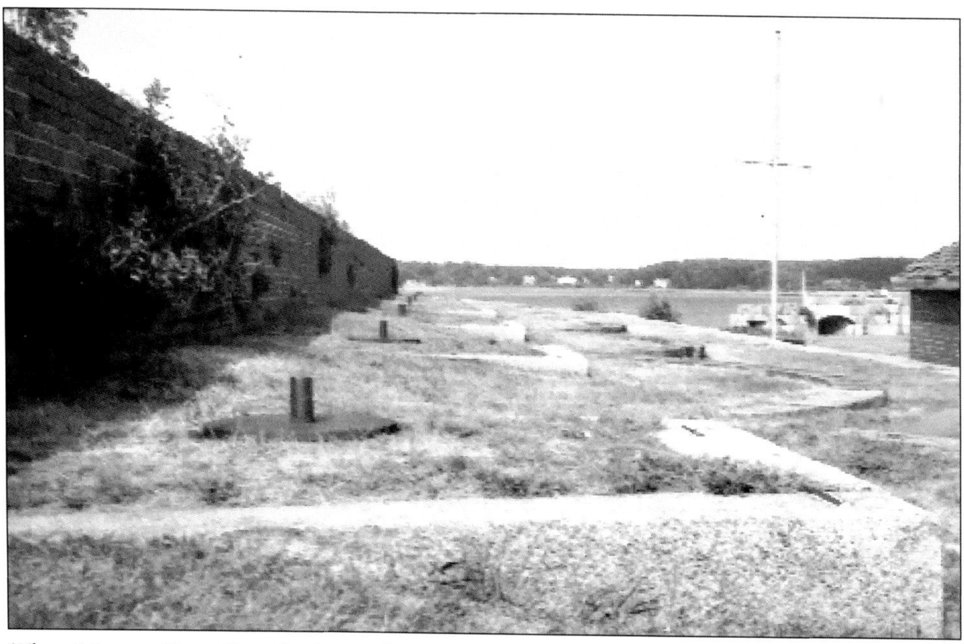

The visitor to Fort Constitution today sees the remains of pintles once used to mount and position huge artillery. These date from the Civil War. (Photo by Benjamin Lawson.)

During all of these fascinating years Charles Brewster surveyed, there were a few great moments that all Portsmouth residents recalled and cherished. The attack in 1774 on Fort William and Mary was one, and the launch of the *America* another. Who could forget the reading of the Declaration of Independence when it arrived in the summer of 1776 or the adoption of the Constitution and resulting parade through the streets of Portsmouth? Who could forget Washington's visit? For many years after, two members of the same family, brother and sister, talked of the day they met President Washington. It was November 3, 1789. Washington walked to Tobias Lear's boyhood home, where Mrs. Lear, Tobias' mother, lived with her sister and brother-in-law, Samuel Storer. When Washington arrived:

> he was introduced to and cordially greeted every member of the family—the venerable mother, her children, and her grand-children. Of the latter might be seen a bright little girl of three or four years, sitting upon his knee and giving him a kiss. No other lady now living in our state can probably bring up a like reminiscence. That lady, Miss Mary L. Storer, still occupies the mansion. There is also a babe presented, who has been christened "George Washington." The President places his hand gently upon the infant's head, and expresses the wish that he may "be a better man than the one whose name he bears."

That parlor in the Lear home, according to Brewster, became a museum, as it were; visitors were taken on a tour and shown where the great man sat, etc. The highlight of the tour, on the wall of the parlor, was "a piece of black satin, of eight by ten inches, . . . framed and glassed." It was a sampler "wrought . . . in a handsome manner, in Roman letters, by the lady who then sat upon Washington's knee. It read:

> (This is worked with our Illustrious and beloved General) George Washington's Hair:
>
> Which covered his
exalted head;
But now enrolled
among the dead,
Yet wears a crown
above the skies,
In realms of bliss
which never dies.

Brewster recorded another memorable moment when a great American visited Portsmouth. This time it was Daniel Webster, the famous American statesmen, returning to Portsmouth in his old age, recalling the time that he spent as a young lawyer just starting out. Webster, a native of Salisbury, New Hampshire, graduate of Phillips Exeter Academy and of Dartmouth, opened his law practice in Portsmouth;

his office was at Market Square. During these years from 1807 to 1816 young Webster married, established himself as an attorney, and entered politics. After almost a decade in Portsmouth, Webster moved to Massachusetts to involve himself more fully in national politics, becoming one of the leaders of the Whig Party. The hero returned in May 1844 to be honored at one ceremony given at Jefferson Hall where he made a brief speech, and another at the "Cameneum," where he:

> stood, not as the statesman or the politician, but as the citizen, the neighbor, the old townsman, who after a long absence had returned to greet his friends. The scene was one of touching interest, the house was well filled. Much of the life which animated the meeting could not number in years his absence. Here and there the bright visage which met his eye reminded him of his fond and beautiful daughter, the first here to greet him as a father, who though long reposing in the tomb, was never buried from his thoughts. Here, too, were some of the intimate associates of the bosom companion of his early life, and the associations which arose from this circumstance were not among the least vivid in his recollection. In the senate-chamber he could contend with and unquailingly overcome the most powerful opponent; but no truly great man is so powerful as to overcome the tender sympathies of the heart. In one portion of his short and feeling address he said,—"The nine years of the most active portion of my life spent here, are treasured in my heart with my dearest, my most enduring recollections." It required not words to interpret what was passing in his mind; tears trickled down his cheek and checked his utterance. The imagination of the audience needed not much effort to see passing before him the long procession of his old associates in his various relations in society, who were now resuscitated. After a momentary pause, he went on, expressing in the most feeling manner his warm attachment to the institutions of his native State, and his gratitude for the good feelings which had ever been manifested toward him by our citizens.

Charles Brewster concluded his final Ramble #149 by reflecting on the vast changes to Portsmouth during the 50-year period of his reports and essays in the *Journal*. "There was no imposing factory building in Portsmouth fifty years ago," Brewster wrote, amazed by the transformation during the previous half-century. The Portsmouth Steam Factory, a massive undertaking built in 1840 on what had once been Nathaniel Adams's land, was a six-story brick and stone building that produced cloth items. In 1866, it became known as the Kearsarge Mills. The Portsmouth Steam Factory was, even so, dwarfed by the buildings of the Newmarket Manufacturing Company, upstream at the falls of the Lamprey River. Yet Newmarket had nothing to compare with the Eastern Railroad and its huge station and roundhouse located south of the North Mill Pond. Such advances in production and transportation impelled Brewster to declare that "the changes in the outer world have been as great

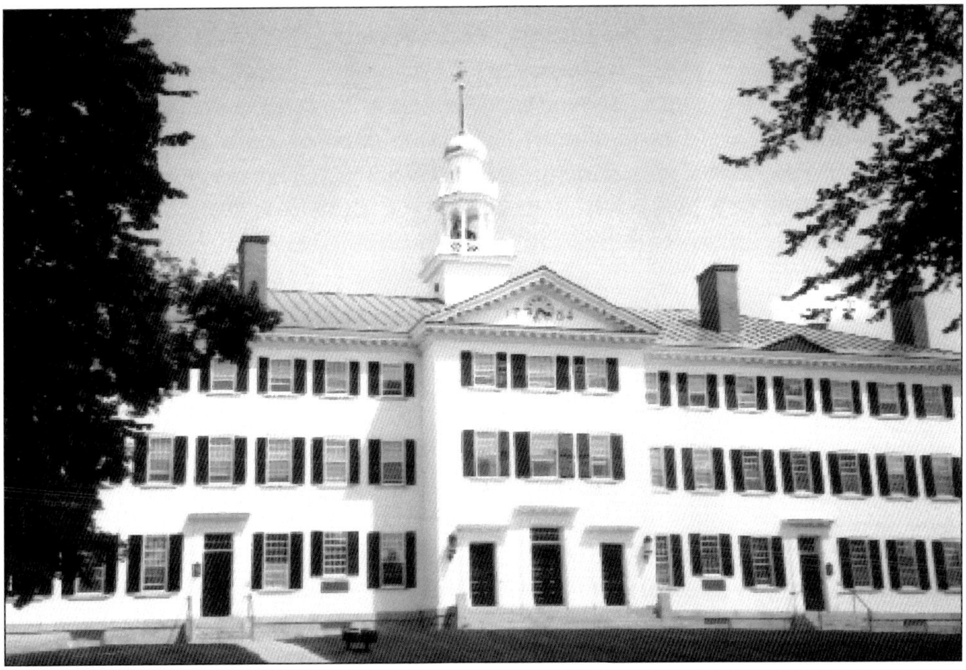

Eleazar Wheelock migrated up the Connecticut River to found Dartmouth College in 1769. The land upon which the college was built was set aside by Governor John Wentworth during the same year. (Photo by Benjamin Lawson.)

as in any half-century since the flood." The advances in printing alone persuaded the historian that "the progress of Printing in the last fifty years has been greater than from the time of its discovery in 1492 to 1818." The printing press had gone from a rate of "300 impressions per hour" in 1818 to "30,000 impressions . . . per hour" and "600 impressions per minute" in 1868.

Communications were also enhanced by the discovery of the telegraph, the development of lithography, the invention of photography by the Frenchman Daguerre, and the implementation of steam power to travel. The orientation toward steam was rapidly forcing Piscataqua shipbuilders to convert their efforts from sleek clipper ships to lumbering yet more steady steamships. The Portsmouth Naval Shipyard, of course, had to accommodate such changes as well. During the Civil War the shipyard produced three ironclad ships, the last of which was the U.S.S. *Agamenticus*.

From 1818 to 1868 there were many explorers who criss-crossed the continent seeking wealth, fame, excitement, an extension of their own knowledge in particular and human knowledge in general, and the expansion in the territory and power of the United States. Many such adventurers were New Englanders, such as Francis Parkman, who traveled west following the Oregon Trail, and Eastwick Evans, who published in 1819 *A Pedestrious Tour, of Four Thousand Miles, through the Western States and Territories, during the Winter and Spring of 1818*.

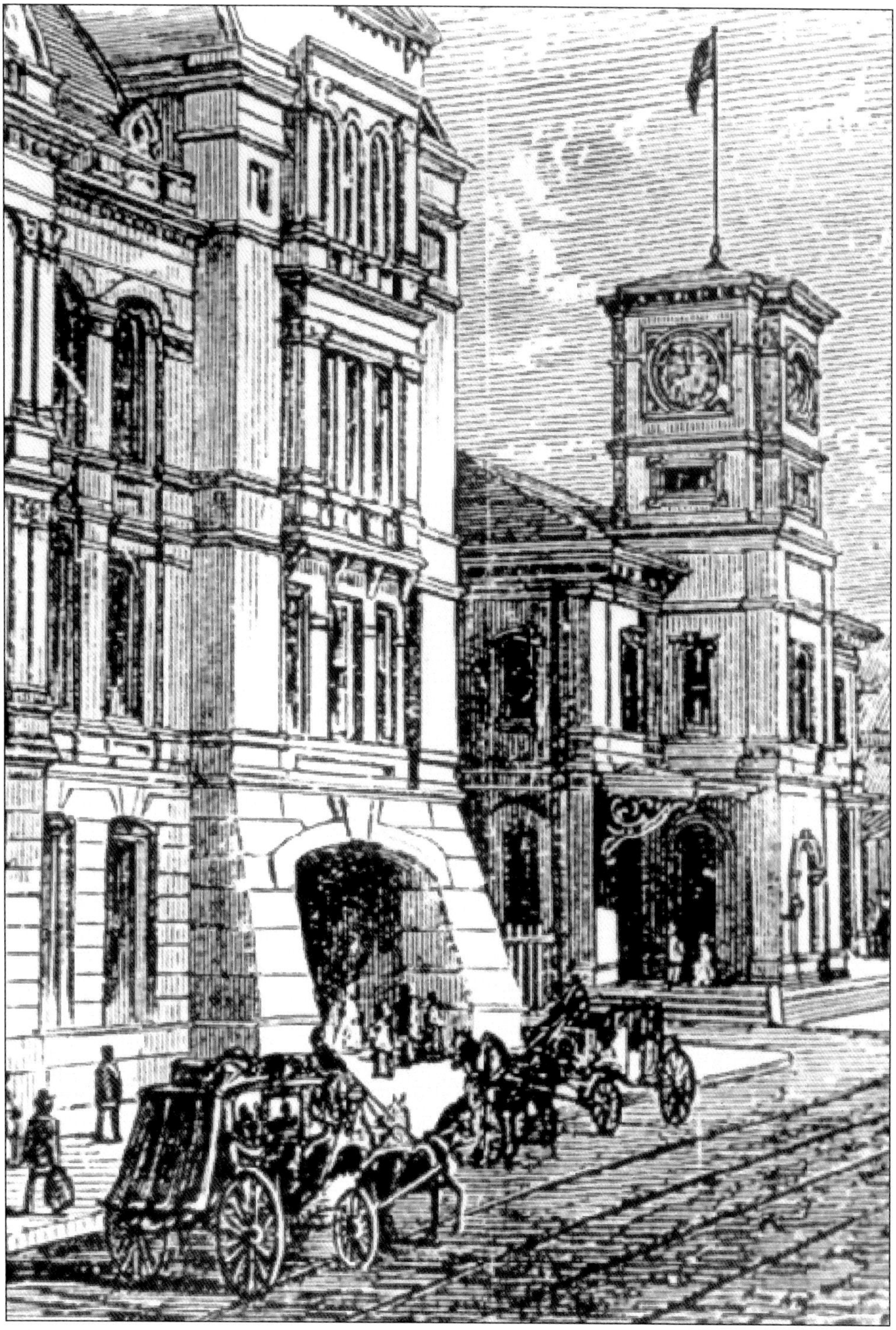

The sights and sounds of the Great East, the Eastern Railroad, was a common sight near the North Mill Pond in mid-nineteenth-century Portsmouth. The Boston Terminal of the Eastern Railroad is shown in this drawing from Boston Illustrated.

Evans was a near contemporary of Brewster, born and raised in Portsmouth during the late eighteenth and early nineteenth centuries. Quick of mind and spirit, Evans studied law and practiced briefly as an attorney before wanderlust convinced him to dress in buffalo skin and set out from New Hampshire in the dead of winter. He crossed the icy White Mountains, traveled through Vermont to upstate New York, then west through Ohio to the Michigan Territory. From there he descended the Mississippi River to New Orleans, then returned to Portsmouth by boat.

Evans saw and recorded the vast differences in landscape, flora, fauna, and peoples of America, but one wonders whether or not Brewster would have felt that his own efforts and travels were diminished in any way compared to Eastwick Evans. In his final Ramble #149, Charles Brewster wrote that his walking commute from home to office (2,300 feet) over 50 years resulted in "27,150 miles in one beaten track, compassing more than a circuit round the world." If he had not seen the Ohio Valley, Detroit in its infancy, the shores of the Mississippi, or the willows of Louisiana, he had seen "the changes of the seasons present in the hundred and twenty trees daily passed, the bud, the blossom, the full foliage, the autumnal tinges, and the strong and muscular bare limbs of the winter months. They are all company to him in their associations." Portsmouth was sufficient for Charles W. Brewster.

Brewster fashioned the mold of the rambler. Subsequent reflective types, natives as well as visitors, who found themselves wandering the streets of Portsmouth followed Brewster's call, took up his cause, and imitated his style. Portsmouth is one of the unique places where the vast layers of the past nestle comfortably next to the present. The appeal of the ramble is to experience simultaneously different times all at once, to bring together if anachronistically two or three centuries. Brewster's rambles were wanderings into the past. So, too, were the digressions of Thomas Bailey Aldrich.

Aldrich was a well-known fiction writer who had spent part of his childhood in Portsmouth. He returned in 1892 to reflect on his youth and resurrect old memories. His ruminations led to a brief historical ramble that he christened *An Old Town by the Sea*. "I call it an old town, but it is only relatively old," he began the book. In the entire run of humanity, Portsmouth's past is indeed brief. Yet it did seem quite some time ago that Martin Pring sailed up the Piscataqua River in search of sassafras. Aldrich stood on the same spot almost 300 years later and wondered what Pring and his men experienced:

> The explorers found themselves on the edge of a vast forest of oak, hemlock, maple, and pine; but they saw no sassafras-trees to speak of.... Here and there were discoverable the scattered ashes of fires where the Indians had encamped earlier in the spring; they were absent now, at the silvery falls, higher up the stream, where fish abounded at that season. The soft June breeze, laden with the delicate breath of wild-flowers and the pungent odors of spruce and pine, ruffled the duplicate sky in the

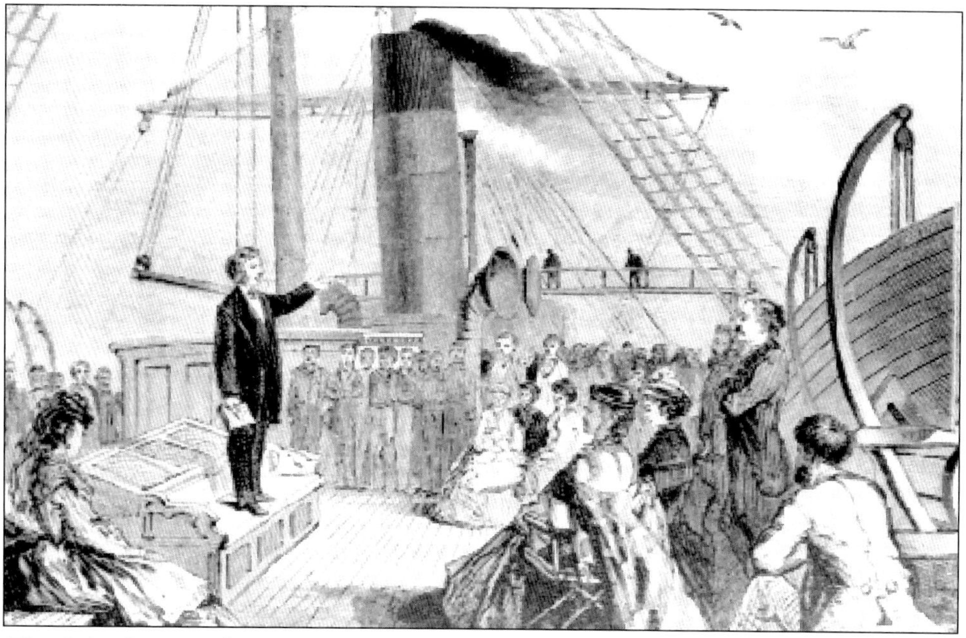

The deck of a steamship sometimes hosted speeches, sermons, and polite conversation. Even ladies braved the elements of the upper deck to listen to a particularly good speaker. (From Around the Tea-Table.)

> water; the new leaves lisped pleasantly in the tree tops, and the birds were singing as if they had gone mad. No ruder sound or movement of life disturbed the primeval solitude. Master Pring would scarcely recognize the spot were he to land there to-day.

Captain John Smith, "the modern Jason," made his peregrinations along the New England coast 11 years later. Aldrich correctly assessed Smith's significance, that his writings (such as *Description of New England*) and map of New England inspired Ferdinando Gorges and Captain John Mason to locate "the Laconia Company" on "the banks of the Piscataqua."

Aldrich, tongue in cheek, proposed at the end of chapter one that he would "take the reader" of his book on a tour of the town, though beware the "flitting ghost of some old-time worthy, on a staircase or at a lonely street corner." Aldrich's ghosts were shades of past memory. Nathaniel Hawthorne on the other hand, who had once frequented the Piscataqua region and had written about its historical delights, thought the ghosts were quite real.

Aldrich admired the selection of the original site of settlement, the "Pilgrims' Rock of New Hampshire," by the agents of the Laconia Company, who chose a spot convenient for trade and fishing. Aldrich, however, was entranced by its overwhelming beauty. "The stream broadens suddenly at" Strawbery Banke, "and at flood tide, lying without a ripple in a basin formed by the interlocked islands and the mainland, it looks more like an inland lake than a river. To the unaccustomed eye there is no visible outlet." Part of the romance of the place was "the worm-eaten wharves, some of them covered by a sparse, unhealthy beard of grass, and the weather-stained, unoccupied warehouses," and other signs of "antiquity" that nestled uncomfortably amid factories and breweries. The harbor appeared depressed, however, as Aldrich saw few sights and sounds of the marine economy that once existed in an earlier century. "Portsmouth," Aldrich lamented, "remains the interesting widow of a once very lively commerce." And yet its decay, the ruins that signified past greatness were, like the ruins of the Roman Forum, the Athenian Acropolis, charming. Portsmouth increasingly survived on its past, its anniversaries, such as its 250th in 1873, when "the lines of pilgrims took up their march from every corner of the globe, and swept down with the music and banners on the motherly old town."

In 1892 Aldrich was content to reminisce lazily about the past as he strolled along the unhurried, slumbering harbor:

> The sunshine seems to lie a foot deep on the planks of the dusty wharf, which yields up to the warmth a vague perfume of the cargoes of rum,

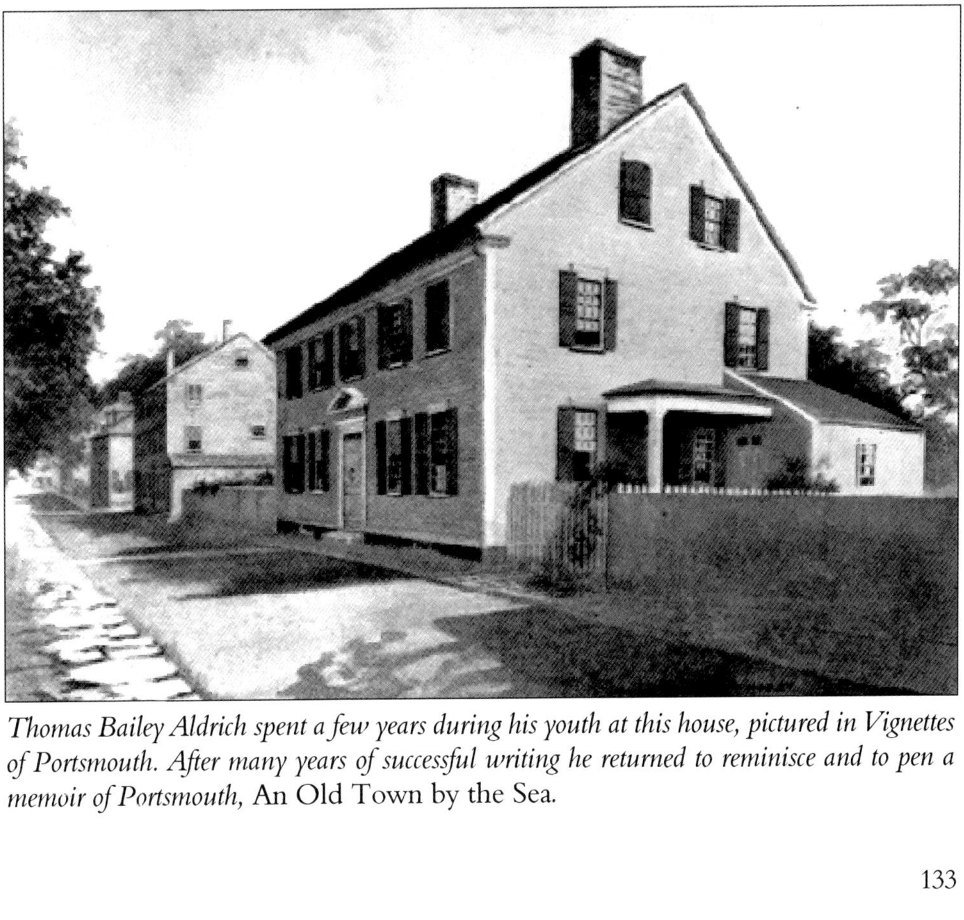

Thomas Bailey Aldrich spent a few years during his youth at this house, pictured in Vignettes of Portsmouth. After many years of successful writing he returned to reminisce and to pen a memoir of Portsmouth, An Old Town by the Sea.

> molasses, and spice that used to be piled upon it. The river is as blue as the inside of a harebell. The opposite shore, in the strangely shifting magic lights of sky and water, stretches along like the silvery coast of fairyland. . . . On your right lies a cluster of small islands,—there are a dozen or more in the harbor—on the most extensive of which you see the fading-away remains of some earthworks. [In the Narrows] perhaps a bark or a sloop-of-war is making up to town; the hulk is hidden among the islands, and the topmasts have the effect of sweeping across the dry land. On your left is a long bridge, more than a quarter of a mile in length, set upon piles where the water is twenty or thirty feet deep, leading to the navy yard and Kittery.

Aldrich went on to describe the hypnotizing effect of the water, the sounds, smells, and dreams. As beautiful were the trees that lined the lanes where the great mansions of Portsmouth stood side by side.

The manor of John Langdon, for example, "stands back a decorous distance from the street, under the shadows of some gigantic oaks or elms, and presents an imposing appearance as you approach it over the tessellated marble walk."

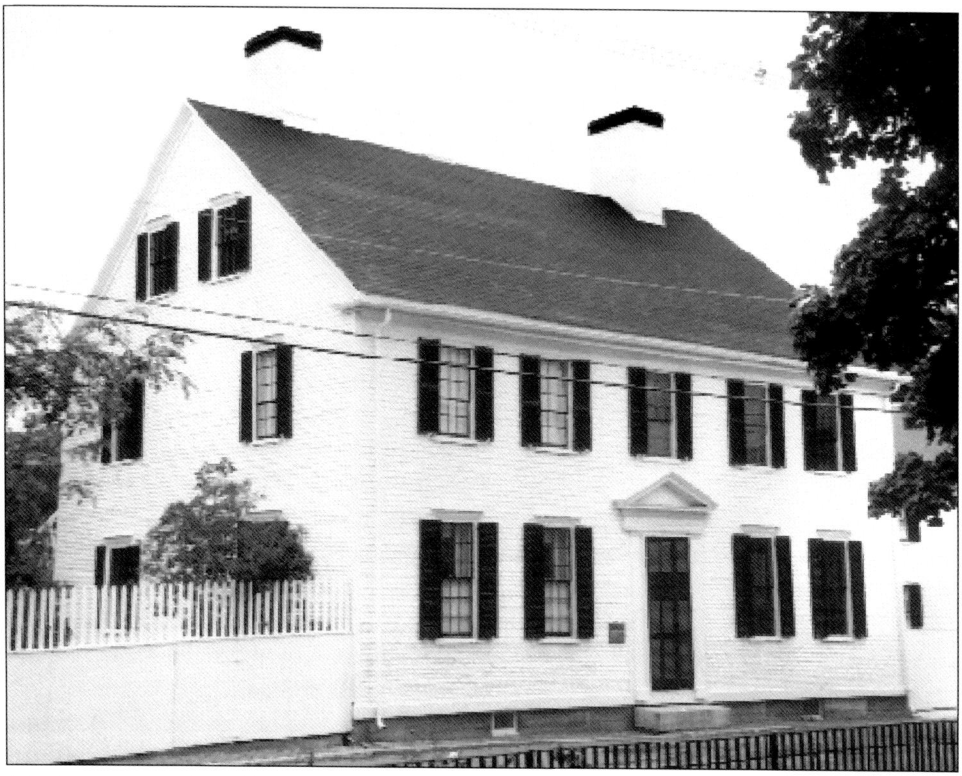

The Thomas Bailey Aldrich home is preserved at Strawbery Banke Museum. The house has scarcely changed in well over a century. (Photo by Benjamin Lawson.)

The "chestnuts . . . in blossom" made Aldrich imagine himself "in a garden in fairyland." More wonderful was:

> the spectacle which certain streets in Portsmouth present in midwinter after a heavy snowstorm. You may walk for miles under wonderful silvery arches formed by the overhanging and interlaced boughs of the trees, festooned with a drapery even more graceful and dazzling than springtime gives them.

Aldrich realized one clear day while surveying the city and its environs from the vantage of the roof of the Athenaeum that Portsmouth was as dependent on trees as the sea. "Glancing down on the town nestled in foliage, it seems like a town dropped by chance in the midst of a forest."

In Aldrich's rambles through Portsmouth and its past, contemplating what had been, thinking about the few years half a century ago when he lived in Portsmouth, he realized that although the sights and smells, the lanes and structures of the port city seemed familiar enough, something was missing. The old town by the sea was rapidly disappearing, being replaced by the modern city. The steamship, railroad, telegraph, and telephone brought rapid transportation and quicker, more efficient communications that transcended localities, bringing a greater sense of connection to the world and a national identity instead of a local one. Aldrich saw what made Portsmouth unique—its "local character"—vanishing in the face of modernization. Resisting this transformation of the small town of his youth, Aldrich felt compelled to portray the many eccentric characters of the past, showing the peculiar uniqueness of the old town.

An Old Town by the Sea, like all respectable histories of Portsmouth, has a full description of Washington's visit in 1789. But what struck Aldrich most and stayed in his memory was the ancient woman who kept a room at a decrepit old tenement house. Her lodgings had once been Stavers' Hotel, where Washington lodged during his visit to Portsmouth. "When I was a boy I knew an old lady," Aldrich recalled, "who had known Washington very well. She was a girl in her teens when he came to Portsmouth." After 60 years she still recalled the President's visit and spent her last days endlessly talking about it, trying to convince all who would listen that George Washington, President of the United States, paid "a compliment to her complexion."

Other ancient women of Portsmouth owned the varied "knick-knack establishments" along Portsmouth byways; often they were in the back parlor of the family home. The owners kept their goods in drawers, which opened to the delight of the customer, who saw a dazzling display of the treasures of long ago. "Here was stored almost every small article required by humanity, from an inflamed emery cushion to a peppermint Gibraltar." These old:

> proprietors . . . were the nicest creatures, somehow suggesting venerable doves. They were always aged ladies, sometimes spinsters, sometimes

> relicts of daring mariners, beached long before. They always wore crisp muslin caps and steel-rimmed spectacles; they were not always amiable, and no wonder, for even doves may have their rheumatism; but such as they were, they were cherished in young hearts, and are, I take it, impossible to-day.

Like his contemporary the Boston writer and historian Henry Adams, Thomas Bailey Aldrich believed that his youthful observations witnessed a watershed in American history—the transition from "the cocked hats" of the past to the "railroad" of the future. Fortunately Portsmouth in 1850 had enough "bits of color, certain half obsolete customs and scraps of the past" to interest the lonesome antiquarian yearning for the good old days.

> I was not too late, for example, to catch the last town crier—Nicholas Newman, whom I used to contemplate with awe, and now recall with a sort of affection. Nicholas Newman . . . was a most estimable person, very short, cross-eyed, somewhat bow-legged, and with a bell out of all proportion to his stature . . . . The only thing about him that matched the instrument of his office was his voice. His "Hear All!" still deafens memory's ear. I remember that he had a queer way of sidling up to one, as if nature in shaping him had originally intended a crab, but thought better of it, and made a town-crier.

Other eccentrics included a barber who ran his shop like an "Emporium" and a delivery man who used a "sky-blue wheelbarrow" to deliver his products, often losing half of the contents along the way. One peculiar soul Aldrich remembered seeing as he passed to and from school. It was a "face peering out of a window in the second story of a shambling yellow house situated in Washington Street." Daily he saw the recluse watching the world from his self-imposed hermitage, "with his cheek so close to the window that the nearest pane became permanently blurred with his breath; for after his demise the blurr remained."

Many days Aldrich spent along the harbor near the Point of Graves, where he came upon the same old mariner "boiling lobsters on a little gravelly beach." His weather-beaten face had "the expression of a half-open clam."

When Aldrich penned his book, this part of Portsmouth, Puddle Dock, was very old and very poor, the center of what was once known as Strawbery Banke. The memories of wealth and grandeur had succumbed to declining trade. Puddle Dock had once been host to the wharves of the Portsmouth rich, the grand merchants whose ships sailed the waters of the Atlantic, the Pacific, and the Indian Oceans. A common sight of the early nineteenth century was the flat-bottomed, single-sailed gundalow—the workhorse of the harbor. The rough and ready among Portsmouth's sailors maneuvered these boats, loaded with native timber and produce or wares from foreign lands, in and about the islands of the Piscataqua. When Aldrich wrote *An Old Town by the Sea* gundalows were powered by lateen sails that resembled, to those sailors who had been to the South China Sea, the junks of those waters. However, even the gundalow was vanishing from Portsmouth harbor.

Aldrich, like all Boston Brahmins and others of wealth and rank, feared the growing tide of immigration flowing upon American shores. Eastern and southern Europeans, Russian Jews, and the impoverished of China fled to America, the promised land. Many ended up in New England cities, and Portsmouth became home to many Italian and Jewish immigrants. Although seeking a new life, they were nevertheless poor, renting the worst sort of housing in Portsmouth. Puddle Dock was an important haven for these newcomers, yet it was succumbing to change. By the turn of the century, Puddle Dock was the town dump. The accumulating rubbish eventually displaced the water and filled Puddle Dock as the years passed, which was indicative of the area's declining importance in Portsmouth social and economic affairs.

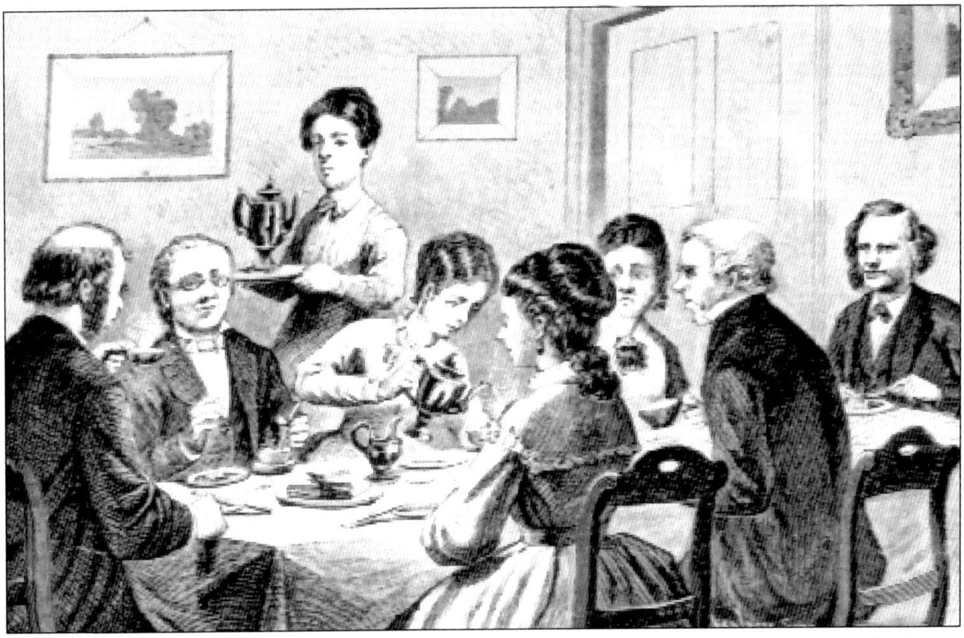

Tea-time was a daily ritual in middle class Portsmouth homes of the 1800s. Tea, which was served several hours after dinner, included a small snack, which would hold one until the light supper before bedtime. (From Around the Tea-Table.*)*

7. Strawbery Banke

Portsmouth today is still a wonderful place for the inquisitive rambler in search of the past. Much has changed since Aldrich penned his portrait of the town in the 1890s and Brewster rambled back and forth to his office during the first half of the nineteenth century. In some ways they would be hard put to recognize today's Portsmouth, which is expansive, busy, and reconstructed. The west side by 1900 had become the center of the manufacturing sector; north of which was a large retail area that today features shopping malls and a busy trade port (what used to be Pease Air Force Base). Portsmouth's North End has in recent decades become an upscale restaurant and hotel sector, whereas a century ago it was an old tired neighborhood of European immigrants. Urban renewal schemes of the 1950s and 1960s reshaped the area, bringing in wealth and attractive architecture while angering Italian-Americans and others whose houses were destroyed and lives altered.

The South End area, once known as Strawbery Banke and later Puddle Dock, has been transformed as well. In 1900, it was a decaying and impoverished ethnic neighborhood. Houses of ill repute and cheap rooms in crowded tenant houses attracted transients and ne'er-do-wells. Crime followed close on the heels of poverty and the busy wharves and gundalows disappeared in the wake of Portsmouth's declining trade. Puddle Dock became a town landfill; mechanics working in garages repairing autos and dealers in scrap metal and junk replaced merchants and ship captains. In time, the urban landscape of the neighborhood hid all remnants of its golden age during the late 1700s and early 1800s.

Reflecting America's industrial economy, the vast number of residents in the old Puddle Dock neighborhood were laborers employed by Portsmouth factories and the Naval Shipyard across the river. Fortunately for the local economy, the Shipyard had weathered bad times and had been reinvented several times to accommodate America's turn to steam and steel, as well as the demand for warships and naval transports during World War I.

The war was a consequence of the competitive, industrial might of European countries such as England and Germany. Industrialization required raw materials from all over the world and international markets. The most powerful countries competed for colonies to supply the former and access to ports to satisfy the latter. Portsmouth briefly was at the center of international competition when it hosted a peace conference to settle the differences between Russia and Japan. President Theodore Roosevelt brokered a treaty between the two rival countries—the Portsmouth Treaty of 1905—for which he received the Nobel Peace Prize in 1906.

But in 1914 there were different circumstances, and the United States had a different president when the Axis powers of Germany, Austria-Hungary, and Turkey went to war against the Triple Entente of England, France, and Russia. At first, the United States stayed out of the war. German aggression to shipping in the North Atlantic and refusal to respect the rights of noncombatants and neutrals eventually compelled the Congress to declare war on Germany in 1917. American "doughboys" went to war. Piscataqua shipyards contributed massive transport ships, such as the *Baboosic*, which illustrates the cover of this book, to bring American soldiers safely to Europe. Within 19 months of America's entry into the war, Germany surrendered and the world was once again, if briefly, at peace.

During this first "Great War," the success of German submarines showed American war planners that the United States needed to turn its attention to building efficient submarines for a future time of renewed hostilities.

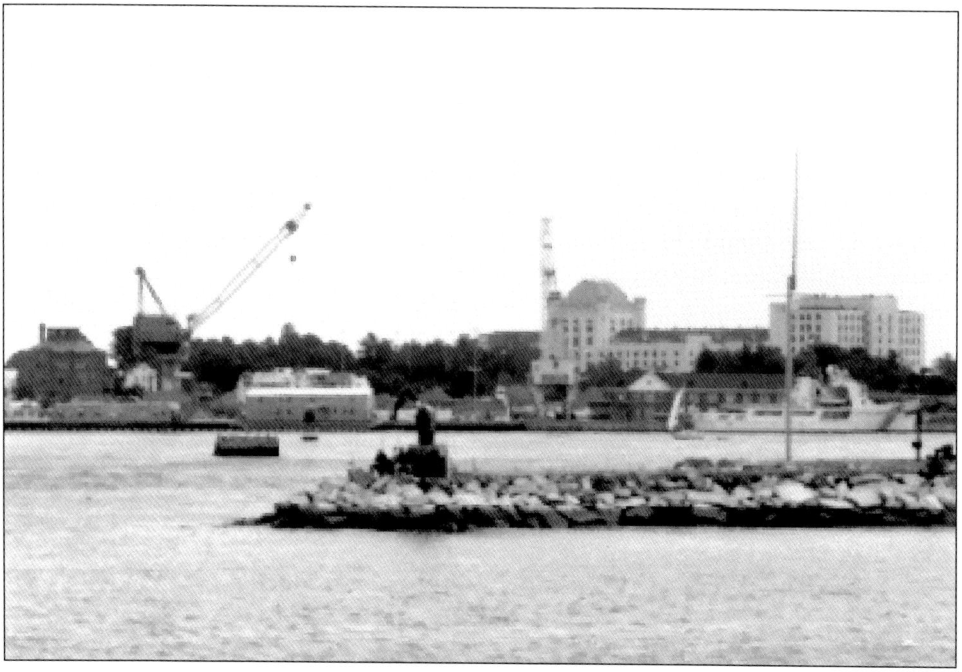

This photo of Portsmouth harbor (by Benjamin Lawson) provides a view of the old navy prison, Portsmouth Naval Shipyard, and U.S. Coast Guard cutter. The Coast Guard maintains a base at Newcastle adjacent to Fort Constitution.

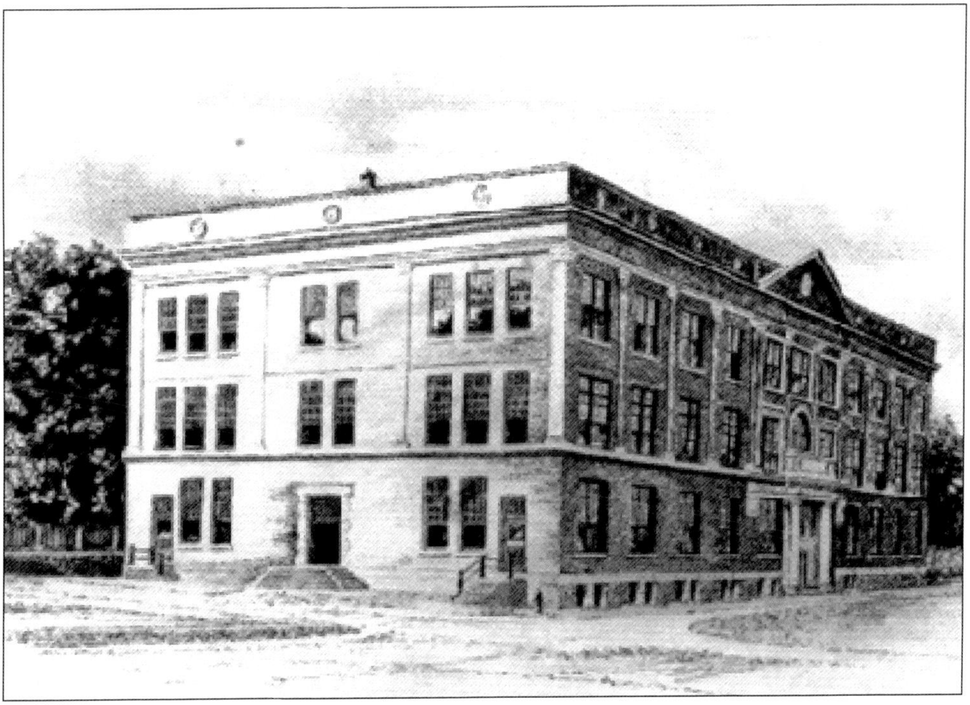

At the Peace Conference Building, Portsmouth hosted representatives from Japan and Russia to settle their differences and bring an end to the Russo-Japanese War. The resulting treaty led to President Theodore Roosevelt receiving the Nobel Peace Prize for his role as broker. (From Vignettes of Portsmouth.*)*

The Portsmouth Naval Shipyard adapted itself to the demands of a new kind of naval warfare, turning its attention to the construction and repair of submarines. This activity accelerated with the onset of World War II in 1939 and America's participation in the war after the Japanese attack on Pearl Harbor in December 1941.

Portsmouth harbor was naturally a strategic location that required defense from possible enemy incursions. Military batteries were set up at Odiorne Point, guarding the mouth of the Piscataqua. Underwater nets stretched across the river's mouth to prevent undetected invasion by enemy submarines. At the end of the war Piscataqua residents witnessed the strange phenomenon of German U-boats sailing into Portsmouth harbor to surrender.

The end of war brought new problems to world affairs. The arms race waged between the United States and the Soviet Union from 1945 to 1991 during the Cold War included the construction of new classes of submarines. The shipyard contributed work on experimental subs, such as the *Albacore*, the unique design of which allowed for greater depth, speed, and time underwater. The Shipyard was one of many yards throughout the United States to begin the tireless work of developing nuclear submarines. After the

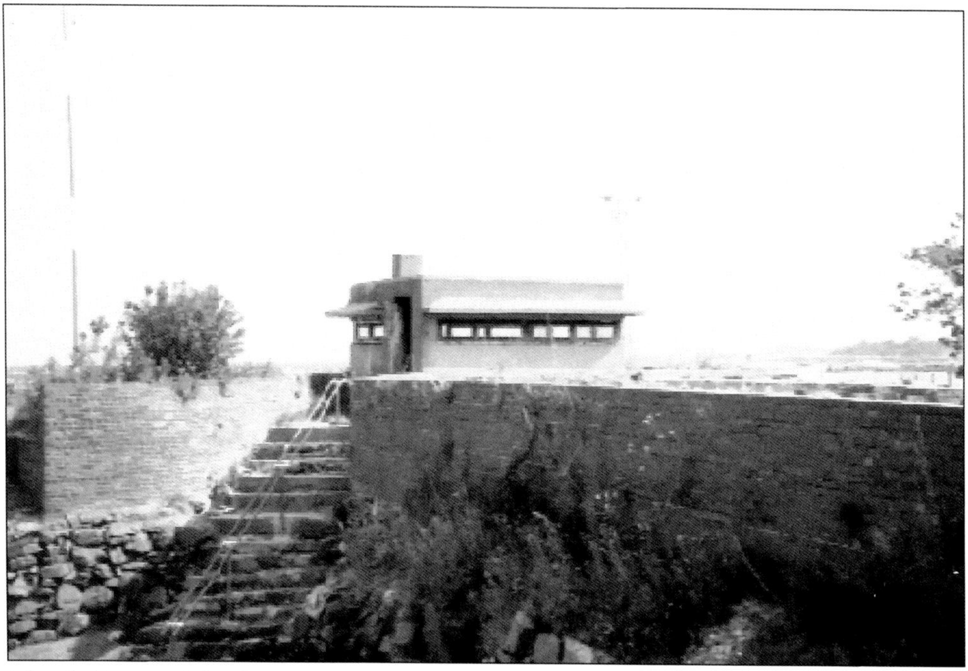

This lookout and fortified post at Fort Constitution was part of the defensive preparations of World War II. From this post lookouts were able to scan the entire harbor and mouth of the Piscataqua. (Photo by Benjamin Lawson.)

1950s, the Portsmouth Naval Shipyard increasingly focused on the repair and maintenance of nuclear subs.

Residents at Puddle Dock were able to keep track of the frequent changes and the comings and goings of ships and submarines at the Shipyard throughout the twentieth century. The lives of Puddle Dock residents were typified by the Abbots. Walter and Bertha Abbott worked as laborers after their marriage in 1896 and they bought a house on Jefferson Street after the First World War. Walter transformed the 200-year old home into a comfortable residence with an adjoining variety store that had a large inviting window. They christened their new source of livelihood "The Little Corner Store;" it was a variety store not unlike those one still finds in small New Hampshire towns. Walter died in 1938, but Bertha kept the store going throughout World War II when Portsmouth's population experienced a minor boom with the increased activity at the Shipyard. Bertha welcomed the end of the war and the rationing of food items, even though postwar prosperity would threaten the existence of small variety stores trying to compete with supermarket chains.

As typical were the lives of the Gormans and Shapiros. Charles and Lena Gorman and Abraham and Shiva Shapiro were Eastern European Jewish immigrants who came to Portsmouth, as did many others, in the 1890s and early 1900s. The Shapiros moved to Puddle Dock after their marriage in 1905.

They owned the house once occupied by Dr. John Jackson, physician and son of the famous eighteenth–century doctor Hall Jackson. Abraham worked in the shoe industry and owned a small pawn shop while Shiva raised Molly, their only child, in a strict orthodox environment. The nearby Temple of Israel served the religious needs of the Shapiros, Gormans, and the many other Jewish families who lived in the Puddle Dock neighborhood. Charles and Lena Gorman were part of this neighborhood. Charles had departed an increasingly anti-Semitic Russia just before the start of World War I. He had family living in the Boston area, but job opportunities in shoe manufacturing north of Boston drew Charles to Portsmouth. After marrying Lena, they established a scrap metal business in Portsmouth on Newton Avenue at Puddle Dock and resided nearby on Court Street. As the Gorman family grew, the business occupied the attention of the father, mother, and daughters. After World War II, the daughters married and left home and the Gorman's scrap metal business eventually closed after the city bought the land for urban renewal.

The Gorman's garage on Newton Street, as well as the Shapiro's former dwelling on Jefferson Street, became part of a successful attempt by concerned Portsmouth citizens to save some of the old homes, particularly those at Puddle Dock, from

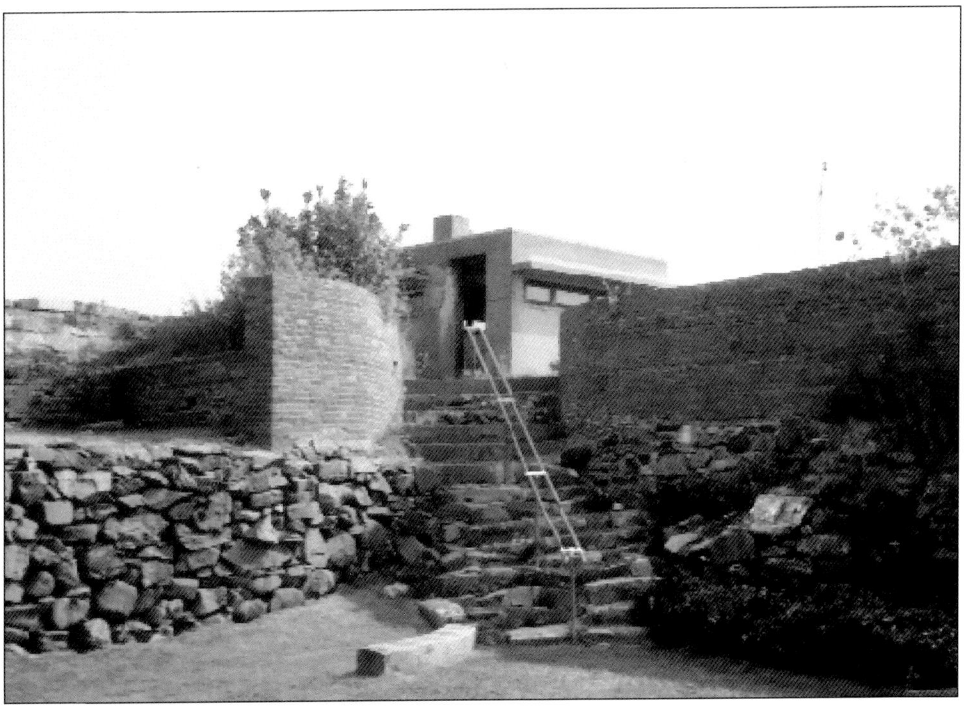

Several periods of Portsmouth history merge at Fort Constitution. The fort has served to protect Portsmouth during the initial settlements of the colonial period, and throughout the conflicts of the American Revolution, War of 1812, the Civil War, Spanish-American War, World War I, and World War II. (Photo by Benjamin Lawson.)

urban renewal. Strawbery Banke Incorporated, a museum neighborhood, opened in 1965 to help renovate and restore the homes of merchants, seamen, and others who had been part of Puddle Dock history over a 300-year period. Strawbery Banke has been an evolving museum, greeting visitors as a work in progress. Archaeological digs, gardens from various times in the past, and craftsmen using the tools of eighteenth- and nineteenth-century coopers and shipwrights to build casks and boats are all significant exhibits at the museum. It has restored Puddle Dock structures as well as others from around the city that were relocated to Strawbery Banke.

To spend a sunny afternoon rambling in and about the lanes and houses of Strawbery Banke is to re-enter, as it were, the past. The museum is encompassed by Hancock, Washington, and Court streets. The main entrance is on Marcy Street, south of which is the site of the First Parish. Next to the entrance is the site of the original Liberty Pole, set up by patriots in 1765 protesting the Stamp Act. The current Liberty Pole, erected in 1824, marks the entrance to Prescott Park, where besides musical and dramatic performances one can spy old wharves and the seaweed and barnacles of the harbor. The ubiquitous cry of seagulls is frequently interrupted by the siren on the Memorial Bridge heralding an incoming or outgoing tanker, cruise ship, or mast ship under sail. The engines of fishing trawlers roar and the smell of burning diesel fuel competes unpleasantly with the otherwise fresh and crisp salty sea air.

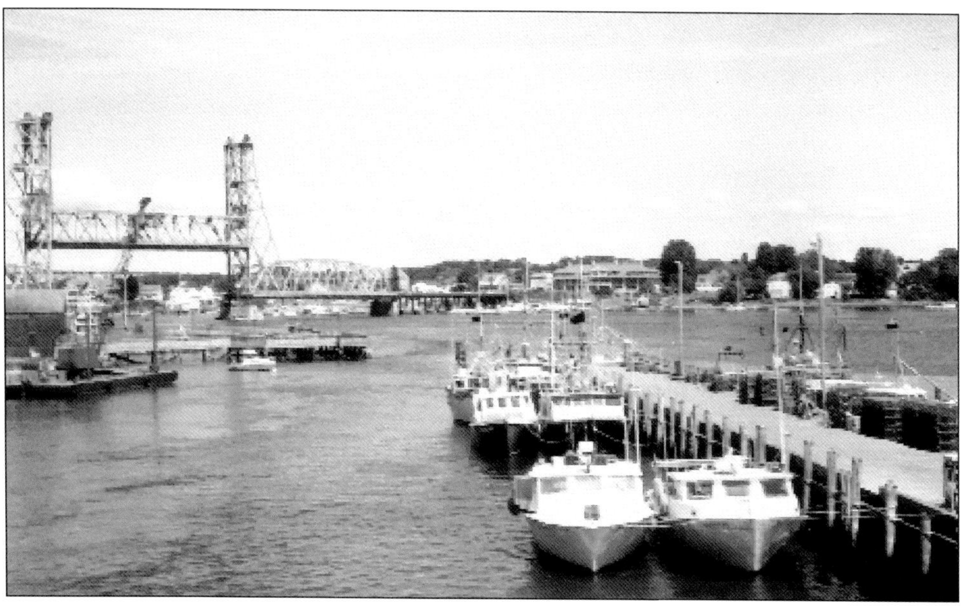

Portsmouth harbor is busy with the comings and goings of pleasure craft and commercial vessels. In the background of this photo (by Benjamin Lawson) the Memorial Bridge is open to allow a passing tall ship.

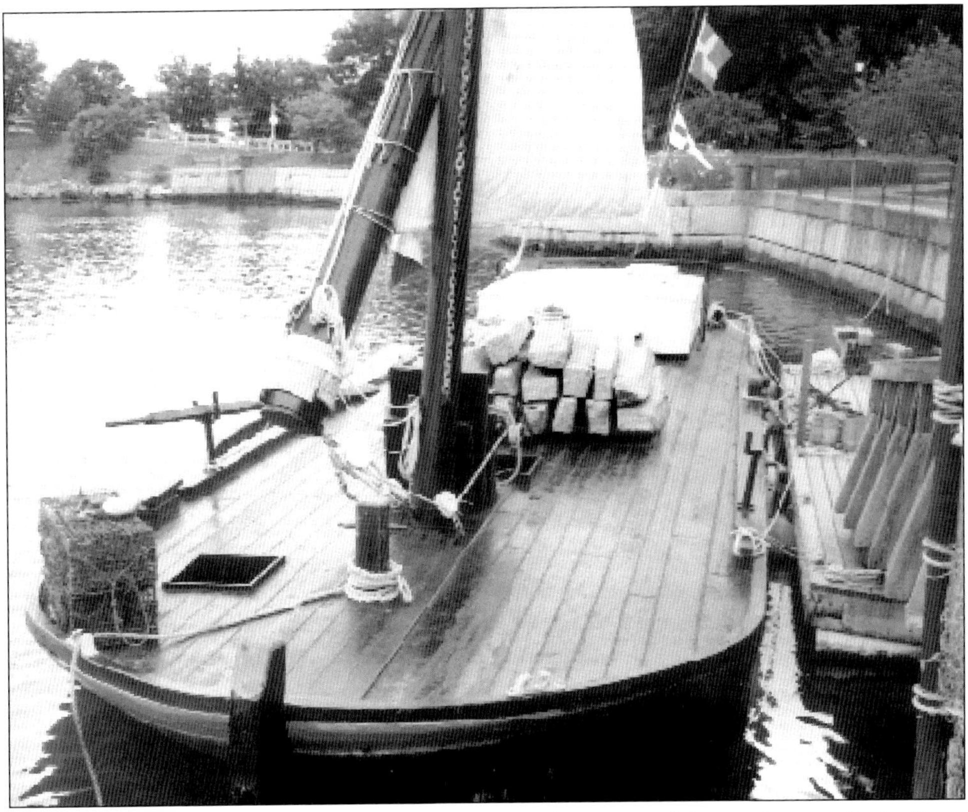

The Portsmouth Gundalow Project, featuring a reproduction gundalow, at Prescott Park allows visitors to inspect the workhorse of Portsmouth harbor for most of its history. Gundalows were rigged with a single lateen sail for maneuverability in tight spots. Their shallow draft allowed them to carry cargo to and from Puddle Dock wharves. (Photo by Benjamin Lawson.)

One spies in the distance the restful Point of Graves, which is in stark contrast to the busy traffic on narrow streets. Wealthy tourists ask questions and cause commotion, but there is much to see. The Portsmouth Naval Shipyard dominates the opposite shore; look closely and one might see a nuclear submarine being repaired. Gulls, pigeons, doves, and cormorants seem unconcerned with such imposing technology and destructive power, and are content to enjoy the sweet murmuring of the river as it slowly moves toward the sea.

The antiquarian spirits of Nathaniel Adams, Charles Brewster, and Thomas Bailey Aldrich join visitors entering Strawbery Banke Museum from Marcy Street. Puddle Dock has long since vanished, but one feels its watery presence nevertheless in the open grassy space and remnants of wharves, such as the Sherburne Wharf, which dates back to the late 1600s. Overlooking the wharf is the Sherburne House, built at the end of the seventeenth century. It is wonderfully old, with a clapboard exterior and two imposing gables, a central chimney, and a massive central beam. It seems a perfect dwelling for

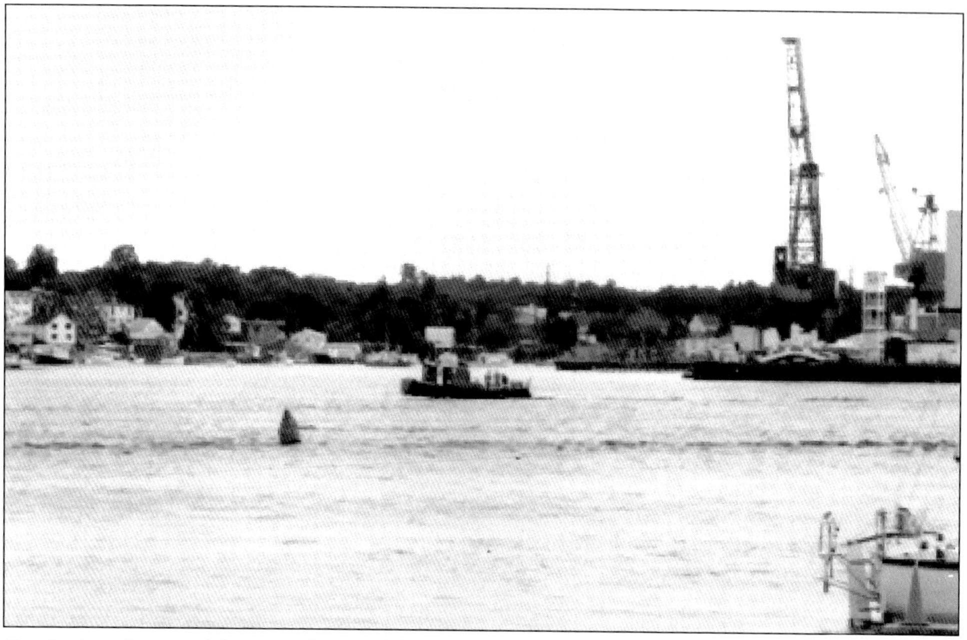

Replacing the gundalow as the workhorse of Portsmouth harbor is the tugboat. Tugs are in constant use escorting freighters and tankers to and from Portsmouth harbor. (Photo by Benjamin Lawson.)

an Elizabethan inhabitant of Tudor England. Captain Sherburne and his wife Mary perhaps inaugurated an herb garden that still produces plants of reputed medicinal quality.

Colonial Americans learned from hearsay and Native Americans that certain plants, imported from Europe or elsewhere or native to America, could be used to combat a variety of diseases. One native herb that decorated most colonial gardens was the Spotted Geranium, which blooms into wonderful purple wildflowers in the early spring. The Geranium was thought to prevent or relieve all sorts of stomach ailments, and was even thought to cure cancer. An imported herb, *Chrysanthemum Parthenium*, was colloquially known as "Feverfew," though it was more effective at preventing migraine headaches.

Puddle Dockers enjoyed the beauty of the hyssop growing in herb gardens. Those well-versed in the Old Testament know that the ancient Hebrews used hyssop. Colonial Americans believed hyssop helped with rheumatism, sore throats, and could fight infections and viruses. Soapwart was another popular herb, used not only for cleaning, as its name implies, but for a variety of diseases as well, ranging from treating acne and boils to soothing the rashes caused by poison ivy; it reputedly even helps to combat breast cancer. Early explorers discovered wild strawberries growing along the area and discovered from native Algonquians the many medicinal uses of the berry, especially when the roots and leaves are boiled in water to make tea. Seamen who lived at the Banke often chewed Wormwood leaves for seasickness, though in so doing they might appear seasick on land, as the herb has a narcotic effect.

The widespread use of herbs proves that Puddle Dockers of the colonial period were cognizant of what worked to bring order to their existence. Indeed, the lanes of Puddle Dock, laid out in right angles, show a regularity not always found among other Portsmouth neighborhoods. These rectangular lots reflect the order and reason of the eighteenth-century Enlightenment. The early settlers of Strawbery Banke also built functional homes and lived on lanes with no-nonsense names. Mast Lane led directly to the wharf, while Puddle Lane paralleled the inlet.

At the end of Puddle Lane stood a house that in 1796 Joshua Jones purchased to pursue his dream of becoming an active merchant at Puddle Dock. The house is large and functional but not ornate, befitting Jones himself. After a long day of speculating in goods, Jones, requiring refreshment, had but a short distance down Atkinson Street to reach the William Pitt Tavern. Owned by John Stavers, the tavern was a central gathering place for business transactions, politics, meetings of groups such as the Masons, and important events. One could also get a mug of ale or rum. The William Pitt Tavern was not the only stately structure on Court Street.

At the corner of Court and Washington stands the Chase House, an inviting Georgian mansion that attracts the visitor today as it drew General Washington to visit merchant Stephen Chase, his wife, and children. The General's ramblings that November day in 1789 perchance took him by other homes of Portsmouth merchants, mariners, and town leaders. Mostly President Washington judged Puddle Dock dwellings to be "plain," which would be

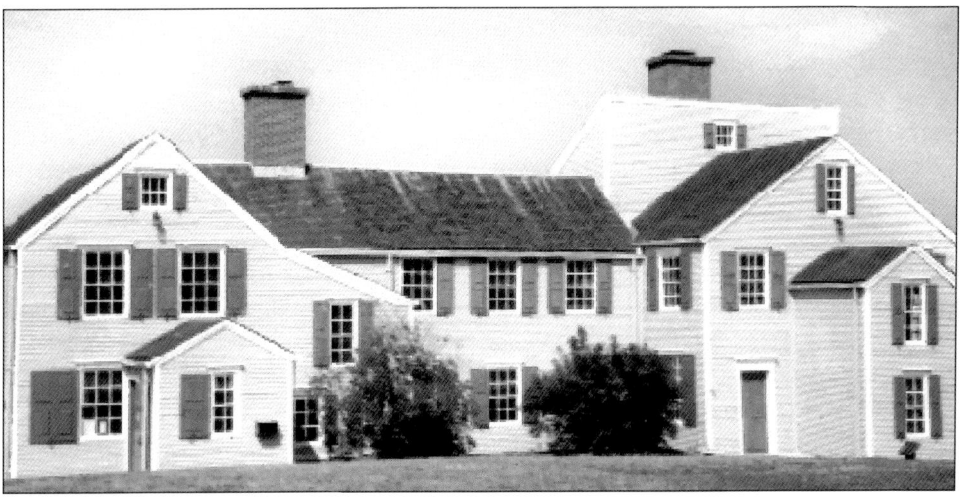

The Wentworth-Coolidge Mansion is operated by the New Hampshire Division of Parks. During summer months tourists can roam the same grounds and rooms as did Governor Benning Wentworth. (Photo by Benjamin Lawson.)

an apt description of the home owned by one of Stephen Chase's neighbors, Samuel Jackson. Jackson was a tanner, hence of middling status, and his home was a structure of functional simplicity perfect for the family of an eighteenth-century craftsman. Notwithstanding Portsmouth's historic pretense to wealth and grandeur, most residents, then and now, are of humble roots living normal, simple lives.

Should one today follow in the footsteps of George Washington and walk the old streets of Puddle Dock, the pedestrian will find many dwellings that were built at, or brought to, the neighborhood in the years after 1789. The 30 years that separated the American Revolution from the War of 1812 were prosperous for Portsmouth merchants, mariners, and craftsmen. Befitting this prosperity, many homes were built such as the Walsh House on Washington Street. Keyran Walsh was a successful mariner and merchant who bought this home and put his personal stamp on it, making it a fine representative of the Federal style of late eighteenth- and early nineteenth-century dwellings.

Other structures at Strawbery Banke were relocated at Puddle Dock in more recent years. This is true of the quaint saltbox home of Judge Samuel Penhallow, which is just down the lane from the Chase residence (having been moved from Pleasant Street to Washington Street). Penhallow came from an old and illustrious family, rich in history, which the Judge undoubtedly

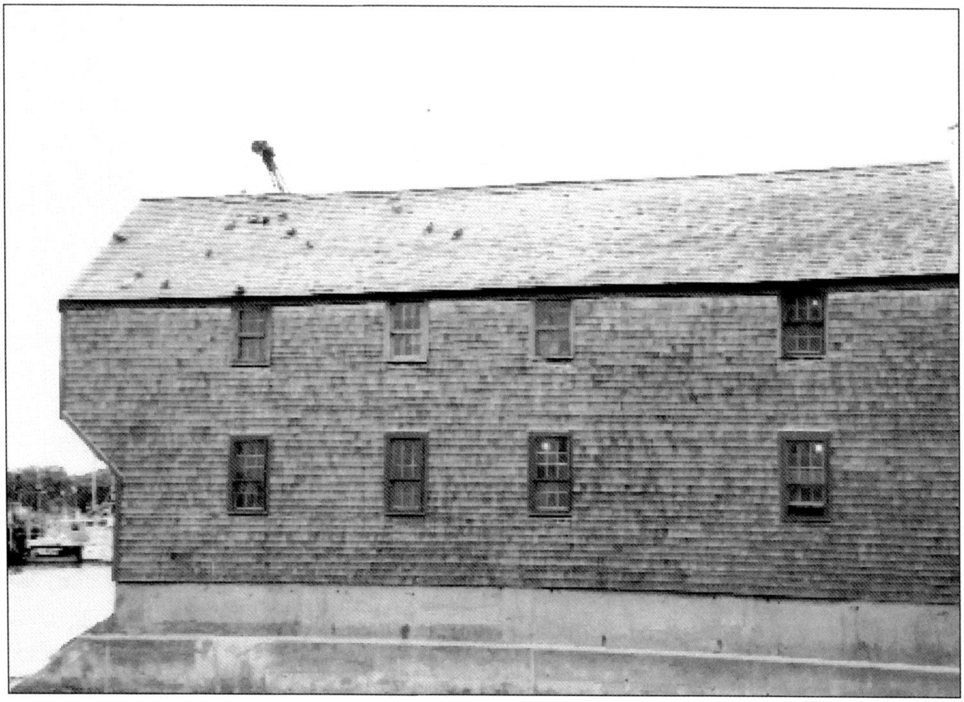

The Sheafe Warehouse is over 300 years old. It is located at Prescott Park adjacent to Portsmouth harbor. (Photo by Benjamin Lawson.)

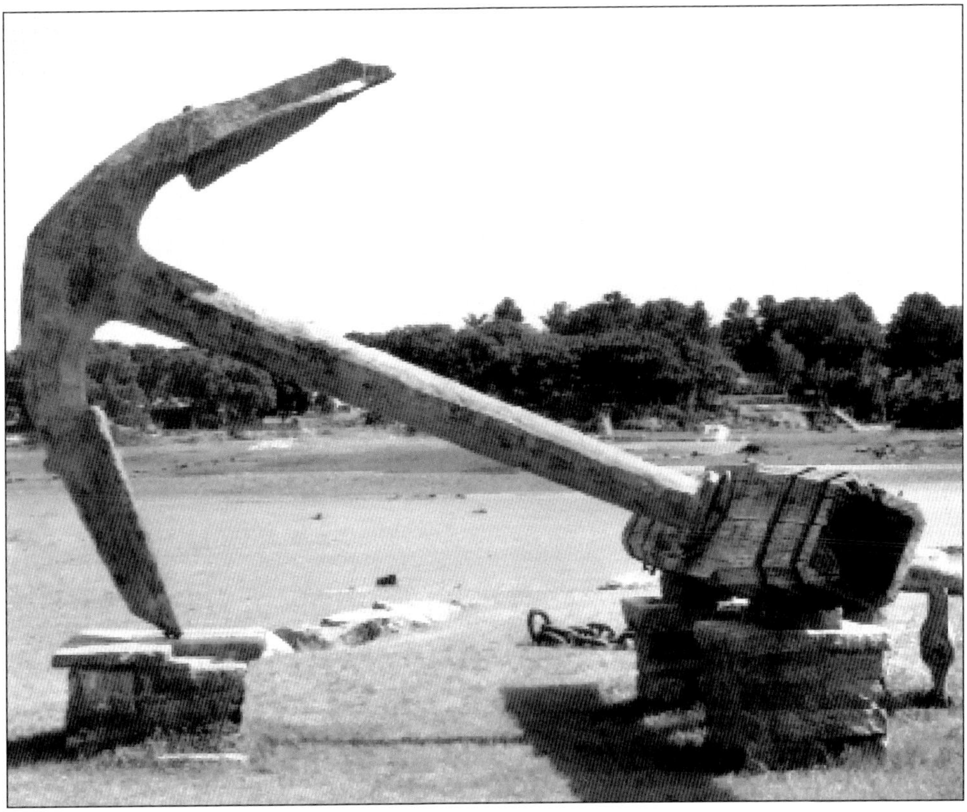

An old anchor lies at rest on the grounds of the Wentworth-Coolidge Mansion. An arm of the Piscataqua River is in the background. (Photo by Benjamin Lawson.)

knew well since his grandfather was the famous historian Samuel Penhallow. Judge Penhallow was also a deacon at the North Parish, serving under Reverend Joseph Buckminster.

One of the most imposing structures at Puddle Dock was moved to Strawbery Banke in 1963 from its original location on Islington Street. This beautiful federal mansion was once the home of Governor Ichabod Goodwin and his wife Sarah. Goodwin became governor of New Hampshire on the eve of the Civil War, in 1859. He was an important leader of the recently organized Republican party, the party of Abraham Lincoln. Lincoln campaigned in New Hampshire in 1860, seeking the Republican nomination for President. Goodwin was present in February when Lincoln spoke to an audience at Concord, the capitol. The Republicans emerged in the 1850s from the old Whig party, one of the leaders of which had been Daniel Webster. The Webster home, originally located on High Street, when threatened with destruction, ended up at Puddle Dock in 1961.

Another important landmark, Stoodley's Tavern, was also relocated during the 1960s to prevent it from succumbing to urban renewal. James Stoodley was a warm patriot who accommodated many a meeting among revolutionaries in the

1760s and 1770s. Like the William Pitt Tavern, Stoodley's was a gambrel-roofed structure. The two-story building was constructed by the same builder of Bell's Tavern on Congress Street. Taverns served as informal meeting places for men, especially those who were restless, disaffected, or otherwise distraught by their lives and current events of their town and country. Such taverns as Stoodley's and Stavers' played important roles in the American Revolution.

The historical consciousness of modern Portsmouth is illustrated in other museums besides Strawbery Banke. The Children's Museum up Marcy Street from Strawbery Banke is housed in the Old South Meetinghouse. Across from Strawbery Banke at Prescott Park, Sheafe's Warehouse still exists after 300 years. A replica of a nineteenth-century gundalow is tied to a wharf at the park as well. Across from Prescott Park, the Point of Graves still attracts visitors interested in the lives of those who lived in the distant past.

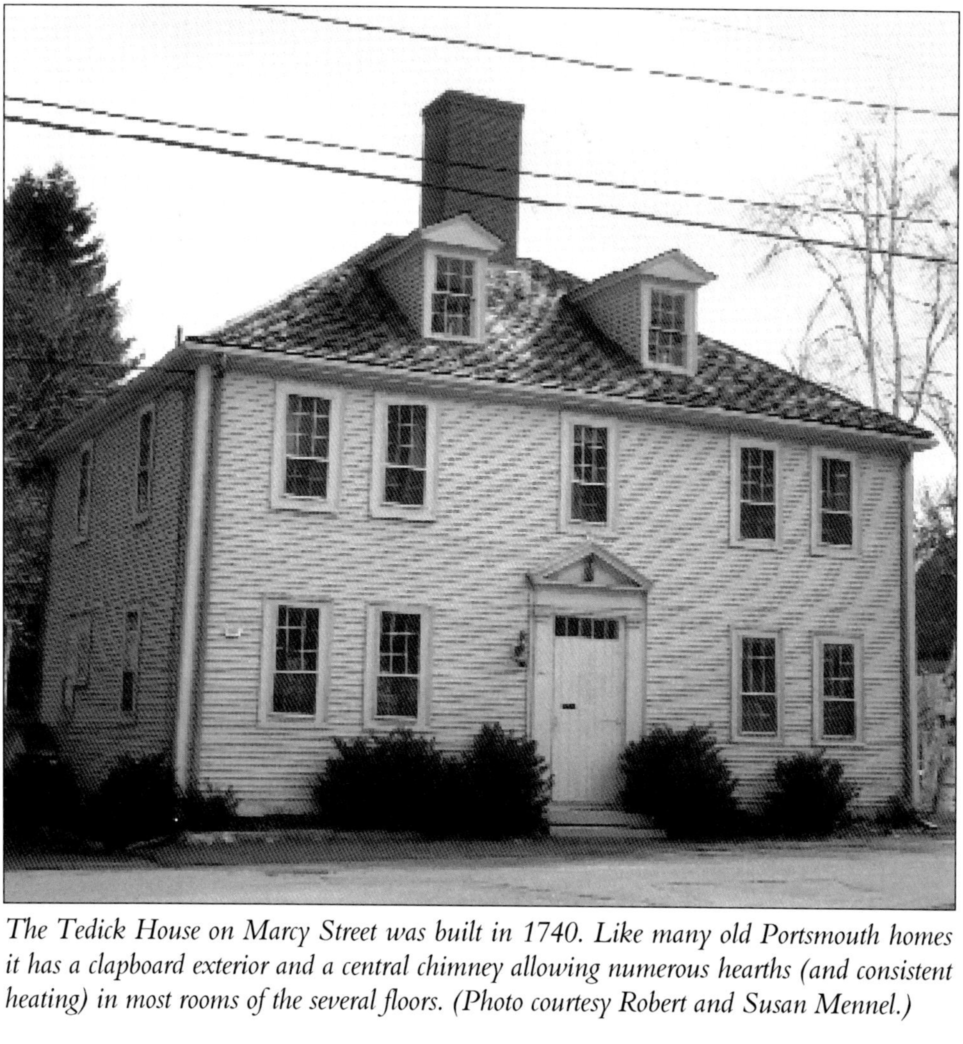

The Tedick House on Marcy Street was built in 1740. Like many old Portsmouth homes it has a clapboard exterior and a central chimney allowing numerous hearths (and consistent heating) in most rooms of the several floors. (Photo courtesy Robert and Susan Mennel.)

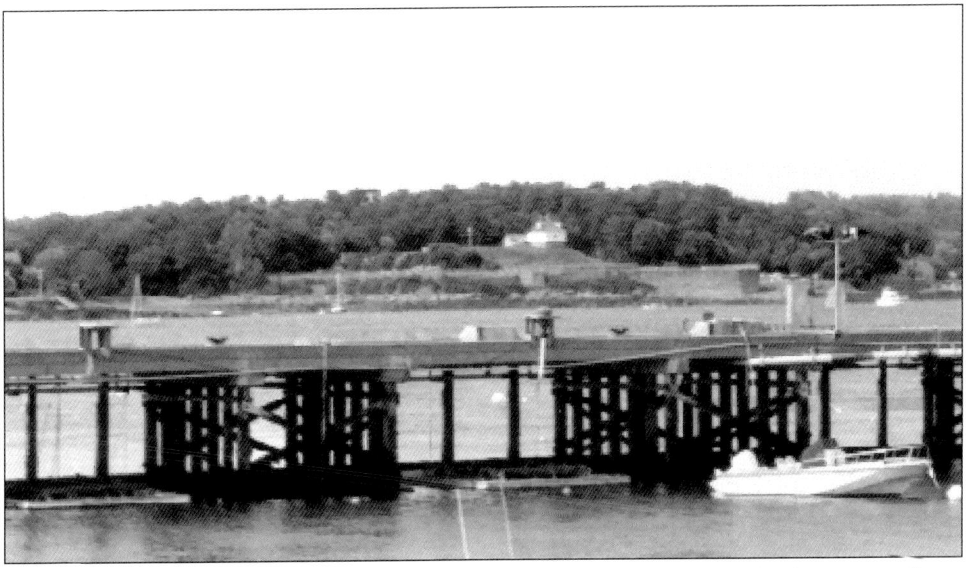

Fort McClary commands a bluff at Kittery Point overlooking Portsmouth harbor. Sir William Pepperrell had considerable influence in maintaining and manning the fort in the years before the Revolution. The current structure dates from the mid-1800s. (Photo by Benjamin Lawson.)

This area of the South End has many important houses besides those at Strawbery Banke. Noteworthy are the Langdon House on Court Street, the Lear House on Hunking Lane, the Wentworth-Gardner House on Mechanic Street, and far to the south, the Wentworth-Coolidge Mansion. Marcy Street is a wonderfully narrow lane that features many old houses that are today private residences; the Tedick House is a good example. William Tedick built it about 1740 and his son (also William) inherited the house, but was away at sea quite often, leaving his wife Martha and their two young children to fend for themselves. Captain Tedick departed for good in the early 1800s when he was lost at sea; his widow lived on until 1875.

At the North End, one may visit the Warner House, built by Captain Archibald Macphaedris in the early 1700s. His daughter married Colonel Jonathan Warner and for years they lived in the most imposing house of the Queen's Chapel neighborhood. Nearby is another imposing structure, the Moffatt-Ladd House on Market Street, constructed in 1763 by Captain John Moffatt. The Warner and Moffatt-Ladd houses, like many revolutionary homes, feature wonderful English and Dutch tiles surrounding the fireplaces.

At Market Square is the Athenaeum, built in 1803, which houses a wonderful collection of books and ship models to interest the inquisitive visitor. The rambler who walks west on Congress Street finds other historical delights, such as the Portsmouth Library, which was at one time the Portsmouth Academy. It was built in 1806 under the direction of the famous Boston architect Charles Bulfinch. Nearby is the John Paul Jones house, and then east on State

Street one finds the Joseph Whipple Mansion, where the Collector of Customs lived and worked.

If the rambler retraces his steps to Middle Street and proceeds south, he is rewarded with a series of Georgian and Federalist mansions of the late eighteenth- and early nineteenth-century Portsmouth elite. Several of these homes have the stamp of Charles Bullfinch, such as the Langley-Boardman House and the Larken-Rice House. James Rundlet in 1806 constructed the Rundlet-May House, a beautiful white Georgian mansion with black shudders enclosing the several dozen windows.

The modern rambler finds, in short, that Portsmouth simply exudes history. Local and state private and public bodies assist those inquisitive about the past with such sites open to the public as Fort Constitution. Several periods of Portsmouth history merge at Fort Constitution. One discovers old stone walls of eighteenth-century Fort William and Mary and the buildings and fortifications of the War of 1812, Civil War, and Spanish-American War. The fort was last used for defense during World War II.

The remains of another old military site open to the public are found across the Piscataqua at Kittery Point. Fort McClary was initially named Fort Pepperrell then Fort William in honor of Sir William Pepperrell, who was the local war hero of the mid-1700s, and his family. The first William Pepperrell bought the land and fortified it. His son, who led local militia in the capture of Louisburg, continued the family influence at Fort William. Patriots took control of the fort during the War for Independence, the Pepperrells having stayed loyal to the king. The U.S. government acquired the land in the early 1800s and renamed it Fort McClary. The current structures date from the period before and during the Civil War.

The city's modern naval accomplishments are accurately represented at Albacore Park, where the USS *Albacore* is open to the public for viewing. The *Albacore* was built at the Portsmouth Naval Shipyard and launched in 1953. She was built for experimental purposes and was used to test sub design, depths, and speed. She was decommissioned in the 1970s and put in dry-dock in the 1980s to serve as a hands-on museum for the curious.

Notwithstanding such plentiful museums, libraries, historic sites, and houses, the rambling historian discovers that the best source of the history of Portsmouth is Portsmouth itself. Stroll its streets, walk its lanes, wander about Strawbery Banke, spend time at Prescott Park looking out upon the harbor: one concludes from such experiences that Portsmouth is still an old town by the sea.

Indeed, the publication of *Portsmouth: An Old Town by the Sea* coincides with the quadricentennial of the first known English reconnoiter of the Piscataqua and Strawbery Banke that resulted in the initial settlements of the 1620s and the establishment of a town in the 1630s. Four hundred years ago this summer, Martin Pring captained one of two tall ships that sailed into Portsmouth harbor. This in itself was no mean accomplishment considering the hazards of shoals and currents that have always marked the Piscataqua.

Pring came at a time when there were no port authorities, harbor masters, or custom officials. His simple boats went where the whimsical winds and currents took them. Neither foghorns nor lighthouses existed to guide sailors entering an unknown land. Clear eyes and a quick response were the only means of avoiding rocks and sandbars.

Precisely who lived in this unknown land was a secondary concern to Pring and his men. First, could they navigate their way to land and find secure moorings? Good anchorage was found by Pring and so many others who journeyed across the Atlantic, south from the rocky Maine coast or north from the sandy shores and crowded harbors of New Hampshire and Massachusetts. The Piscataqua still invites those seeking its singular beauty: the narrow, shoal- and island-ridden passage upstream that opens to a broad, deep harbor; the thick, enchanting, blinding fogs; the rocky points jutting into river and sea; the fresh and cool salt air. It is difficult to depart, having breathed such air, as the English of the early seventeenth century showed. In Pring's wake came John Smith, David Thomson, Walter Neal, and others who were delighted to find amid the wild strawberries an ideal location for fishing and trade. For 400 years this has been the story of Portsmouth: the wayfarer in search of a safe harbor unexpectedly finds it at the port near the river's mouth.

ESSAY ON SOURCES

The historian intent on reconstructing the Portsmouth past finds the way less imposing because of the variety of original documents and town records preserved at the Portsmouth Library, Strawbery Banke Museum, the Portsmouth Athenaeum, the Dimond Library at the University of New Hampshire, town and provincial records at the New Hampshire Historical Society, and records at the City Hall. The Portsmouth Town Records, upon which much of this book is based, provide a wonderful glimpse into the life of early Portsmouth during its heyday from the mid-1600s to the early 1800s. I used the typescript copy found at the Portsmouth Public Library. Other important primary sources on Portsmouth history are church records, the Selectman's Book (1728–1736), tax records, deeds, probate, city directories, maps, newspapers such as the *New Hampshire Gazette*, and antiquarian accounts. Of these, Charles Brewster's *Rambles About Portsmouth*, Nathaniel Adams's *Annals of Portsmouth*, Thomas Bailey Aldrich's *An Old Town by the Sea*, and John Jenness's *The Isles of Shoals* stand out. Another outstanding source is Jeremy Belknap, *History of New-Hampshire*, published in three volumes in 1784, 1791, and 1792. Belknap founded the Massachusetts Historical Society in 1791, the papers and published *Collections* of which are also invaluable sources for early Portsmouth. The *Collections* of the Maine Historical Society are also useful for retracing early Portsmouth. Early historians and writers such as John Josselyn (*Two Voyages to New-England*), William Hubbard (*General History of New England*), John Smith (*Description of New England*), and Portsmouth native Samuel Penhallow (*The History of the Wars of New-England with the Eastern Indians*) are also good.

There are as well many good histories by modern historians of Portsmouth and the Piscataqua. Many focus on Portsmouth after 1800. *Portsmouth: An Old Town by the Sea* helps to fill a gap in the story of daily life in colonial Portsmouth. Other important works are Charles E. Clark, *The Eastern Frontier: The Settlement of Northern New England*; Jere Daniell, *Colonial New Hampshire*; Ola Winslow, *Portsmouth: The Life of a Town*; Robert Whittaker, *Land of Lost Content*; Robert Gilmore and Bruce Ingmire, *The Seacoast New Hampshire: A Visual History*; James Dolph and Ronan Donohoe, *Around Portsmouth in the Victorian Era*; Matthew Thomas, *Rockingham County*; Glenn Knoblock, *Historic Burial Grounds of the New Hampshire Seacoast*; Samuel Chamberlain, *Portsmouth New Hampshire*; the works of Raymond Brighton, such as *They Came to Fish* and *Tallships of the Piscataqua*; the works of Richard Winslow, such as *The Piscataqua Gundalow*; and William G. Saltonstall, *Ports of Piscataqua*.

Useful specialized studies include Timothy Alden, "Account of Religious Societies in Portsmouth," *Collections of the Massachusetts Historical Society*, vol. 10; Lawrence Shaw Mayo, *John Langdon and New Hampshire*; Edwin Page, *George Washington in New Hampshire*; Josiah Henry Benton, *Warning Out in New England*; Samuel Eliot Morison, *John Paul Jones: A Sailor's Biography*; Carl Bridenbaugh, *Cities in the Wilderness* and *Cities in Revolt*; Donald Cole, *Jacksonian Democracy in New Hampshire*; M.O. Hall, *Rambles About Greenland in Rhyme*; Charles Burroughs, *Discourse Delivered in the Chapel of the New Almshouse, in Portsmouth New Hampshire* (1835); Lawrence Craig, *Three Centuries of Religious Living: A History of the South Church and Parish*; *The Rules and Regulations &c. of the Portsmouth Female Asylum* (1815); Helen Pearson, *Vignettes of Portsmouth*; Laurel Thatcher Ulrich, *A Midwife's Tale*; Louis Wright, *The Cultural Life of the American Colonies*; Richard Bushman, *From Puritan to Yankee*; David Van Deventer, *The Emergence of Provincial New Hampshire*; Byron Fairchild, *Messrs. William Pepperrell: Merchants at Piscataqua*; my own *Passaconaway's Realm: Captain John Evans and the Exploration of Mount Washington* and *The American Plutarch: Jeremy Belknap and the Historian's Dialogue with the Past*; and the excellent web pages of Strawbery Banke, Inc., and SeacoastNH.com.

Illustrations from Usher Parsons, *Life of Sir William Peperrell*, Eliza Buckminster Lee, *Memoirs of Rev. Joseph Buckminster*, and Helen Pearson, *Vignettes of Portsmouth*, are courtesy the Portsmouth Public Library. Unless otherwise noted, all photographs and illustrations in *Portsmouth: An Old Town by the Sea* are courtesy of Benjamin A. Lawson.

INDEX